Capital and Uncertainty

Capital and Uncertainty

The Capital Investment Process in a Market Economy

Ian Runge

Director, Capital Strategy Pty Ltd, Australia

THE LOCKE INSTITUTE

Edward Elgar

Cheltenham, UK • Northampton, MA, USA

Published by
Edward Elgar Publishing Limited
Glensanda House
Montpellier Parade
Cheltenham
Glos GL50 1UA
UK

Edward Elgar Publishing, Inc.
136 West Street
Suite 202
Northampton
Massachusetts 01060
USA

A catalogue record for this book
is available from the British Library

Library of Congress Cataloguing in Publication Data
Runge, Ian C. (Ian Charles), 1952–
    Capital and uncertainty: the capital investment process in a market economy / Ian Runge.
        p. cm. — (The Locke Institute series)
    Includes bibliographical references (p.) and index.
    1. Capital investments—Decision making. 2. Uncertainty. I. Title. II. Series

    HG4028.C4 R82 2000
    332.6—dc21   00-035345

ISBN 1 84064 288 2

Printed and bound in Great Britain by MPG Books Ltd, Bodmin, Cornwall

Contents

Figures

Tables

Preface

The standard tools of neoclassical economics have proved successful in modelling many areas of market economies. In finance markets and in the consumer goods industries, for example, market participants learn quickly, and the assumptions of low transactions cost and perfect information are not unrealistic. In these fields, the use of standard neoclassical tools yields results that closely reflect the real world. Capital, and capital investment choice, on the other hand, is much less successfully explained by the narrowly defined assumptions of these models. Costly reversibility, costly information, imperfect expectations and uncertain intertemporal valuation introduce elements that, if overlooked, yield results far from reality. This book addresses the impact of these non-equilibrium elements on the capital investment decision process.

The book has two components. First, it examines and develops a theoretical model of choice under uncertainty. Second, it applies this model to the capital investment decision process within a firm. The issue is addressed following the opportunity cost tradition, characterized by scholars such as Hayek, Coase and Shackle and the London School of Economics tradition of the mid-twentieth century, and by American scholars such as Buchanan and Alchian.

A model of the capital investment process within a firm is developed. The model incorporates individual choice under uncertainty, the impact of institutional structures to accommodate and reduce the uncertainty, and the impact of costly information on the choice process.

The analysis promises significant advancement in the way capital investment decisions are understood and in the way these decisions are made within firms. By explicitly analysing uncertainty and identifying where uncertainty translates into risk, the theory and tools set out in the text provide a framework for choice between alternatives with differing risk and return profiles. By focusing on opportunity cost as a primary ingredient in strategic choice the model demonstrates scope for improved decision-making leading to choices with lower overall risk, higher returns and increased value.

Ian Runge is Executive Director of Capital Strategy Pty Ltd, an international advisory firm specializing in business strategy for capital-intensive industry. He may be contacted at <irunge@runge.com>.

1. Introduction

Economics defines investment as the act of incurring an immediate cost in the expectation of future rewards.[1] Investment, or *capital* investment, is concerned with decisions to build new ports, roads, mines or factories, acquire new or upgraded equipment, increase the quantity of trading stock held in inventory, or acquire an education – to name just a few economic activities that qualify under this universal label.

When one investment is chosen over some other alternative course of action that might have been followed, the process is – at least at one level of abstraction – no different to the choice a consumer makes in choosing apples over oranges. From revealed preference we can conclude only that, at the moment of choice, the subjective valuation of the actor ranked one (*the option chosen*) more highly than the other (*the most valuable alternative foregone*). Even then, revealed preference may be silent on precisely what the foregone alternative was.

At another level of abstraction there is a substantial difference. The value of apples or oranges is well understood from past experience, and past experience is a reliable guide to the future. Value materializes quickly. The actions of others influence this value only peripherally. Capital investment choice on the other hand is open-ended. It is a choice to follow a certain path into the future, and this path itself involves follow-on choice influenced by the initial path chosen. Few elements of the choice can be reversed if this future turns out to be different to expectations. Value materializes only slowly over time and is directly influenced by the actions of others pursuing their like plans. Initial choice must consider these follow-on actions and the actions of others over whom only limited control can be exercised. It takes time for the value in these diverse choices to be understood.

The primary contribution of this book is in analysing capital investment choice as a *process* – the process of how an individual actor, an entrepreneur, or an institution comes to understand 'value' prior to making the choice. Uncertainty over future value, coupled with limited market structures to serve as benchmarks for value, means that privately arrived at and understood *subjective* value informs decision-making far more than the calculus of simple neoclassical choice suggests.

The understanding of capital investment choice as a process has required significant modifications or extension to the standard neoclassical economic tools. These advancements involve:

- An extended model of rational choice. This model – the temporal utility model – recognizes that value in the mind of an actor comes to be understood only through time. In this model 'value' is not the outcome of some *simultaneous* weighting of all of the attributes of each choice alternative, but is a *sequential* process where the attributes are reconciled (in an expectational sense) in rank order from important to less important.

- The application of the model to capital investment choice under uncertainty. In this application, results are different to the standard neoclassical choice model in two areas: in choice between alternatives having *different* uncertainty characteristics, and in the valuing of information prior to choice. Both of these areas are examined at length.

- Examination of the way choices are understood within institutions. When the rank-ordering of choice attributes considered sequentially is combined with successive rounds of evaluation, over time, the final outcome is path dependent.[2] Profit-maximizing results (in the traditional sense of the term) do not necessarily follow.

- The modelling of a production process with indivisibility in capital. Uncertainty in capital investment choice means uncertainty in the *expectation* that returns to investment will materialize as planned. There is a fundamental difference between investments involving irreversible capital, and the capital rental model of neoclassical economics.

Dixit and Pindyck (1994) suggest that the most important elements of investment decisions are the *irreversibility* of the investment, *uncertainty* over future value and the *timing* of the investment. Each of these elements is subject to analysis throughout the book. From a methodological viewpoint, there is a fourth difference. Within a firm, capital investment decisions are never arrived at instantaneously. Lengthy procedures involving successive rounds of technical evaluation, financing and approval in a highly institutionalized environment provide an unusually open laboratory to study the choice process. Within this process, decisions to invest in information and decisions to reject alternatives from further consideration are predicated on valuations not yet evident by revealed preference. This process highlights the vital elements of any model of choice under uncertainty.

THE PROBLEM TO BE ADDRESSED

After two decades of direct involvement in major capital investment decisions within large corporations, I am convinced that the model of choice in the neoclassical[3] literature is simply not a useful tool for understanding this style of choice. Too many effects are left unexplained, and 'profit maximization' as typically defined does *not* characterize much decision-making in this environment.

This observation is not unique, and in itself does not invalidate the neoclassical model. Summers (1987a, b) showed hurdle rates[4] ranging from 8 to 30 per cent in businesses where the real cost of capital was only one-quarter to one-fifth of this amount. Such *average* expected returns do not necessarily imply that marginal returns do not equate to the marginal cost of capital, although they do imply a situation far from the perfect information model of general equilibrium. Other observers, for example Williamson (1964), Crew *et al.* (1971), Fama (1980), and Fama and Jensen (1983), have also recognized the inadequacy of the profit-maximization assumption of neoclassical economics, and have provided explanations based on agency issues and the compatibility of incentives. Agents (*the firm's managers*) are still assumed to be rational utility-maximizers, but their utility functions include arguments that are not necessarily consistent with profit maximization at the level of the firm.

All of these approaches have considerable explanatory value. Yet there remain many characteristics of corporate decision behaviour not captured in these models. The identification of these characteristics is complicated by the time it takes for the decision process to come to fruition, and by the problem that, *ex post*, when empirical data can be meaningfully sought, the nature of the problem has changed. Not only is the opportunity cost then unobservable, but the basic elements that gave rise to this displaced alternative are rarely still evident and available for comparative analysis.

The theory set out in this book adds substance to the elements of irreversibility (or sunk costs), uncertainty and timing that recognizes the observed non-profit-maximizing outcomes within an expanded framework of rational choice, but distinct from the well-developed, incentive-compatibility approach to the problem.

OBSERVED PRACTICE

The model of profit maximization (or, as usually framed, maximization of shareholder value) is rarely questioned in the finance world. Firms rarely acknowledge that their choices are directed at any other objective. To do so is to invite market reaction whose cost would surely be substantial.

To complicate the issue, the proposition that 'profit maximization' is *not* the practice when closely observed is confounded by empirical ambiguity. Actors can be faithfully following a process that they believe to be profit maximizing, yet the process itself does not ensure such a result. Moreover, actors making capital investment decisions on other grounds must still *present* results according to the profit-maximizing objective. Alternatives are always replanned and recalculated with changing guidelines until the favoured choice is shown to be superior by the criteria that the firm *says* it uses. Support for the idea that profit maximizing is *not* normal practice requires more than just superficial examination.

Every decision is influenced by agency considerations. To some extent individuals always act according to their own objective unaligned with the corporate objective. Nevertheless, agency issues, to the extent that they influence choice in any direct way, are usually easy to identify.[5] If one participant has a primary interest in protecting the firm from potential losses rather than seeking higher expected returns (even returns to counterbalance potential losses) is this an agency problem, or is he or she simply more risk averse? A view through a normative lens could conclude that there are agency problems everywhere. A positive view cannot reach this conclusion as readily. Pure agency explanations account for only a small proportion of choice differing from the profit-maximizing optimum.

The starting point of this model, consistent with my experience, is that most participants in the corporate decision process *do* faithfully attempt to choose according to the true wishes of shareholders (to the extent that such an aggregate opinion could even be ascertained), yet even by so doing this is not the result that follows.[6] Actual choices are only rarely profit maximizing, even *ex ante*.

Even in the absence of agency problems, and even taking into account the discipline of the share market, economic incentives do not guarantee such a result. Actors, behaving rationally throughout the process of decision-making, do not automatically arrive at the profit-maximizing choice. If the process can be better understood, then there is scope for achievement of superior outcomes.

This problem has not gone unnoticed in the economics literature. Alchian (1950) sees it as one of 'making a decision (selecting an action) whose potential outcome *distribution* is preferable, that is, choosing an action with the *optimum distribution,* since there is no such thing as a *maximizing* distribution'. The representation of such choice problems in terms of subjective distributions adds considerable insight to the problem at hand, but to reduce it to one of choice only between *distributions* is to over-simplify the process.

VALUATION AS A PROCESS

Valuation is a *process*. The process is hardly observable in consumer choice. The process is distinct and clearly observable in capital investment choice. Progressive reconciliation of value, abandonment of alternatives with limited scope for value enhancement and resolution of uncertainty are the key components of this process.

Consider a proposition to build a new factory. Alternatives include different physical locations, different technologies and different outputs. For any one alternative, there is a range of possible outcomes. Alertness to some highly negative or highly positive potential outcome triggers consideration of a whole new set of alternatives. It also triggers a re-rating of the rules of evaluation, with objectives previously considered minor sometimes assuming major importance, and vice versa.

Reconciliation of the value attaching to the various potential outcomes is not something that is done *simultaneously*, as implied by the preference functional model of neoclassical economics.[7] High-value potential outcomes may not even be considered until the risk is reduced to some acceptable level. *Simultaneous* evaluation across the full distribution of potential value is only possible during some penultimate stage of the evaluation – and by this stage the sub-set of alternatives under consideration may exclude high-value options that were eliminated when the focus of valuation was more narrowly defined.

Faced with uncertainty in outcomes, the focus of attention of a rational actor (what constitutes 'utility' for the time being) changes during the valuation process. 'Risk of loss', 'profit potential', and 'adaptability' are just three likely foci. The institutionalized corporate decision environment adds asymmetric economic forces to this choice process. With the arrival of information through the evaluation process, alternatives that indicate high value at the start can be subject to progressive erosion of this value, but alternatives that indicate low value at the start are no longer examined and do not benefit from increased value that new information may demonstrate. The outcome from this process is a choice that may be far from the profit-maximizing one if all information were available from the start and all alternatives were considered simultaneously.

In addition, in such an institutionalized environment there is rarely the scope to balance the positive subjective values of one participant with the negative values of some other participant to achieve a result that balances these valuations. The changing focus during the choice process, coupled with choices having differing attributes, presents even a unified set of actors with a dilemma similar to the Arrow critique[8] of voting behaviour.

Without loss of generality, experience suggests that this process 'weighs up' (compares the value of) alternatives initially with the focus only on some risk-related objective.[9] Different actors of course have different tastes for how much risk is acceptable and how much knowledge is needed for these elements to be understood. The satisfaction or reconciliation of this 'risk-related' criterion eliminates a number of alternatives from the choice set – even before some attributes associated with these alternatives have been explored.

For the remaining choice set, and in the progression through the final stages of the choice process, the focus of valuation changes to one of maximizing profit or some similar objective. The key observation remains, however, that during the initial (risk focus) stage, no information that demonstrates up-side potential (scope for high-utility outcomes) is considered. There is no weighting of 'utilities' whilst there is scope for more important preferences to remain unsatisfied or unreconciled.

OUTLINE

The book proceeds in 12 chapters. Chapter 2 provides a brief introduction to the theory of capital and the nature of capital investment decisions within a firm. It establishes an introductory framework for the characterization of the choice process that follows.

Chapter 3 characterizes this choice process and defines risk and uncertainty in context. Most elements of the neoclassical paradigm have been retained: for example, the assumption that rational individual actors pursue choice to the point where marginal benefit equals marginal cost. Some important elements of the neoclassical paradigm do not fit the world of entrepreneurship and capital investment choice and are therefore excluded from the model. In particular, the general equilibrium framework (at least as typically defined) is inconsistent with entrepreneurship and the style of capital investment choice in this book.[10]

The literature of rational choice is reviewed in Chapter 4. The starting point for this chapter is the standard neoclassical model. Under conditions of perfect information, known preferences and well defined choice sets, this 'pure logic of choice' as it was referred to by Hayek (1945), has little to fault it. In intertemporal choice, perfect information is impossible, choice sets are much harder to define and 'choice' is essentially between *strategies* – each strategy itself implying follow-up choices and constraints. The strengths, weaknesses and successes of the neoclassical models and the relative contributions of alternative models are examined in so far as they apply to the problem being addressed.

Chapter 5 is the first of two chapters that lay the groundwork for the model of choice under uncertainty developed in Chapter 7. It examines intertemporal valuation and entrepreneurship within a market setting. It characterizes entrepreneurship and the capital choice decision in terms of changes in capital value. Since changes in capital value can only occur outside the general equilibrium model, this chapter uses some alternative conceptual frameworks to highlight elements of uncertainty and how they influence the choice problem.

Chapter 6 examines intertemporal valuation from an individual perspective. It proceeds in three parts. The first part examines the economic basis for rational capital investment decisions and reframes the decision problem that the book aims to address. In particular, it introduces a translation mechanism between the corporate concept of value (shareholder value) and 'utility' in the mind of the individuals involved in the choice process. The second part looks at changes in value over time and their influence on entrepreneurial expectations as the defining characteristics of entrepreneurial choice. The third part develops support for and extends the model of intertemporal valuation from an economic perspective.

A model of cost and choice under uncertainty, labelled the *temporal utility model*, is set out in Chapter 7. This model postulates a *process* of value formation in cases of uncertainty wherein the information pertaining to choices and the rules for evaluating choices are subject to continual refinement. Following this process, the outcome of choice under uncertainty is found to be consistent with the neoclassical model for many cases – even cases involving *substantial* uncertainty. Conversely, capital decisions and other cases involving intertemporal valuation show results quite unlike the neoclassical result.

The economic environment within which capital decisions take place in a firm is characterized by knowledge dispersed amongst many actors. No one actor is well enough informed to direct choice alone. Knowledge changes during the decision process and values held in this process influence decisions to seek out further knowledge. Any model of such choice is therefore incomplete unless placed within some institutional framework that takes cognizance of this dispersed knowledge arriving over time. Chapter 8 addresses this issue. It characterizes choice as a process involving progressive generation followed by elimination of alternatives, and generation followed by confirmation of the rules governing choice. Alternatives are not 'chosen' in this model – less valued options are rejected.

A model of capital investment within a firm is developed and applied in Chapters 9, 10 and 11. Chapter 9 introduces the model, extending from a purely value-based definition of capital, and examines the potential for loss of value as the 'real' risk in capital investment choices. It draws a contrast between the fully competitive case characterized by contestable market theory and 'real' risk cases that involve potential for loss in value. The expectations of the future conditions that inform choice include the likelihood of such losses.

Chapter 10 sets out a model of capital investment choice highlighting the influence of capital heterogeneities and complementarities. The model is built on a foundation of indivisibility of capital within the production process, and the loss in value (sunk cost) in the event of actual conditions turning out different to the plan. To highlight the capital decision process, this model assumes an amount of capital associated with a certain technology ('primary' capital, involving a high proportion of sunk cost), coupled with additional capital ('secondary' capital, involving a lesser proportion of sunk cost), and purely variable costs.

Chapter 11 examines implications of the model and, in particular, highlights expectations (and *confidence* in expectations) as primarily important in capital investment decisions. Further, it examines real options, and the value of these options for decision-making. The results of this analysis suggest, for example, that only minor importance attaches to price and interest rate variables in capital investment decisions. This chapter also demonstrates empirical support for the influence of uncertainty on capital investment decisions in a market economy.

Chapter 12 summarizes the essential results of this book. References are appended at the end of the text.

NOTES:

1. Dixit and Pindyck (1994, 3)
2. In their 1982 bestseller, *In Search of Excellence*, Peters and Waterman (1982) attempt to define what makes certain companies into 'can do' organizations that far outperform competitors. The assumption is that most companies are following the profit-maximization model of neoclassical economics, but that these 'excellent' companies are doing something different. They suggest some form of managerial 'native art'. The model in this book suggests that the 'excellent' companies are merely 'profit maximizing' in the neoclassical sense, and other organizations (even without agency problems) are falling short of this assumed goal. The shortcomings of these companies stem from institutional structures and path dependencies in the valuation process that constrain and bias rational consideration of choices subject to uncertainty.
3. The term 'neoclassical economics' is used in this book to refer to the core theory of microeconomics, most of which is used and supported even where actions are accompanied by substantial uncertainty. The two elements of this core theory that are most relevant, and

unsupported, in this context are (a) the general equilibrium framework, and (b) actors with well-defined, stable preferences (utility functions) who engage in maximizing behaviour.

4. The hurdle rate is a guideline applied by corporate finance departments to exclude from consideration projects with inadequate returns. It represents the return at the margin of the last dollar of investment funds (the marginal cost of capital from an opportunity cost perspective). It suggests that investment opportunities which have an expected return in excess of this rate will always take up the full amount of investment funds available.

5. This is an observation from participation in a large number of board room discussions over a 20-year period. In this environment, *significant* conflict of interest issues are usually well known to participants or quickly become known. Less significant and less well understood conflicts of interest are relevant not so much because of their direct influence on choice, but through their influence on the rules applied to arrive at the choice. This 'agency affect' on the rules is considered in part in Chapter 8.

6. I am not suggesting that 'profit maximization' (or 'shareholder value', or some like measure) *should not* be the objective – indeed, my view is that this *should* be the objective.

7. By 'simultaneous' assessment I refer to the process in the mind of the actor. Actual comparative value may of course come from elements that are temporally separated: the 'event' may not occur simultaneously, but assessment of it can. Preference functional models that do not use continuous functions would not necessarily be subject to this critique.

8. Arrow (1950) demonstrated cycling of choices where at least three actors, each with transitive preference orderings, are called upon to select amongst three or more options by progressive pair-wise elimination. The final option chosen is a function of the order of pair-wise choice. The same result can occur in a corporate environment where *all* actors may prefer one choice over another from a profit-maximization perspective, but this option may be eliminated in some earlier round of assessment when the focus of valuation was centred on risk.

9. The meaning of risk and opportunity cost is discussed in greater detail in Chapter 3.

10. 'The theory of social interaction, of the mutual adjustment among the plans of separate human beings, is different in kind from the theory of planning, the maximization of some objective function by a conceptualized omniscient being' and 'There are properties or characteristics of equilibria in markets that seem superficially to be equivalent to those attainable by the idealized optimization carried out by the planner' (Buchanan, 1981, 5). In this book, models of *consumer choice*, involving no intertemporal valuation, are seen to be closer to these market equilibria (and are treated as such by way of comparison) than is the model of capital investment choice. Indeed, the model of capital investment choice in this book, built strongly upon incentives offering scope for entrepreneurial profits, could not exist in such an equilibrium framework.

2. The nature of capital investment decisions

This chapter provides a brief introduction to capital and the nature of capital investment decisions. It establishes an introductory framework for the characterization of the choice process that follows.

In economics there is probably no concept that has been subject to more confusion through time than the concept of capital.[1] Writers extending from Adam Smith (1776) and Böhm-Bawerk (1921) through to the present have associated capital with something that yields value in the future, but typically such constructs have limited the definition to 'groups of accumulated goods' or 'produced means of production', thereby excluding from analysis some of the most important elements necessary for the understanding of the subject. The first section of this chapter, 'Capital', defines and examines capital in value-based terms.

To bring capital into being is to forego certain near-term alternatives in the expectation of receiving greater value from outcomes continuing over some more extensive and more distant time period. In the second section, 'Capital Investment Choice', the components of value associated with this capital investment choice are introduced and dissected in a way that focuses on the potential loss in value as the primary determinant of choice.

Arguably, the primary objective of most individuals banding together into organizational forms for business purposes ('firms') is to facilitate direction or redirection of capital from liquid form (*that is, as money*) into and out of less homogeneous forms of capital in a way that facilitates maximum creation of wealth. The institutional environment developed to achieve this is introduced in the final section, 'Capital Decisions within the Firm', highlighting where knowledge issues and progressive resolution of uncertainties over time influence choice.

CAPITAL

'Capital' is the essence of intertemporal valuation. It is the value, assessed in the present, attaching to something envisaged in the future. The value is attached to certain goods (capital goods) combined with resources, institutional structures and a plan within some market framework that, combined, represent the ingredients in bringing this future to realization.

Physical goods (tools, machinery and the like) may be part of this valuation, but, following Mises (1966, 514), capital itself is 'nowhere but in the minds of planning men'.

Whilst not popularly thought of in this way, even consumer goods, purchased with the intent (*a plan*) for later consumption represent capital. 'Capital', according to Irving Fisher,[2] 'includes all wealth in existence, without exception of any kind.' Such a value-based definition admits a wide range of economic goods rarely addressed by early authors. An *education* represents human capital to the extent that the mind of the actor envisages future value above the future value that would materialize in its absence. *Knowledge* is capital to the extent that its input to the plan contributes to increased envisaged future value compared to any alternative which lacks such knowledge.

Ordinary consumer choice (oranges versus apples) has a very evident connection between the good or activity in question and the value as envisaged by the actor. With goods or activity spanning a larger temporal spectrum the connection is much more tenuous. 'Value' is strongly linked to an individual actor's ability and confidence in envisaging such futures, and, in a choice situation, his or her ability to influence the realization of such value.

Two key attributes of capital follow from this definition:

1. Capital is in 'the minds of planning men', but until interaction in a market setting the plan that gives rise to value in the mind of one market participant cannot be presumed consistent with the plan of any other participant. Unlike consumer choice, where the high degree of market interaction and frequency of market participation serves to align values at the margin, alignment mechanisms with capital are far more problematic. Only in the presence of highly institutionalized arrangements for alignment of expectations can some general intertemporal equilibrium be meaningfully thought of with respect to capital.

2. Capital may be created or destroyed with no physical change. The admission of new private knowledge can enhance capital value. The widespread dispersal of knowledge or sudden recognition that previously private knowledge has now become public can reduce capital value.

Beer barrels and blast furnaces, harbour installations and hotel-room furniture are capital not by virtue of their physical properties but by virtue of their economic functions. Something is capital because the market, the consensus of entrepreneurial minds, regards it as capable of yielding an income. (Lachmann, 1978)[3]

CAPITAL INVESTMENT CHOICE

Capital investment choice is about the decision to bring *into* being these beer barrels and blast furnaces, harbour installations and hotel-room furniture.

To paraphrase Lachmann (1978) again, this choice is integrally linked to the explanation of why capital resources are used in the way they are; why in a given situation some alternatives are rejected, others selected; what governs the choice or rejection of alternative uses when unexpected change compels a revision of plan; and the extent to which the likelihood of capital value change influences choice.

Every capital investment can be conceptually divided into two components:

1. There is a component of value that is well recognized in the market place. For this component there is little difference between the owners' valuation and the market valuation. A pick-up truck operating around a processing plant may be an integral part of the plant, but it is valued according to the market value of similar pick-up trucks operating anywhere else in the economy under the assumption of no transaction costs of substituting it by or for its alternative use. The pick-up truck is still 'capital', but its homogeneity in use means that its value is independent of the success or otherwise of the overall investment plan of which it is a part.

2. There is a component of value that comes about through *proprietary* knowledge or influences. This component is integral to the success of the plan. When the investment is in full production and the output has a market value, this component can be valued externally through its assumed contribution to actual output. Prior to this, the general market lacks a reliable benchmark for such value and with less than full information there is less than full market valuation. This component represents the entrepreneurial element of the capital, and its heterogeneity in use means that its value is directly dependent on the success or otherwise of the overall investment of which it is a part.

Whilst the example of the pick-up truck *does* represent a physical item of capital, this conceptual division of capital requires no such distinction based on physical characteristics. A custom-built lathe may be valued at $50,000 in the overall investment, but may still be worth $20,000 if turned to another purpose. The market-determined or alternative use value constitutes the former element of capital value, whilst the difference (*$30,000*) represents the entrepreneurial capital component – the component whose value is *totally* sensitive to the realization of value *within the plan*.[4]

The significance of this value-based division of capital will be expanded upon in Chapters 9, 10 and 11. Nevertheless, foreshadowing this discussion, it can be seen that decision-making with respect to value falling into the former (non-risk) division represents no difficulty. It is only the scope for *loss in value* – the entrepreneurial or risk element of capital that lies outside of the market-based valuation – that complicates choice.

CAPITAL DECISIONS WITHIN THE FIRM

No choice is instantaneous. However, any choice that can be reversed with no loss in value can be made instantaneously with no risk. Institutional arrangements to ensure the correctness of such choice can be minimal. Even within a firm decisions can be made by just one person.

If there is potential for loss in value following choice, then the *expected* value must be high enough to compensate for this potential loss. The extent of potential loss has an impact on the time and resources necessary to understand the nature of the choice. Institutional arrangements to ensure the correctness of such choice must be more substantial.

The nature of capital decisions is such that all available knowledge pertaining to the choice is not given to any one person or even just one team. Moreover, a team that best understands one alternative is frequently not the same team that best understands some mutually exclusive alternative that is the subject of the choice.

Within a firm, institutional arrangements provide the mechanism for assimilation of data and guidelines for the assessment of such alternatives. These institutional arrangements provide, *inter alia*:

- guidelines (rules) for the style of capital investment opportunity that the firm is prepared to entertain;
- guidelines (rules) for reducing all the data pertaining to each choice into a sub-set deemed most important for comparative evaluation. The sub-set might include, for example, the total funding requirements, the net present value, internal rate of return, payback period, and the sensitivity of these items to changes in various inputs;
- progressive consideration, elimination and eventual selection of capital investment choices.

The outcome of this process cannot be presumed equivalent to that of an omniscient profit-maximizing individual. Moreover, sequential assessment processes, agenda control and valuation criteria that are themselves defined within the process promote results that are not necessarily a balanced weighting of the views of the individual participants in the decision. The institutional arrangements leading to capital investment choice are set out in more detail in Chapter 8.

NOTES

1. 'When economists reach agreement on the theory of capital they will shortly reach agreement on everything. Happily for those who enjoy a diversity of views and beliefs, there is little danger of this outcome' (Bliss, 1975).
2. Quoted by Böhm-Bawerk ([1921]1959), drawing primarily on Fisher (1906).
3. Lachmann is consistent with Fisher and Mises in that 'capital' exists only through an expectation in (someone's) mind that it is capable of yielding an income. But a consensus of entrepreneurial minds is *not* necessary. Private capital requires only one entrepreneurial mind. Of course, entrepreneurial profits follow only when there is more than one entrepreneurial mind and a market environment, and in large measure the capital investment process is itself one of translating private capital value into 'market recognized' value. To *start* from the point where capital is already valued through such a consensus is to pass over an important part of the capital investment process – the most important part – since such a consensus implies diversifiable risk. The whole capital choice problem is about valuing risks that are *not* diversifiable.
4. A distinction is made here between capital value, in its alternative use, and sunk costs. Sunk costs typically imply irreversibility in a physical not a value sense. An underground excavation developed for the purposes of mining is a sunk cost as traditionally defined. None of the cost can be recovered. But if it can be turned to some other purpose (such as water storage) that has a value in this application of half the original expenditure, then only half of the original expenditure is at risk and only half of the value of the original investment is sensitive to realization of value within the plan.

3. Choice, risk and uncertainty

This chapter does two things. First, it sets out the background to the theory of cost and choice viewed through an 'uncertainty' lens. This exposition starts from some fundamental characteristics of human action and establishes the mandatory elements for rational choice within this context. It follows the opportunity cost tradition, particularly drawing from Alchian (1968) and Buchanan (1969).

Second, it establishes the framework for discussion of the terms risk and uncertainty. Following Knight (1921) these terms have received prominent treatment in the economics literature. Much of the development subsequent to Knight has been undertaken within the general equilibrium framework, with the result that certain terms that are synonymous and used interchangeably in this context become inappropriate once there is a departure from this framework. This section starts from the Knightian definition, but reframes some of the more modern uses of the terms into a form more applicable to the capital investment process.

PREREQUISITES FOR HUMAN ACTION

Human action is synonymous with choice. *No* action, in a situation where action is possible, is still a choice – a choice in favour of the status quo.

The three prerequisites for action, paraphrased from Mises (1966) and Locke ([1693]1995) are:

1. Dissatisfaction or uneasiness with the current state of affairs, or the state of affairs as they are envisaged to materialize in the absence of action.[1]

2. An imagined set of conditions which are more satisfactory.

3. The expectation that purposeful behaviour directed towards bringing about the imagined set of conditions has the power to remove or at least alleviate the felt uneasiness.[2]

Note that the first condition and the quotation in note 1 differentiates 'the greater good in view' (the availability of some improved set of conditions) as an incentive for action, from 'some uneasiness'. According to Locke, uneasiness is a prerequisite for action. An envisaged 'better state of affairs' is not a sufficient condition to generate this uneasiness: an actor may be perfectly content with the current state of affairs even whilst envisaging something better. In the first part of this book, the difference is overlooked; however, the discussion starting from Chapter 5 and followed up in the remainder of the book demonstrates that the difference is fundamental.

The three conditions can be defined more precisely from an economic, opportunity cost perspective. Put into standard economic terminology, the first condition – uneasiness with the current state of affairs – defines the *expected utility* of the status quo, or some less-than-certain chance of it materializing. The second condition – the imagined set of conditions – amounts to the *expected utility* of the envisaged alternative. The third condition characterizes the *uncertainty* or *riskiness* attaching to the alternative.

The Misesian construct can be reframed into a simpler formulation:

• one alternative (*the 'default', or status quo*), which has some envisaged value or *expected* utility, *and* some uncertainty concerning the extent to which this envisaged value will materialize (in the absence of action); and

• some other alternative which also has some envisaged value and some uncertainty over the extent value will materialize.

At the moment of choice, the subjective value of the alternative which is *not* acted upon gets named the *opportunity cost*.[3]

Action is therefore the outcome of choice between alternatives *each of which* has an *expected value* and each of which has some *uncertainty* that this value will materialize. Under uncertainty, 'utility' has at least two dimensions. A frequent failing in theoretical analysis of choice under uncertainty is the implicit assumption that the default option is subject to *no* uncertainty. Additionally, since 'choice' typically means selection of the alternative other than the status quo, the implicit assumption is that the opportunity cost (the 'value' of the status quo) is well defined and uncertainty-free.

A further characteristic frequently overlooked or simply assumed is the mechanism for the formulation of alternatives that facilitate choice. On the one hand, *default alternatives* are self-evident. Nevertheless, to be rationally evaluated they still require some expectational mechanism. The mind of the actor has to envisage the future set of conditions that are likely to transpire in the absence of action.

On the other hand, *new alternatives* involve a two-fold and more difficult expectational problem. Actors have first to envisage something that does not exist but which through their actions might conceivably be brought into existence; second, they have to envisage how this alternative might be fitted into the existing framework and the future set of conditions that are likely to transpire in this framework. This is a non-trivial and frequently overlooked issue which will be taken up again from Chapter 5.

Whilst not explicitly focusing on the uncertainty aspects of the choice decision, Buchanan (1969) set out to reconcile the genuinely scientific theory of economic *behaviour* and the pure logic of *choice* applied through the neoclassical framework. This reconciliation employed the notion of opportunity cost as the analytical coupling device.

In the remainder of this chapter the model set out in Buchanan (1969) and Buchanan and Thirlby (1981) is followed to highlight costs and choice in an environment of uncertainty, again using opportunity cost as the analytical coupling device.

RISK AND UNCERTAINTY

Challenges to the neoclassical model revolve around its treatment of uncertainty. In a world with no uncertainty – known utility functions, perfect information and foresight, deterministic choices – the model remains unchallenged. Departures from the neoclassical model are therefore best understood in a framework characterized by such uncertainty.

The lack of a relatively consistent world-view in the area of uncertainty is no better illustrated than in the definition of the terms risk and uncertainty themselves. Knight (1921) distinguishes between events that are capable of actuarial treatment (which he called risks) and events not capable of such treatment (which he called uncertainty). Neoclassical economic theory is almost always concerned with risk according to the Knightian definition, and has very little to say about events that are not capable of actuarial assessment.

In this book, the neoclassical neglect of events 'not capable of actuarial assessment' cannot be overlooked, since it is the objective to examine choice decisions precisely of this type. Two approaches could conceptually be adopted:

1. *A Bayesian approach* Proponents of the Bayesian methodology argue that the process of estimation is not one of deducing the values of fixed parameters, but rather of continually updating and sharpening our subjective beliefs about the state of the world.[4] The language of probability theory applies, but each representation combines observed values with a term that represents some 'prior' beliefs of the observer.

2. *A Shackelian approach* This approach eschews any appeal to probabilistic methods where the value associated with choice derives from something envisaged in the future.[5]

Both these approaches have merit. Yet even acknowledging that the future is unknowable, the imagined futures attaching to capital investment choice include elements that are at least conceptually knowable. Part of the process leading to valuation is the discernment of those elements that are conceptually knowable and those residual elements that cannot be so classified. In the final analysis, the process involves a balance between the uncertainty attaching to unknowable elements and the reduction in uncertainty through further search or study of those elements that are conceptually knowable. For this endeavour, the language of probability theory – of Bayesian constructs and subjective valuations – still provides a useful mental tool, even with no possibility of actuarial treatment.

Despite the popular use of the terms risk and uncertainty to mean different things than they mean in the Knightian definition, the Knightian view of risk is still supported in many strands of the economic and finance literature. In this literature, risk or the riskiness of an investment is synonymous with the statistical variance of a financial instrument (stock or bond) compared to the market average. Yet, even in this literature, there is inconsistency in application of the terms. For example, apparently anomalous statistical results from empirical work on stock market performance suggest insufficient cognizance of the differences between *diversifiable* risk and *non-diversifiable* risk. In an advanced market economy, diversifiable risk equates to Knight's concept of risk. Non-diversifiable risk is similar to Knight's concept of uncertainty. Some of these anomalies in the understanding of the finance markets have been highlighted by Brealey and Myers (1991).[6]

Outside the Knightian definition, the layman's concept of risk – call it *real* risk – is integrally bound up with the scope to make a wrong decision and the premium sought to expose oneself to the outcome resulting therefrom. The dictionary definition of 'exposure to the chance of injury or loss' is quite different to just an outcome 'capable of actuarial treatment'. An outcome that leaves one better off by some amount uniformly distributed between $1 million and $2 million is still a risk under the Knightian definition, but involves no exposure to the chance of injury or loss.

Knight's definition of risk associated with some outcome does not require knowledge of what the alternative choice might be. 'Real' risk *does* require knowledge of the alternative. It presupposes an alternative (the opportunity cost) that has less risk. If the alternative to the outcome above is a guaranteed $1.25 million, then the choice of the alternative that involves some uncertainty in final outcome *does* involve risk. The choice of the alternative that has an *expected value* of $1.5 million also involves a 25 per cent chance of loss *compared* to the other alternative. The difference in expected values between the option under consideration and the alternative choice is balanced against the difference in risk.

The Knightian concept of risk is definable independent of choice. 'Real' risk requires choice. 'Real' risk is a meaningless concept independent of the opportunity cost.

In an advanced market economy with actuarially assessable events, actors are presented with an opportunity set that covers a broad spectrum of risk and return. Assuming risk-averse actors, arbitrage ensures that opportunities with the same expected value but lesser variance in potential outcomes are *ceteris paribus* valued more highly than opportunities with greater variance. In this environment – with established markets and actuarially assessable events – risk and variance *are* synonyms: '[I]f we look in areas where poaching is easy, prices and quantities will be arbitraged into relationships predicted by rational formulations. The stock market will look pretty good on this basis' (Zeckhauser, 1986, 260). This model – of the stock market, or any other market where choices have such well-defined characteristics – is *not* the subject of study in this book.

Where events are not actuarially assessable and uncertainty derives from ill-defined future action, risk is not synonymous with variance. There is no (actuarially assessable) 'variance'. Arbitrage, even where it exists, cannot guarantee consistency across the spectrum of return versus riskiness.[7,8] Private knowledge is as much a determinant of riskiness or the perceived lack thereof as are the inherent characteristics that might be observable and assessable by a third party. This (third party) observability and knowledge is a necessary condition for arbitrage to play a meaningful role. Capital investment within firms, activities that are outcomes of the political or legal process, and such things as career choice decisions are examples of economic activity characterized by this model.

In these models, variability in the outcome – even if it could be quantified – is not synonymous with risk, since there can be no presupposition about the characteristics of the opportunity cost. Variability is relevant to the extent that it impacts on the scope for an outcome valued less than the opportunity cost, but only then does it imply risk. Heterogeneous, ill-defined opportunities employing proprietary knowledge may offer substantial premiums over the next most valued opportunity that itself may be characterized by substantial (or even greater) variability.

The neoclassical definitions are appropriate for many of the purposes for which they are commonly used. Nevertheless, for this book some refinement is demanded. The following definitions have been adopted.

Uncertainty Uncertainty refers to some outcome whose value is not definitely known or cannot be determined in advance. Uncertainty may arise on economic grounds because information is not free – an additional drillhole to resolve some uncertainty in orebody definition may not yield knowledge enough to offset the cost. Alternatively, uncertainty may be an inherent

characteristic unable to be resolved by known technology or additional
expenditure (due to the weather, for instance). Uncertainty may or may not
be assessable in some actuarial manner. Further, since 'value' is a subjective
concept, *outcomes* with no uncertainty can yield uncertain *value* where an
actor is unsure how the pursuit of some choice will translate into utility for
him- or herself. Uncertainty is characterized by some distribution of potential
values, rather than one unique value.

Risk Risk is the potential exposure associated with an outcome whose value
falls short of some minimum expectation. Even with a great deal of
uncertainty, there is not necessarily risk if the value resulting from all the
possible outcomes still exceeds this minimum. On the distribution of values
characterizing uncertainty, an outcome involving risk is one that falls on the
adverse side of some 'reservation' line – a line denoting satisfaction or
continued satisfaction of certain preferences corresponding to some
minimum utility of the actor.

Figure 3.1 shows the characterization of risk and uncertainty. Uncertainty
is represented by the distribution of values. Value (or 'utility') is represented
on the x-axis, and the relative likelihood of occurrence on the y-axis. The
outcomes whose value falls to the left of the reservation line represent risk.

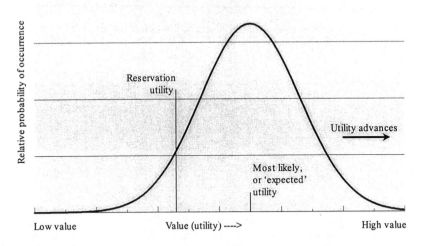

Figure 3.1: Distribution of values, risk and uncertainty

Figure 3.1 helps illustrate the popular concept of profits as the reward for
risk-taking. The difference between the *expected* utility and the reservation
utility represents 'profit' (or *expected* profit) at least in some non-economic
sense. A decision to engage in the activity characterized by Figure 3.1

involves some trade-off between this profit and the risk. Whilst this difference (between the *expected* utility and the reservation utility) may indeed represent some psychic concept of 'profit', expected *economic* profit will not be the same thing unless the reservation line represents the opportunity cost and is itself uncertainty-free. In the kinds of economic activity that are primarily under study in this book this is not necessarily so.

NOTES

1. 'What is it that determines the will in regard to our actions? ... [it] is not, as is generally supposed, the greater good in view, but some ... uneasiness a man is at present under. This is what successively determines the will, and sets us upon those actions we perform' (Locke ([1693]1995, 176).
2. See Mises (1966, 14).
3. Buchanan (1969).
4. See, for example, Greene (1993, 255).
5. 'If thoughts can be absolute originations in some part of their character, if choices can be in some respects absolved and exempt from entire governance by cause, the content of time-to-come is not merely unknown but non-existent, and the notion of foreknowledge of human affairs is vacuous. Then the effort to gather enough data to establish a unique path of history-to-come can be renounced in favour of the discipline of possibility. We ask, not what will take place but what can take place on condition of our acting thus or thus. This is an essentially different posture of thought from that which regards unknowledge as a deficiency, a falling-short, a failure of search and study' (Shackle, 1983).
6. For example: 'the capital asset pricing model is an enormous step towards understanding the effect of risk on the value of an asset, but there are many puzzles left, some statistical and some theoretical ... The statistical problems arise because the capital asset pricing model is hard to prove or dis-prove conclusively. It appears that average returns from low-beta stocks are too high (that is, higher than the capital asset pricing model predicts), and those from high-beta stocks are too low' and 'some tests indicate that average return has been related to diversifiable risk as well as beta' (Brealey and Myers, 1991, 919).
7. Choi (1993) provides an example derived from Arrow (1974) about 'an important class of intertemporal markets [which] shows systematic deviations from individual rational behavior'. Arrow cites case studies indicating that people do not always take advantage of obvious gains: 'for example, when the US government was willing to provide flood insurance at rates well below their actuarial value, very few took advantage of the offer, despite the readily available information about its benefits. In this instance, the "high costs of information" will not suffice to rescue the expected utility maximization model from this predictive failure' (Choi, 1993, 20-21). Presumably, the insurance offer was framed in a way that prohibited arbitrage.

   Zeckhauser (1986) gives a similar example of behaviour which, under efficient market conditions, adherents to the 'substantive rationality' viewpoint would suggest couldn't exist. The example concerns professors at Harvard not considering some highly favourable retirement programs. 'But', says Zeckhauser, 'it is hard to see how one could make a profit capitalizing on the irrationality of the Harvard professors who failed to consider their retirement plans adequately'.
8. Knight (1921) denies this characterization (that there exist substantial sectors of the economy unaffected by arbitrage): 'The fact is that while a single situation involving a known risk may be regarded as 'uncertain,' this uncertainty is *easily* converted to *effective* certainty; for in a considerable number of such cases the results become predictable in accordance with the laws of chance, and the error in such prediction approaches zero as the number of cases is increased. Hence it is *simply a matter of an elementary development of*

business organization to combine a sufficient number of cases to reduce the uncertainty to any desired limits.' (ibid., 46, emphasis added). If it were possible 'to combine a sufficient number of cases' uncertainty would definitely be reduced. Investors can spread their portfolios over many firms engaged in certain types of activities. But this is a separate choice problem to when an actor (an employee, a board member) in one of these firms decides on an individual investment where success or failure impacts on him or her privately. Indeed, the neoclassical literature pertaining to agency issues in the theory of the firm *demands* such incentive compatibility for rational choice in such an environment.

4. Rational choice

Every argument in economics must proceed from some conception of how humans act, and the study of rational choice (so called) is as old as the study of economics itself. This chapter reviews some of this history and highlights the contribution, strengths and weaknesses of the major strands of thought towards the problem of capital investment under uncertainty.

The first section sets out the background and contrasts purely economic underpinnings of the choice problem with motivating forces drawn from other sources. The second section, 'Rational Choice Paradigms and Models', categorizes the various schools of thought and the styles of model deriving from them. The mainstream model of choice under uncertainty – the current positive model which is the benchmark from which departures are normally measured – is described in the section 'Expected Utility Model'.

Gambling and similar games of chance constitute the major areas of research into uncertainty within the economic tradition. This form of uncertainty is distinctly different to the capital investment decision-making that is the subject of this book. However, there are insights from this strand of thought that offer considerable assistance. These similarities are discussed in the fourth section.

The standard neoclassical model has had a long history of controversy, not the least of which has come from scholars focused on subjective value. This tradition of thought, which also offers insight into the capital investment problem is followed up in the final section.

BACKGROUND

The study of economics is underpinned by the assumption that humans act in a rational manner. An actor is making a rational choice in the economic sense if the actions chosen are purposely directed to the achievement of some ends. Rational behaviour means behaviour held to be consistent according to some simple axioms and directed towards some ordering of alternatives in terms of relative desirability.

To make analysis tractable most economic models use a more restrictive definition of rationality. Decision-makers are typically said to behave rationally when behaviour conforms or can be interpreted to conform to the

neoclassical rational choice paradigm. This paradigm is examined in
'Rational Choice Paradigms and Models' (pp. 26–8). In the neoclassical
context, rational actors choose on the basis of maximizing their subjectively
understood *expected* utility.

The rational choice paradigm provides economics with a disciplinary
unity that is lacking in other social sciences and, even with acknowledged
shortcomings, allows advances that are envied by other branches of scientific
endeavour which lack such a unifying, easily identifiable and relatively
consistent world-view (see Hogarth and Reder, 1986, 4).

Reviewing the state of development in the formalization of the theory of
choice under uncertainty in 1951, Arrow described three seminal
developments that, at the time, promised significant advance. The most
important of these was the axiomatic treatment of choice among probability
distributions (by von Neumann and Morgenstern, 1947), but Arrow also
included the theory of statistical inference, by Neyman and Pearson (1933)
and Wald (1939, 1950), and the formulation of the whole problem of
uncertain anticipation and actions based on them, due to Shackle (1949).

In the half-century since Arrow suggested that these developments 'have
given hopes of a much clearer understanding of the problem' the
understanding has probably not turned out to be as clear as Arrow then
hoped. Reviewing the mainstream perspective on uncertainty 36 years after
Arrow, Machina (1987, 121) summarized it thus:

> Fifteen years ago, the theory of choice under uncertainty could be considered one
> of the 'success stories' of economic analysis: it rested on solid axiomatic
> foundations, it had seen important breakthroughs in the analysis of risk, risk
> aversion and their applications to economic issues, and it stood ready to provide
> the theoretical underpinnings for the newly emerging 'information revolution' in
> economics. Today choice under uncertainty is a field in flux: the standard theory is
> being challenged on several grounds from both within and outside economics.

Unfortunately for this book, the 'standard' theory – the mainstream
perspective referred to – equates 'choice under uncertainty' with 'choice
under (probabilistic) risk'. Under mainstream analysis, if the variability of an
outcome cannot be quantified in some way – or characterized as such – the
problem is of little interest. Capital investment choices usually *cannot* be so
quantified. A neoclassical observer may still not find this restrictive; for
many applications it just demands some auxiliary assumption. For our
purposes, however, the auxiliary 'assumption' could not be 'an assumption'.
The extended characterization of the choice problem is in fact the problem.

Not all observers following the mainstream approach to the problem
would agree that the field of choice under uncertainty is a field in flux.
Whilst explanation of many choices under uncertainty requires auxiliary
factual assumptions beyond the narrow utility-maximization approach,

substantial advances in economics have undoubtedly been made directly through such extensions (see, for example, Becker 1981). Nevertheless, in many cases the conclusions depend not on the assumptions of optimization but on the (untested) auxiliary assumptions, and utility maximization is neither a necessary nor a sufficient condition for the behaviour being modelled (Simon, 1986, 30). Hence the apparent robustness of the neoclassical model for many observers is not due to the model itself, but due to 'other' factors whose robustness may well be questionable.[1]

Much of the debate involves a contrast between the 'substantive rationality' approach built on the positivist tradition (Friedman, 1953) compared to an approach grounded more in psychology. In the former the predictive power of the model takes precedence, whereas in the latter the validity of the assumptions is paramount. Simon (1986) draws the distinction thus:

> If we accept values as given and consistent, if we postulate an objective description of the world as it really is, and if we assume that the decision maker's computational powers are unlimited, then two important consequences follow. First, we do not need to distinguish between the real world and the decision maker's perception of it: he or she perceives the world as it really is. Second, we can predict the choices that will be made by a rational decision maker entirely from our knowledge of the real world and without a knowledge of the decision maker's perceptions or modes of calculation. (We do, of course, have to know his or her utility function.)

This is the rational person of neoclassical economics. Decisions are made objectively and predictably in terms of the given utility function. As Pareto (1909) put it, once we have obtained 'a photograph of his tastes ... the individual may disappear' (quoted in Schoemaker, 1980, 2).

Alternatively:

> [if] we accept the proposition that both the knowledge and the computational power of the decision maker are severely limited, then we must distinguish between the real world and the actor's perception of it and reasoning about it. That is to say, we must construct a theory ... of the processes of decision. Our theory must include not only the reasoning processes but also the processes that generate the actor's subjective representation of the decision problem (Simon, 1986, 27).

This is the rational person of cognitive psychology – what Simon calls 'Procedural Rationality'. Decisions are made only within the limits of available knowledge and computation.

In a world of little uncertainty and scope for learning and adaptation, it is not hard to see the success of the neoclassical rational man. In some aggregate sense where market outcomes cancel out opposing differences between individuals, this model may similarly be quite valid. The extension of the model as called for by Simon arguably adds very little explanatory power.

Conversely, in a world of uncertainty where we are trying to understand *individual* behaviour, not the outcome of some aggregate set of individual behaviours, the rational person of neoclassical economics is found wanting. Counterbalancing forces which can be ignored in any aggregation of behaviour cannot be overlooked when modelling individual choice. The argument then is: how much extra support is needed in this model to make analysis tractable?

The conclusion in this book is that the neoclassical model of rationality applied to an individual can be made workable in an environment of uncertainty without resorting to the procedural rationality model. The extension to achieve this is set out in Chapter 7. Even though such a model constitutes only a minor extension to the neoclassical case, the difference is quite significant in the case of capital investment and intertemporal choice.

Another discord with the neoclassical world concerns aggregation. Results from this extended model must be passed through some institutional framework before they are meaningful in any aggregated sense (that is, for the purposes of decision-making at the level of the firm). This framework is set out in Chapter 8.

RATIONAL CHOICE PARADIGMS AND MODELS

. A critical issue in any analysis of rational choice centres on what economists mean by the concept of rational choice behaviour. In the broad definition of rationality, economists are referring to a paradigm rather than any particular theory (see Hogarth and Reder, 1986, 2). This paradigm – the world-view adopted in most of the neoclassical literature – has three elements:

1. It supposes that an individual decision-maker has a known utility function. This function defines the subjective value that an individual attaches to alternative uses of the resources with which he or she is endowed.

2. There is a set of constraints on the possible choices available.

3. The decision-maker solves a constrained maximization problem to determine which resources are devoted to each of the possible uses.

In this form, the rational choice paradigm is really an heuristic device for interpreting behaviour under assumptions of minimal uncertainty. Nevertheless, as a model of the real world it has proved remarkably resilient. Individual actors *do* frequently behave as if they were solving a constrained maximization problem, even if this narrow model must be supplemented by specific auxiliary assumptions for particular applications. There are good reasons why this result does frequently hold: people learn; individuals copy others whose actions achieve more; institutional structures develop to reduce uncertainty.

Outside of this world the model lacks specificity, since it assumes an actor with a known utility function, deterministic choices and no uncertainty. Clearly, much real world action cannot be so characterized. Individuals frequently do not know their likes and dislikes until confronted with them in a choice situation. Learning through trial and error or imitation is often difficult. The relationship between cause and effect is often unclear. Market activity involves real actors interacting with real other actors, and, given strategic behaviour, even rational actors do not necessarily arrive at optimal outcomes. Institutional structures are often slow to develop.

Models of rational choice under uncertainty extend at least from Cramer (1728), and have been based on a wide range of criteria. In addition to the *maximum expected utility* criteria (see below, p. 28) of von Neumann and Morgenstern and others, criteria have involved *survival* (Cramer, 1930), *range and mode* (Lange, 1943), *mean and semi-variance* (Markowitz, 1970), *focus value and surprise* (Shackle, 1952) and various other modifications and extensions.

Following Sinn (1989), three classification criteria encompassing the range of rational choice models are set out below. The classification system is fairly comprehensive (though perhaps disputed by some authors), but the models identified with each classification are chosen for their representativeness, not their exhaustiveness:

Expected utility criterion	By means of a given utility function the end-of-period wealth distribution is transformed into a distribution of utilities whose mathematical expectation serves as the preference functional (Example: von Neumann and Morgenstern, 1947).
Lexicographic criterion	A preference function is formulated to evaluate the probabilities of wealth exceeding some critical levels (Examples: Cramer, 1930; Roy 1952).
Two-parametric substitutive criterion	From the probability distribution, two characteristic numbers are generated to indicate 'risk' and 'return'. The numbers are evaluated by means of a substitutive preference function (Examples: Hicks, 1933; Markowitz, 1952, 1970; Shackle, 1952).

Figure 4.1 shows a distribution of values to illustrate components of choice under uncertainty adopted by different authors. Depending on the style of model, either axis may represent 'objective' data or subjective values. The figure highlights the mean value, modal value, standard

deviation, and other elements of uncertainty. The *y*-axis represents the likelihood of occurrence (either relative or absolute). The dual *x*-axis provides for the representation of Shackle which eschews 'utility' in favour of a 'degree of surprise' function. The named parts of the distribution shown in Figure 4.1 are referred to in some of the discussion in the following parts of this chapter.

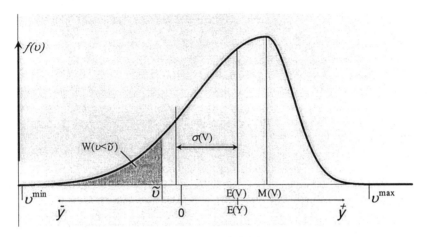

Figure 4.1: Distribution: models of choice under uncertainty

The most widely accepted of these alternative models is due to von Neumann and Morgenstern (1947) who extended the deterministic model to include subjective *expected* utility – an extension that provides explanatory power for risk aversion due to declining marginal utility of wealth. In cases of uncertain outcomes, the neoclassical paradigm can be said to include this von Neumann and Morgenstern extension, even though such recognition depends on strong assumptions of a psychological nature avoided in the standard (deterministic) model.

Whilst much criticism has been levelled at this model, it remains the only model of rational behaviour under uncertainty with widespread acceptance in the mainstream economic community. It is therefore the benchmark against which alternative models must be compared.

EXPECTED UTILITY MODEL

The expected utility model[2] attempts to account for the *expected utility* associated with variable outcomes rather than the utility of an *expected outcome*.

Mathematically, the attractiveness of a gamble offering the payoffs $(x_1, \ldots, x_n)$ with probabilities $(p_1, \ldots, p_n)$ is given by its expected value $\bar{x} = \sum x_i p_i$. Yet it has long been recognized that risk-averse individuals prefer the (certain) sum $\bar{x}$ to the mathematically equivalent probability of receiving this expected value $\bar{x} = \sum x_i p_i$.

Attempting to resolve this paradox,[3] Bernoulli (1738, quoted in Arrow, 1951) argued that a gain of say \$200 is not necessarily 'worth' twice as much as a gain of \$100. Bernoulli postulated what is now termed a *von Neumann–Morgenstern utility function* (U(•)). Rather than using expected *value* $\bar{x} = \sum x_i p_i$, the expected utility model assumes choice is based on expected *utility:* $\bar{u} = \sum U(x_i) p_i$.

Thus the sure gain β which will yield the same utility as the results of the above gamble, i.e. the certainty equivalent of the gamble, is determined by the equation:

$$U(W + \beta) = p_1 U(W + x_1) + p_2 U(W + x_2) + \ldots + p_n U(W + x_n)$$

where W is the individual's current wealth, and $\sum p_i = 1$.

Notice in this formulation that probabilities $(p_1, \ldots, p_n)$ are linearly weighted.

Figure 4.2 shows a utility function as typically represented in the expected utility model. Increases in wealth are associated with declines in the marginal utility of wealth. Hence, in von Neumann–Morgenstern utility terms, an increase in wealth by an amount μ above some existing level does not result in utility change (increase) as much as a decrease by an amount μ results in decreased utility.

Although it shares the name 'utility,' the von Neumann–Morgenstern utility function U(•) is quite distinct from the ordinal utility function of standard consumer theory. While the latter can be subjected to any monotonic transformation, a von Neumann–Morgenstern utility function is cardinal in that it can only be subjected to transformations of the form: $aU(x) + b$, (with $a > 0$), that is, transformations which change the origin or scale of the vertical axis, but do not affect the 'shape' of the function (see Machina, 1987, 123).

The simple application of the model is also demonstrated in Figure 4.2. An uncertain event whose outcome may be x', or x'' but with an *expected* value of $\bar{x}$ does not result in utility $U(\bar{x})$. The concavity of the von Neumann–Morgenstern utility function associated with declining marginal utility in wealth reduces the expected utility to $\overline{U}$.

The von Neumann–Morgenstern construct means that any probability distribution of outcomes can be mapped into a distribution of utilities. From the assumption of transitivity of preferences any distribution of utilities can

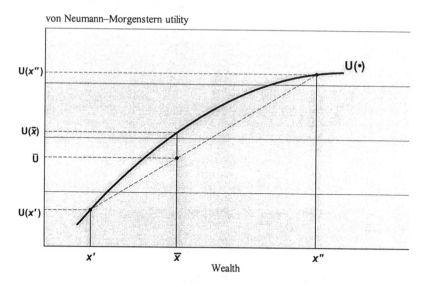

von Neumann–Morgenstern utility

Figure 4.2: Utility function, expected utility model

also be equated to a single 'utility' falling within the range of the distribution. Variable outcomes reduce to a single utility.

Whilst the von Neumann–Morgenstern model certainly provides helpful insights into economic behaviour where choice can be characterized by such distributions, increasingly the relevance of it for real-world application is being brought into question. The defence of this favoured position of rationality according to the paradigm is built on a set of bolstering assumptions that are themselves under attack. In particular, it is commonly assumed that substantial violations of the standard model are restricted to insignificant choice problems, quickly eliminated by learning, or irrelevant to economics because of the corrective function of market forces (Tversky and Kahneman, 1986, 89).

These issues will be addressed further in the succeeding sections; however, it is worth noting that the particular areas of concern in this book are those that are not subject to adaptation or correction through learning, and which, by the indeterminateness of their variability, cannot relieve decision-makers of risk versus return trade-offs through subjection to the forces of the market.

GAMBLING

If the characteristics of the uncertainty are not definable – the major area of interest in this book – the neoclassical model offers very little assistance. But if the characteristics of the uncertainty *are* definable (for example, gambling and lotteries), the limits of reliance on the traditional economic tools can at least be tested. This area of research offers some insights for the more ambitious task in the main part of the book.

Many of the challenges referred to by Machina (1987) have been derived from experimental work having to do with just this area of inquiry: gambling and lotteries. In this work stochastic characteristics of available choices are frequently known in advance. Despite this, empirical work shows that many actors still choose on grounds inconsistent with the neoclassical model. Such challenges therefore escape many of the defences which might otherwise be employable where empirical work contradicts established theory.

Models in this category are broadly termed non-expected utility models of preference and this class of models is the logical extension of the subjective expected utility models based on the pure logic of choice.

All the models under this heading work with known choice sets and defined probabilities so they are of limited use for the cases under study. Nevertheless, some of the results (and terminology adopted to describe the effects) are common to observations on capital investment under uncertainty within firms. The following observations set out some of these common areas and reasons for likely similarity and differences in result. Where generalizations about the models have been made, the comments apply to what is arguably the primary model used in this work: the models using the Marschak–Machina triangle.[4]

Restricted Choice Sets

Whilst notionally based on complete choice sets, the completeness in these models is only within certain bounds. Actors must choose either the red ball or the black ball. The option of *not playing* the game is excluded from the choice set. Any one choice therefore implicitly defines the opportunity cost (the alternate choice) because choice sets are complete and mutually exclusive. For many studies in gambling, this poses a dilemma: *all* choices have a negative *expected* value, with some (small) probability of a strongly positive result. This is almost the opposite of the real world of entrepreneurial capital investment choice, where all choices would have positive *expected* values, but varying degrees of probability of a negative result.

Opportunity Cost

An empirically demonstrated result from these models is that aggregate utility apparently cannot be arrived at by just a linear combination of the probabilities multiplied by their respective utilities.[5] The dependence between probabilities and payoffs (referred to as *common consequence effects* and *stochastic dominance*[6]) leads model-makers to postulate preference relationships (or indifference curves) in probability. Yet such indifference curves (and the phenomenon of 'fanning out') do have counterparts in real life once opportunity cost is explicitly introduced. If the only alternative to a loss-making option is another loss-making option, then behaviour which aims to maximize the *expected* value will apply only to the extent that all cases have a high probability of loss. If there is a different probability of loss, then actions may be directed at minimizing the maximum loss[7].

Whilst not explicitly related to these models, two other characteristics of choice under uncertainty relevant to capital choice are well recognized. The first such grouping has to do with preference reversal and framing effects. This effect – sometimes ignored in the economics literature as a psychological issue – has to do with how the subject comes to understand the problem at hand; and if the same problem is presented in two different ways it can result in two different results, even if the subject is aware of the framing. A similar situation arises with preference reversal. In the simplest of these cases, relative preferences over two choice alternatives that become available at different times in the future may change through time, even with no change in information. Specifically, the alternative that becomes available first may have the lower rank ordering when viewed 'from afar' but the higher rank ordering when its availability is imminent.

Both these effects can be understood through an opportunity cost approach. 'Framing' in the psychological work means focusing the actors attention on what the alternative might be to some proposed course of action. Value is always assessed against this 'cost'. Yet opportunity cost is a private cost – only the actors themselves could know the value of the alternative choices open to them at the moment of choice. *From an action/economics point of view, preference reversal due to a change in the opportunity cost is not an anomaly.*

As a partial explanation of entrepreneurship, the preference reversal phenomena is visited again in Chapter 6 under 'Defining Characteristics of Entrepreneurial Choice.' It too can be understood using an opportunity cost approach. When viewed from a long time in advance, the valuing of two choices includes (in the actor's mind) the value of other options that might materialize in the intervening period. Even if there is no uncertainty about the two alternatives narrowly defined, the *value* of these alternatives also depends on the other components of the actor's opportunity set and there may be substantial uncertainty within this set. When one alternative is imminent, its value is subject to no uncertainty, whereas the value of the still-distant second alternative remains more uncertain. Thus the *value* of the foregone alternative changes, representing a change in opportunity cost. Again, from an action/economics viewpoint, preference reversal due to this cause is not an anomaly.

The second area of inquiry concerns adaptive behaviour. Theorists focusing on the impact of adaptive behaviour suggest that much of what economists study with respect to choice under uncertainty is not 'choice' as such, but decision rules which have had the benefit of continual review, revision and trial-and-error adaptation. This disqualifies many models for choice in situations where adaptation and refinement of decision rules are impossible. Real-world choices clearly involve learning and adaptation, and an understanding of these is an important part of any comprehensive model of choice under uncertainty. In this book, the model of choice is treated separately from the examination of these decision rules.[8]

CHOICE IN A SUBJECTIVE VALUE FRAMEWORK

All of the models previously discussed relate to uncertainty in outcomes, but no uncertainty in performance or in the individuals utility function. Furthermore, they make the assumption that the uncertainty in outcomes may be considered in probabilistic terms. Most models reduce the problem to a comparison between alternatives, with value expressed as a single ordinal or cardinal number in a unidimensional utility space.

Whilst many insights can be gained from these models their application to the capital investment process is limited. Decisions regarding capital are decisions regarding the value of following uncertain strategies into the future. Whilst the future remains an unknown, this style of choice can be valued only in a *subjective* way. Models of choice following this subjective value approach therefore hold promise of illuminating the problem in ways that the more quantitative models can never do. Two areas of interest emerge from these models.

The first of these recognizes that capital investment is not just a single choice decision but in fact a series of decisions. Uncertainty in performance is directly connected to the decision environment faced by actors themselves during the life of the project in question – a decision environment where sunk costs change the incentive structure even to the detriment of the investors themselves.

A second area of interest has to do with how values are formed and how values change across choice sets and across time. There is no mutual exclusivity of outcomes in capital investment, since the actor her- or himself is a participant in bringing the envisaged result to fruition, and acting on one approach (if chosen) does not preclude acting on a different approach if it happens to be chosen. Of all alternatives under consideration, the sum of probabilities of occurrence does not have to equate to one. In addition, decisions where value materializes over time are particularly prone to changes in expectations and changes in preferences, and the *ex ante* valuation must also consider the uncertainty of such value scales.

Subjective uncertainty models see the choice problem beyond unidimensional utility space. Keynes (1921) considered conduct that is guided not only by the expectation of utility but also by some measure of risk. Shackle (1949) used a similar two-dimensional characterization, combining the value (expected 'utility') with a 'degree of potential surprise' function. Shackle's formulation rejects all probability elements in favour of 'possibility'. For Shackle, 'probability' implies that if one outcome is more likely, then other outcomes are less likely. 'Possibility' recognizes that more than one course of action leading to the future could have 100 per cent chance (in the mind of the actor) of being brought to fruition if that was the course decided upon. The actor her- or himself is not remote from the event being considered. Similar two-dimensional, subjectively based concepts can be inferred to underpin the models used by Keynes with respect to businessmen making investment decisions at the time of his writing in the 1930s.

In view of the fact that both he and Keynes particularly addressed the capital investment problem, the model by Shackle is worthy of examination. He develops the model from a conception of choice similar to Figure 4.1, except that in the Shackelian model the horizontal axis does not represent 'utility' but some measure of desiredness or counter-desiredness. Nevertheless, many arguments still hold even with this axis representing utility (a neoclassical economist would merely include additional arguments in the person's utility function). Two distributions of value associated with two potential investment choices are shown in Figure 4.3.

In Figure 4.3, the *x*-axis represents utility, and the *y*-axis a measure of *possibility* (or *relative* probability). The first contribution by Shackle is the recognition that somewhere along the *x*-axis is a neutral point. A guaranteed outcome exactly at this point leaves the actor indifferent to proceeding or not proceeding.

To be indifferent to proceeding, the assumption is that the actor has some sure alternative that will guarantee this result. Outcomes to the right of this neutral point leave the actor better off than this sure alternative, and the aggregated set of outcomes to the right of the neutral point represent the (positive) economic forces favouring the overall proposition. Outcomes to the left of the neutral point leave the actor worse off, and taken in aggregate are the (negative) forces against the proposition. In Figure 4.3 the neutral point is the point of indifference on the utility axis. Within a firm the neutral point is the marginal cost of capital on the return-on-investment axis.

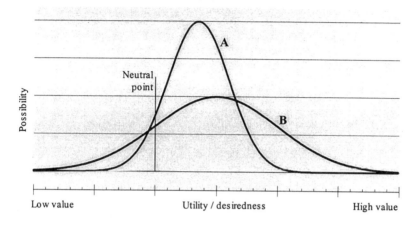

Figure 4.3: Distributions of value under uncertainty

Following Shackle, choice under uncertainty means balancing the positive value of the outcomes that are to the right of the neutral point with the negative value outcomes to the left.

Figure 4.4 shows how 'possibility' is combined with desiredness. In this construct, 'possibility' has been used synonymously with *relative* probability since relative probabilities do not have to sum to unity. A function incorporating the distance from the neutral point and the relative probability (possibility) of occurrence translates the outcomes with utility greater than and less than the utility at the point of indifference (the neutral point) into some weighted probability terms (positive and negative).[9] The two extreme values of the function – the maxima (labelled F") and minima (labelled F'), which 'attract the greater part of the individuals attention' are called the *focus-values*.

How are choices made under this model? This is the second contribution from Shackle and the contribution that highlights the inapplicability of any approach that attempts to reduce the two dimensions of utility into just a unidimensional number.

After eliminating clearly inferior options (where both the positive and negative focus-values are inferior, for example) the model suggests that the

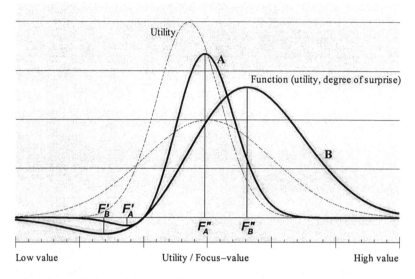

Figure 4.4: Shackelian choice model, focus-values

preferred choice is the one with the highest relative return. In this case, the relative return is the ratio of the positive focus-value over the (absolute value of the) negative focus-value – both values being expressed by their distance from the neutral point. In the example shown, curve A has a maximum focus-value 4.8 per cent higher than the neutral value and a minimum focus-value 1.3 per cent less than the neutral value, for a relative return of 3.69. The corresponding values for curve B are 8.1 per cent and –3.1 per cent for a relative return of 2.61. The alternative represented by curve A would be selected.

Thus, in the end, although dressed up in strongly subjective language, the Shackelian model reduces to a unidimensional outcome driving choice. Intuitively appealing though it is to take the last step – turning the maximum and minimum focus values into some sort of ratio – it is this step that introduces the difficulty. The difficulty is best illustrated in a case where one option has no scope for losses (but perhaps only very small scope for gain). Then this option is *always* favoured over other outcomes that have some (even just a small) possibility of loss even if these other outcomes offer very high expected returns.

Hence a choice with an expected value of 100 units and a 1 per cent chance of a small loss is passed over for a choice with an expected and guaranteed value of just 1 unit. Intuitively and empirically such outcomes cannot be supported and, short of some discontinuous function to do the translation, choice between certain and uncertain alternatives will always favour the certain case using any ratio-based formulation.

Other observers (for example, Ford, 1987) have made extensions to the Shackelian model but, even with reframing the model in various forms, the reduction of the final decision criteria into some unidimensional 'utility' has not proved advantageous.

NOTES

1. Debate on this issue is limited. In an early example, Becker (1962) indicates that he denotes as irrational 'any deviation from utility maximization'. Thus, the bounded rationality of observers such as Simon and Williamson is irrationality in this tradition. Winter (1975) challenges the extent to which theoretical propositions should be limited by the 'as if' principle; and, in reply, Lucas (presumably as an exemplar of the positivist tradition) 'leaves a door open ... for those who advocate more explicit reliance on empirically grounded behavioural generalizations at the foundations of economic theory' (Lucas, 1986; Winter, 1986, 244).
2. For a comprehensive but informal description of the axioms contained within the von Neumann–Morgenstern utility theory and how this model differs from the model of Bernoulli, see Schoemaker (1980, 13–15).
3. The immediate example that gave rise to the realization of the problem was a hypothetical bet, now known as the St Petersburg Paradox. A useful illustration of the paradox is given in Machina (1987, 122).
4. The primary contribution of this model (over the subjective expected utility model) is its inclusion of preference relationships in probability. For a description of this model, see, for example, Machina (1987) or Hey (1991).
5. This result is in contrast to the independence axiom of Samuelson (1983). This axiom pertains to an individual's preferences over probability mixtures of lotteries, and implies that the probability of the final outcome is all that influences choice, not the probabilities of intermediate outcomes. Specifically: If the lottery $P*$ is preferred to the lottery P, then the mixture $\alpha P* + (1 - \alpha)P**$ will be preferred to the mixture $\alpha P + (1 - \alpha)P**$ for all $\alpha > 0$ and $P**$.
6. For a description of these effects, see, for example, Tversky and Kahneman (1986).
7. See, for example, Wald (1939, 1950). This criterion is frequently referred to as the minimax principle. This result is also consistent with the model developed in Chapter 7 of this book.
8. The model of choice is described in detail in Chapter 7. The process of refinement of decision rules, learning, and adaptation is set out in Chapter 8.
9. In Shackle's words: 'The degree of enjoyment or distress caused by the thought of any hypothetical outcome will be a function, first, of the degree of success or advantage represented by this hypothesis, and second, of the degree of potential surprise associated with it.' These two arguments are different to the arguments that are described in the text, and also there is no suggestion in the Shackelian model that the function is simple multiplication as used in this example. Nevertheless, I argue that, with no possibility of applying quantitative numbers to any of the arguments, the essence of the Shackelian construct is still captured in the model presented.

5. Entrepreneurship and the market order

This chapter is the first of two chapters that lay the groundwork for the model of choice under uncertainty developed in Chapter 7. It examines value changes associated with entrepreneurial activity in a market-based economy. The following chapter (Chapter 6) examines intertemporal valuation from an individual perspective.

The first section, 'Entrepreneurship and Intertemporal Valuation', extends the concepts introduced in Chapter 3 and reviews intertemporal valuation and entrepreneurship within a market setting. Drawing partly from Böhm-Bawerk's review of capital[1] it develops and characterizes entrepreneurship and the capital choice decision in terms of changes in capital value. Since changes in capital value can only occur outside the general equilibrium model an alternative characterization of the market economy is developed, starting from 'The Market Order' (pp. 41–2). This alternative framework, drawing partly on Alchian (1950), examines this economy from the perspective of changes occurring exogenously (in the third section) and endogenously (in the fourth section). The characteristics of these ideal-type economies are used to draw conclusions regarding the economic forces influencing *individual* decisions. In the final section, the transmission of knowledge through the price system is examined using an example from Hayek (1945), reframing the problem from the perspective of capital investment choice. Clear distinctions emerge between choices influenced by pure chance events and choices influenced by uncertainty that is conceptually quantifiable and/or changing in some logically determinable way.

ENTREPRENEURSHIP AND INTERTEMPORAL VALUATION

Entrepreneurship involves *inter alia* exploitation of differences between market-determined values and private value. Successful entrepreneurship involves demonstrating *to someone else* (the 'market') that the value attached to some private capital exceeds the value that has hitherto been appreciated. The 'market', the consensus of entrepreneurial minds evaluating it from a broader perspective, changes its value of the things that make up this capital – the capital goods, resources, institutional structures and the plan. The demonstration may be through many mechanisms, including promotion, education and production. Changes in capital value associated with this enhanced market realization result in entrepreneurial profits or losses.

Entrepreneurial profits and losses derive from (a) private knowledge, (b) an ability to envisage application of this knowledge within a future market environment evolved to accommodate this application and changes brought about through the actions and reactions of others, (c) purposeful action on the part of the entrepreneur to bring the envisaged future to realization, and (d) mechanisms for others (the 'market') to recognize the value hitherto perceived primarily by the entrepreneur. Such mechanisms result in at least some elements of the private knowledge becoming public.

It is not the objective of this book to develop a comprehensive model of entrepreneurship. Nevertheless, capital investment choice is integrally linked to entrepreneurship via the decision-maker's capacity or lack thereof to envisage the future, or some multiple sets of futures, in a way superior to other market participants. The understanding of this element – this entrepreneurial ability to envisage the future – is vital to the comprehension of the capital investment process. Since capital is valued entirely from a perception of what this future will look like, this value is dependent on how strongly this vision is portrayed and held and on the probability that the envisaged future can be brought into reality.

In Chapter 3, attention was drawn to a quote from Locke wherein the 'greater good in view' as an incentive for action was differentiated from 'some uneasiness'. In this section I examine this distinction and conclude that it is fundamental to an understanding of capital investment choice under uncertainty.

Conventional economics focuses on the 'greater good in view' as an incentive for action. According to this conventional focus, rational actors always pursue utility-maximizing choices. Once attention has been drawn to such possibilities no further economic force is deemed necessary to initiate action. Even perfectly contented individuals, upon being made aware of something that has the potential to make them happier, need no more incentive to pursue this choice. 'Uneasiness' is a sufficient but not a necessary precondition to action in this world.

Yet there is substantial evidence that the presence of utility-maximizing choices on their own is not sufficient to initiate action. Hogarth and Reder (1986b) cite examples from Einhorn and Hogarth (1986), Thaler (1986) and Tversky and Kahneman (1986) in which, contrary to (neoclassical) economic theory, greater economic incentives have been shown to lead to less rather than more 'rational' behaviour.

The standard neoclassical position can of course be rescued through a broader definition of utility which is assumed to include unobservable arguments. Yet as others (for example, Buchanan, 1969) have observed, such an escape risks overlooking important explanatory and predictive elements in these supposedly unobservable arguments and, taken to a logical conclusion, borders on the tautological.[2] Perhaps the most important explanatory element overlooked in this simplification has to do with entrepreneurship.

The Locke position, that 'uneasiness' is *the* driving force for action, is less subject to this criticism. 'Uneasiness' drives action even where rational actors have no imagination and no intertemporal valuation. Rational actors with no imagination and ill-developed faculties for intertemporal valuation will not act under the influence of some 'greater good in view' unless or until the negative shock of unenvisaged futures becomes evident in the present and has a direct impact upon them.

The 'greater good in view' has only an indirect impact upon human action. Through imagination and intertemporal valuation, alternative futures present themselves via uneasiness. For consumer choice, the future (when the value of a particular choice will materialize) and the present (when the choice is being made) are effectively the same. Thus for consumer choice and for many other sectors of a market economy the attributes that differentiate 'uneasiness' from 'the greater good in view' are unimportant. For entrepreneurial or intertemporal choice, they are vital.[3]

Clearly, everyone has some ability to envisage what the future might be like. This ability also varies amongst individuals and may usefully be thought of as some continuum – of anticipation, action and reaction to change. What then is the impact on choice amongst actors at each end of this spectrum?

At one end of the spectrum is a model of pure survival. Action is focused purely on removal of the uneasiness immediately evident. Hunger drives the search for food. Coldness drives the search for warmth. This model assumes little or no cognitive ability beyond learning through evolutionary development and trial and error.

At a slightly more advanced stage is *reactive* entrepreneurship. At this stage action is again driven only through the uneasiness immediately evident rather than that evident from the contemplation of things to come. At this slightly more advanced stage, however, an actor, once alerted[4] to the problem, does not pursue action which is confined only to the removal of felt uneasiness, as in the survivorship model. Learning in an ontogenetic sense means intertemporal valuation in selecting a choice which offers the greatest utility not just for the immediate choice but for a class of circumstances that the actor is now alerted to. Actors following this model do not lack imagination or vision, but are constrained by an institutionalized environment or less-developed faculties in their ability to envisage certain facts unless confronted with the impact of them directly.

The other end of the continuum is *visionary* entrepreneurship. Uneasiness remains the driving force for action, but the uneasiness stems from the contemplation of things to come. The 'greater good in view' in the mind of a powerful visionary may invoke just this uneasiness in a current situation by way of comparison to what might be.

Hence the route from 'a greater good in view' to uneasiness leading to action is an indirect and tortuous one. Vision is the translation mechanism in the mind of the entrepreneur. Competition is the translation mechanism within a well-developed market structure. Where these two translation mechanisms are absent or masked, then action does not necessarily follow the presence of utility-improving options in an actor's choice set. Ultimately it is only time that translates previously envisaged futures into uneasiness in the present when action or entrepreneurship of the purely reactive or survival form takes over.

If capital investment decisions are to be made only when the negative aspects of *not* proceeding are self-evident – the *reactive* or survival case – then the scope for capital gain (maximizing capital value) is limited. Knowledge that is evident to all will already be taken into account in market values. Maximizing capital value through exploitation of private knowledge requires performance that anticipates the general market. The institutionalized environment within a firm determines how much of this gain can be captured.

THE MARKET ORDER

Growth in a market economy is not something that, on its own, is the focus of attention in this book. Nevertheless, growth is in large part an outcome of the successful realization of capital investment plans, and its significance cannot be overlooked in any analysis of capital investment strategies. In this section, the market setting within which capital investment decisions are made is examined and characterized in order to draw some insights into the factors influencing their outcomes and to highlight some of the risks associated with bringing them to fruition.

Successful realization of entrepreneurial plans means that the results of the plans are valued in the market place more than the market place values resources foregone in bringing them to fruition. The entrepreneur has this expectation at the moment of choice. In due course (after implementation, perhaps) others come to the same realization and market values adjust accordingly. The difference in value represents real growth. Nevertheless, there is no one-to-one correspondence between capital investment and growth. Capital investments are predicated on the *expectation* of increases in value, whereas growth is the outcome of *realized* increases in value. Changes in value can also be realized through other means – for instance, *luck*.

In a world where everything happens according to pure chance, entrepreneurial profits do not exist. (There would be windfall profits, however). In the value-static world of general equilibrium where nothing happens by chance, entrepreneurial profits also do not exist. Between these two extremes lies the real world where there is sufficient private knowledge and scope for action unanticipated by the market to allow entrepreneurial profits to exist. Such a world is also conveniently viewed as a spectrum.

On one side of this spectrum is the general equilibrium conception of the world. Perfect information and perfect foresight mean that the market valuation is always in one-to-one correspondence with the valuation of entrepreneurs. Indeed, entrepreneurs do not exist in this model. Capital investment decisions are purely *maintenance* decisions – pre-existing capital replaced to maintain its productive capacity. In this world, be it the neoclassical general equilibrium model or the Misesian evenly rotating economy, value-adding is non-existent. 'Value' (a subjective term) is for practical purposes synonymous with real goods in any definition of capital.

On the other side of the spectrum is the evolutionary model first articulated by Alchian (1950). In this model growth is possible but the forces that govern changes in the economy are outside human control. Entrepreneurial action of the visionary type is ruled out by the complete unpredictability of the future. *Reactive* entrepreneurial action, however, is an allowable and important ingredient of this model.[5] Opportunities for profit appear unpredictably, and entrepreneurial gains follow from their early recognition until their market value is fully realized. Negative 'shocks' also appear unpredictably, and entrepreneurial losses follow from them until resources can be directed away from such activity. If profits exceed losses, then there is an overall increase in value leading to growth.

The analysis of value change across this spectrum is in two parts. The first, 'Entrepreneurial Action in an Economy of Exogenous Change', highlights the elements of individual action necessary for value-adding under conditions of unpredictability and totally exogenous change. The second, 'Entrepreneurial Action in an Economy of Endogenous Change', highlights the elements of individual action necessary for value-adding using private knowledge but under conditions of varying external market unpredictability.

ENTREPRENEURIAL ACTION IN AN ECONOMY OF EXOGENOUS CHANGE

Assume first an economy where the original driving forces for change occur exogenously, and randomly, and where human action is limited to *reacting* to the change. Change could occur over just a very small sector of the economy, with the balance of the world presented to human actors as appearing completely predictable. Alternatively, the exogenous shocks could be widespread throughout the whole economy.

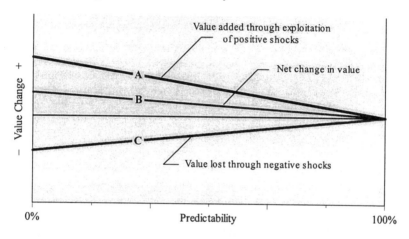

Figure 5.1: Spectrum of value change under exogenous shocks

Figure 5.1 illustrates the spectrum. The right side represents general equilibrium. Everything in the economy is predictable according to the pure logic of choice. The left side represents the pure evolutionary model, with everything unpredictable.

The three lines plotted in Figure 5.1 show changes in value assuming entrepreneurship is just *reactive*. There is no proprietary knowledge and no foresight with respect to future events. Individuals with bad luck (point C) suffer negative exogenous shocks and, until they can direct resources away from their area of activity, there will be a loss of value, as shown by the lower line. Individuals with good luck (point A) enjoy a positive shock which results in an increase in value as shown by the upper line.

As demonstrated by Alchian, even with equivalent negative and positive shocks, resources will be directed or redirected disproportionately towards the positive value-adding areas and withdrawn from other areas.

If the relative magnitude and frequency of exogenous change is less than human ability to adapt to it, then value formation (growth) in some aggregate sense will follow.[6] This aggregate value change is characterized by the middle line in Figure 5.1 where point B does not represent *any* firm but may be some 'representative' firm defined *ex post* in some constructs.

Individual growth cannot be guaranteed and does not necessarily follow this model. Luck is the primary ingredient contributing to individual success. Beyond luck, given a diversity of firm characteristics, the next most important ingredient leading to success is the speed of adaptation. Individuals who recognize changed circumstances early (are more *alert*) and who have a superior capacity to adapt relative to other market participants have the greatest scope to minimize losses and to realize capital gains and growth.

ENTREPRENEURIAL ACTION IN AN ECONOMY OF ENDOGENOUS CHANGE

Consider now an economy where the original driving forces for change are completely endogenous. Human action creates disturbances in an existing market order. Other actors anticipate such disturbances and simultaneously adjust their actions to exploit the circumstance or minimize the negative impact of the changed order. (Actors also *react* to unanticipated change, but this reactivity is excluded from this immediate model.) Again, endogenous change may involve few externalities and might occur over just a very small sector of the economy (the right side of the spectrum), with the balance of the world presented to human actors as appearing completely predictable. Alternatively, change and externalities associated with change could be widespread throughout the whole economy (the left side of the spectrum).

Figure 5.2 shows the same spectrum as Figure 5.1 but in this case showing value changes associated with entrepreneurship following the visionary model. Entrepreneurship in this visionary model means having private knowledge that allows the future to be understood in advance of general market understanding. Action influences the market process – and, to the extent that this is consistent with actions of others in the market, entrepreneurial profits ensue. On the right side of the spectrum, private knowledge cannot be translated into increased value, because action is fully anticipated. This may be a static world. Alternatively it may be the world of rational expectations where physical advances (for example, increased production year by year) are possible, but aggregate value changes cannot be captured, because every change is anticipated.[7]

On the left side, entrepreneurship involving vision is also meaningless. Extreme unpredictability means that private knowledge can influence so small a proportion of the outcome that value enhancement is minimal. Rather

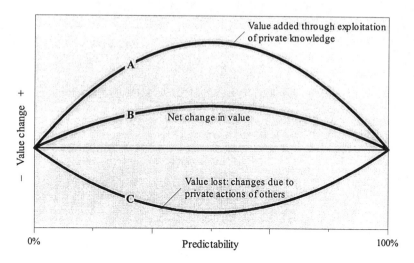

Figure 5.2: Spectrum of value change under endogenous shocks

than directing entrepreneurial action to influence the future, it is more efficient simply to *react* to change as it is encountered.

The model in Figure 5.2 is totally built on private knowledge, but in any one individual's plan there are elements that clash with the elements of other private plans. For any one degree of predictability in the economy, the strongest results (point A) go not to the individual with the most private knowledge, but to the individual whose private knowledge is capitalized on in a way that is most in harmony with the plans of other market participants. The weakest results (point C) fall on the individual whose private plans were most out of harmony with other market participants. Aggregate value change is maximized at some intermediate point in the spectrum. To the right of this maximum, private value is reduced because changes are anticipated 'too quickly' by the market. To the left of this point, value is reduced because of signal extraction problems: entrepreneurs cannot differentiate 'real' market changes induced by other participants from random influences.

In this model, unknown data are at least conceptually knowable – plans of others are discoverable or able to be deduced, and in making investments more information can allow a higher probability of a positive result.

Capital and Uncertainty

ENTREPRENEURSHIP IN A CHANGING MARKET ORDER

The real world economy has elements of both exogenous change *and* endogenous change, and somewhere in the middle of this spectrum is a market environment that allows private value formation to be maximized.

The aggregate value change (the summation of the middle lines from Figure 5.1 and Figure 5.2) is shown in Figure 5.3. This portrays the broad ingredients for success in macroeconomic terms as commonly presented in country-wide GDP statistics or in stock market aggregates. Nevertheless,

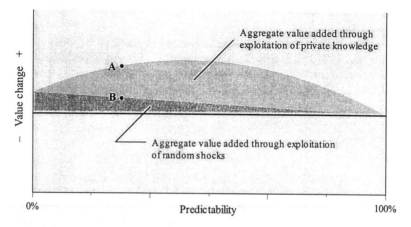

Figure 5.3: Spectrum of aggregate value change after shocks

some important elements that drive the capital investment decision process from an individual or firm perspective can still be inferred from the above model. The elements can best be illustrated with an example, drawn from Hayek (1945):

> Assume that somewhere in the world a new opportunity for the use of some raw material, say tin, has arisen, or that one of the sources of supply of tin has been eliminated. It does not matter for our purpose – and it is very significant that it does not matter – which of these two causes has made tin more scarce. All that the users of tin need to know is that some of the tin they used to consume is now more profitably employed elsewhere, and that in consequence they must economize tin. There is no need for the great majority of them even to know where the more urgent need has arisen, or in favour of what other needs they ought to husband their supply. If only some of them know directly of the new demand, and switch resources over to it, and if the people who are aware of the new gap thus created in turn fill it from still other sources, the effect will rapidly spread throughout the whole economic system and influence not only all the uses of tin, but also those of its substitutes and the substitutes of these substitutes, the supply of all things made of tin, and their substitutes, and so on; and all this without the great majority of

those instrumental in bringing about these substitutions knowing anything at all about the original cause of these changes.

In this classic example of the transmission of knowledge through the price system, Hayek focuses primarily on consumer choice: the *reaction* to unforeseen change. On the assumption that 'the great majority' of users of tin have a relatively elastic demand for the metal, then their insensitivity to this element of the economy means that they perceive little economic value in keeping alert to where more urgent needs might arise or in keeping alert to who else might have greater needs than themselves.

The situation is different in the case of users whose wealth (capital value) is sensitive to the price and availability of tin. Under these circumstances the simple model does not yield such unambiguous results.

Assume first that the source of the shortage of tin is a totally random, unexpected, and unlikely-to-be-repeated occurrence, *and it is known that this is so* (for example, a meteorite strike hitting a major tin producer). This is the situation characterized above in 'Entrepreneurial Action in an Economy of Exogenous Change'. Consumer reaction follows the Hayekian model. The major producer finds himself on the receiving end of the negative shock – point C in Figure 5.1 – suffering a loss in value. Conversely, *other* producers potentially find themselves at point A in Figure 5.1, and are presented with opportunities for gain. The result from this model is that so long as there are no characteristics of the uncertainty that are predictable (across sectors of the economy or across time) then it *doesn't impede capital investment choice*:

- Take first the case of the existing producer who suffers a loss in value. Investors in this plant have indeed made a loss, but the probability of this loss is independent of the project and does not affect future similar projects.[8] Even after suffering a loss, uncertainty associated with *future* capital investment choices is the same across all alternatives and therefore does not impede choice.

- Now consider the other producers contemplating expansion and potential entrepreneurial gains. The reasons for the changed market conditions may have been unpredictable *ex ante*, but the environment of capital investment *reacting* to this is subject to no unpredictability or ambiguity. The cause of the change that gives rise to the new opportunity is subject to no uncertainty. New capital investment to react to the change can proceed without delay.

- The *timing* for new capital investment is also not subject to the uncertainty characterized here. Uncertainty due to this source cannot be reduced by waiting or by additional search. The greatest entrepreneurial gains flow to those investors lucky enough to have the appropriate private knowledge available at the time and who are in a position to react to the changed market conditions the fastest. Random uncertainty where the cause is clearly understood promotes *early* reaction and adjustment.

Of course, capital investment related to the production or consumption of tin may be affected if the (random) uncertainty is perceived to be something characteristic of this industry rather than some other industry, or *increasing* in this industry relative to other industries. But such a characteristic already presupposes something non-random about the uncertainty and is therefore excluded from this first model.

Now assume that the shortage of tin derives from new demand associated with some new technology, *and it is generally known that this is so*. This is the situation characterized above in 'Entrepreneurial Action in an Economy of Endogenous Change'. Consumer reaction again follows the Hayekian model. Producers and consumers whose wealth (capital value) is sensitive to the price or availability of tin seek to protect or enhance that capital value, and their success or otherwise is a function of how well their plans anticipate and mesh with the plans and actions of the rest of the market participants.

- The primary source of the endogenous change – the owner of the newly developed technology – is in the strongest position to understand the impact of his or her increased demand on the market for tin. But this does not mean that the capital value of this new investment is sensitive to the price: tin might be a relatively minor element in the cost of production. Only if the value of the new investment is sensitive to the price of tin will he or she seek to mitigate (via futures markets, forward contracts and so on) a rising price that his or her increased demand is sure to precipitate. Only in this instance can the advance signals necessary for the validity of the Arrow–Debreu (Arrow and Debreu, 1954; and Debreu, 1959) and Rational Expectations models (see, for example, Lucas, 1966; Lucas and Prescott, 1971) be meaningfully presumed to exist. If capital value is insensitive to the market disruption that its introduction is bound to create, then the owner of the planned new technology has an incentive to protect such knowledge from the market place in general to gain comparative advantage in the market that the technology itself is aiming to serve. Disruption to the tin market is a pecuniary externality associated with some completely different market.

- Whilst disruption to one market may indeed be an externality of some other market, this does not mean that it cannot be anticipated. The owners of capital whose value is sensitive to changes in the price 'or availability of input factors or demand characteristics in the product market, have an incentive to monitor *anything* that has the potential to create such a change. Capital value is protected or enhanced to the extent that such change is anticipated and to the extent that adaptation of the capital structure accommodates the change. To the extent that markets are undeveloped or that actors have an incentive for misinformation, any capital investment in this environment is subject to uncertainty. To garner investment, this raises the threshold *expected return* before investment can be proceeded with.

• The *timing* of new capital investment is also subject to uncertainty. In incomplete markets or markets where strategic action is influential, the passage of time and the arrival of more information reduces uncertainty. The same investment delayed by one month represents less risk. If the present value of this lower-risk investment exceeds the value foregone in the intervening month, then new investment can be rationally delayed.

In reality, elements of randomness in the market exist side by side with conceptually predictable change (expected and unexpected) due to human action. Signals from the market place are never so clear that they can be neatly categorized as truly random events or events resulting from the actions of other market participants. Even where signals point strongly to randomness, ambiguity is not eliminated entirely because actors still have to know whether stochastic characteristics are stable or not. Is the weather going through some cyclical pattern, for instance, and is there something that conscious human action can do to understand this pattern better?

It follows that:

1. True chance events that are known to be so have no impact on capital investment choice.[9] If the uncertainty due to chance events is the same in one sector of the economy *vis-à-vis* other sectors of the economy and the underlying probability of such events is unchanging, then all alternatives are subject to the same 'uncertainty' characteristic and choice is unaffected. The same logic holds for choice across time.

2. Actors have to discern which of the factors affecting them are pure chance events and which are the result of human action and at least conceptually discoverable.

3. To the extent that factors influencing capital investment choice *are* due to some underlying random factor independent of the participants in the market, then search is an essential prerequisite. The search aims to establish sufficient confidence that the subjectively understood probability truly reflects the underlying characteristics of the randomness.[10]

4. Once chance events causing uncertainty are separated from events generated by other market participants, then these remaining influences have to be assimilated. All of these influences are conceptually discoverable, but rational strategic action (misinformation) by some

market participants makes discovery of some things impractical. The marginal cost of much information outweighs its marginal benefit. Choice must ultimately be made, given residual uncertainty.

NOTES

1. See: 'The Controversy over the Concept of Capital', in Böhm-Bawerk ([1921]1959).
2. See also Choi (1993): 'If a theory can explain everything, and anything, it is not a theory, but a tautology'. A fully fledged critique of rational choice is outside of the scope of this book; however some of these issues have been taken up in more detail in Chapter 4 above.
3. The difference between consumer choice (where learning and selection play an important role in achieving efficiency) and capital investment choice can be paraphrased from Tversky and Kahneman (1986, 90): 'The necessary feedback is often lacking for the decisions faced by managers, entrepreneurs, and politicians because (i) outcomes are commonly delayed and not easily attributable to a particular action; (ii) variability in the environment degrades the reliability of the feedback, especially where outcomes of low probability are involved; (iii) there is often no information about what the outcome would have been if another decision had been taken; and (iv) most important decisions are unique and therefore provide little opportunity for learning.'
4. The 'alertness' term is an important element of entrepreneurship in Kirzner (1973). This model of *reactive* entrepreneurship bears many similarities to the Kirznerian model of entrepreneurship.
5. Alchian (1950) develops this model from a complete evolutionary perspective and demonstrates that purposeful behaviour beyond 'survival' is not even strictly necessary for the model to hold: 'With a knowledge of the economy's realized requisites for survival and by a comparison of alternative conditions, [the economist] can state what types of firms or behaviour relative to other possible types will be more viable, even though the firms themselves may not know the conditions or even try to achieve them by readjusting to the changed situation if they do know the conditions. It is sufficient if all firms are slightly different so that in the new environmental situation those who have their fixed internal conditions closer to the new, but unknown, optimum position now have a greater probability of survival and growth'; and: 'If these conditions last "very long" the dominant firms will be different ones from those which prevailed or would have prevailed under other conditions.'
6. The last section of Chapter 7 discusses some empirical work which suggests that the aggregate affect of increased uncertainty (reduced predictability) is not value enhancing. This doesn't necessarily show that the aggregate line (line B in Figure 5.1) is declining with reducing predictability, because 'uncertainty' in this work does not separate out exogenous from endogenous causes. Nevertheless, it does suggest that *increased* uncertainty for the economy as a whole is not value-enhancing.
7. This 'rational expectations' equilibrium (one allowing physical change and physical increases in output) is different to the notions of general equilibrium discussed and criticized by (for example) Mises (1966) and Hayek (1941), who were primarily focused on constant real goods and real output rather than constant *value*. Nevertheless, an equilibrium that does not allow changes in value is also an equilibrium that has no scope for entrepreneurship. What is the point of inventing something new if it is to be totally anticipated by the market and entrepreneurial profits fully discounted beforehand?
8. Of course, the occurrence of such an event might cause actors to revise their subjective valuation of the likelihood of such chance events, and any new such valuation may result in changes in the style of projects considered. Shackle considered this style of problem and suggested that 'when an event with high potential surprise has occurred, forcing a revaluation of the uncertainty situation, the effect will not take place all at once but only after an interval of time during which almost every possibility is assigned a low potential

surprise' (Shackle, 1949, 73–5). Since styles of investment and sectors of the economy are influenced to a different degree by chance events, some revision might occur here, too, but changes of this nature are excluded from this model by the assumption of true randomness independent of the perception of the actor.

9. These risks are diversifiable. But since we don't live in a world of complete markets the development of a market for diversification of this risk (where no such market existed previously) *would* represent a change in economic structure of projects subject to this sort of risk.

10. This case (of some underlying distribution 'out there' waiting to be discovered) was extensively examined by Stigler (1961).

6. Intertemporal valuation

This chapter sets out the first part of the theoretical development in the book: a model of individual choice under uncertainty.

This model eschews any *simultaneous* weighting of high and low utility outcomes prior to choice. It postulates and builds the theory to support a process of value formation based on *sequential* assessment of choice attributes against a rank-ordered set of preferences that the actor is seeking to satisfy.

The model pertains to any choice situation. Nevertheless, in most choice situations it yields results no different to the standard neoclassical models. Differences *are* significant in the case of large decisions, where individual decision-makers have a high personal stake in the correctness of the outcome. Decision-making processes of this nature take place over time. During this time, knowledge about each alternative changes. Priorities for information gathering through the process, and for evaluation of alternatives, are governed by the actor's perception of the likely outcomes and how this perception changes through the process.

The model is conceptually simple and builds on two well-recognized but usually overlooked aspects of choice: value formation in the mind of an actor, and how individual preferences come to influence this value when uncertainty is present.

The economics literature is hardly lacking in models of rational choice, but few models (with the notable exception of Shackle's model expounded in Chapter 4) address the 'large decision' issue. Yet this 'large decision' issue is surely the fundamental one. Ordinary consumer choice is a sub-set of the large decision problem wherein certain aspects can be overlooked.

The chapter is arranged in three sections. The first reframes the decision problem that the book aims to address. It paints a scenario of capital investment choice in a corporate context, where risk-averse actors have the objective to maximize shareholder value. 'Choice' is always an individual act, and this section also introduces a translation mechanism from shareholder value into utility in the mind of the decision-maker.

Changes in capital value are the *sine qua non* of entrepreneurial expectations, and these valuations are examined in the second section of the chapter (pp. 62–72).

The third section (pp. 72–7) examines and applies uncertainty to the model of intertemporal valuation from a strictly economic, opportunity-cost viewpoint. It recognizes that any event planned to come to fruition in the future is subject to more uncertainty than the same event not so temporally distant. Also, even *certain* outcomes result in uncertain utility perceived from a distance if the actor can pursue other opportunities in the intervening period and these opportunities also offer utility.

ECONOMIC BASIS OF RATIONAL CAPITAL INVESTMENT DECISIONS

Choice situations analysed in this model are ones where the actor has a high personal stake in the correctness of the outcome. There is scope for an outcome that leaves the actor worse off, in his or her own subjective *ex ante* view, than he or she might be if some alternative path (including the status quo) were followed. This contrasts with ordinary consumer choice where the selection of one alternative does not evidently preclude the next most favoured alternative at some later time. In large decision choice the (opportunity) cost is starkly evident. Something important to the actor is being put 'at risk'.

It is useful in the first instance to characterize the decision-maker in this model as an entrepreneur or a speculator, as opposed to an engineer in the sense of Mises (1966). Using this characterization, an engineer '[knows] everything that is needed for a technologically satisfactory solution', and '[as] far as some fringes of uncertainty are left in his power to control, he tries to eliminate them by taking safety margins'. Alternatively, '[in] the real world acting man is faced with the fact that there are fellow men acting on their own behalf as he himself acts. The necessity to adjust his actions to other people's actions makes him a speculator for whom success and failure depend on his greater or lesser ability to understand the future. Every action is speculation' (Mises, 1966, 112, 113).

Any capital investment choice will involve elements of both of these ideal-type characterizations. Choice alternatives will be structured to 'engineer' as many elements of uncertainty as economically viable so to do. The reduction of uncertainty to effective certainty by combining 'a sufficient number of cases', as referred to by Knight (1921), is one such mechanism. Nevertheless, some residual uncertainty will remain.

This residual uncertainty is one of the undesirable attributes associated with the choice. Responsibility for balancing undesirable attributes with desirable attributes in the choice decision falls to residual claimants whose own future is at least partially aligned with the success or failure of the venture under consideration.

It is also useful in the second instance to recognize that *every* choice is a choice between the *complete future opportunity set* if one path into the future is followed, compared to the complete future opportunity set if some alternative path into the future, perhaps the status quo, is followed. However, elements of the future that are common to all alternatives do not need to enter the evaluation: 'Each choosable course of action must be linked with some imagined sequels, or some combination of imagined sequels, which belong to this course alone' (Shackle, 1983).

Again paraphrasing Shackle, the business of choice of action is conceived to proceed in three phases:

- The first phase is imagination. It is 'the origination of various inceptive modes of use of the chooser's array of means of action, and the conceiving, for each such mode, a skein of rival imagined sequels' (Shackle, 1983, 64).

- The second phase is that of critical examination. 'The sequels which, in such time as his deadline or some exterior signal allows him, the chooser has invented for any one mode, must be tested for possibility. The path of each must be scanned for obstacles. Those sequels which emerge unscathed are the basis of the claim of the particular course of action or mode of inceptive use of resources to be the chosen one' (ibid.).

- The third phase is that of valuation.

The conceptual sub-division of the choice problem into the above three phases is appropriate for this stage of the book. Nevertheless, it is useful here to foreshadow the discussion in Chapter 8 demonstrating that this sub-division does not follow such a strict, linear, step-wise progression. Indeed, the business of choice normally starts from Shackle's third phase, because it is only an 'unsatisfactory' valuation of some perceived default alternative that gives rise to the first phase of imagination concerning other possibilities. The process is an iterative one, traversed many times. Moreover, it may logically be commenced at any of the three steps.

The following sub-section presents an actual though exceptional case study illustrating capital investment choice where many elements of the uncertainty could not be turned into effective certainty via market mechanisms. The subsequent sub-section draws from this example to highlight how desirable and undesirable attributes of each capital investment choice are understood in a way that ultimately allows them to be valued, at least comparatively. This section essentially addresses Shackle's third phase. Some comparative examples from cross-disciplinary literature that lend support to this decision model are described in the third sub-section (p. 59).

Capital Investment Under Uncertainty: An Example

This case study involves the potential investment in a major mining venture in a third world country recently emerged from communist rule. The company involved in the proposed venture, a large multinational corporation listed on the New York Stock Exchange, is experienced in operating mines in the less-developed world. A team of mine planning professionals examined the project. The plan was presented in a 'base case' format – engineered to reduce as many risks as possible through forward sales of product, insurance for certain political and weather-related risks, and conservative project design. For this company, capital investments in the order of $500 million or more are routine.

The proposed venture,[1] involving capital expenditure of $100 million, showed an internal rate of return of over 80 per cent and a net present value of $250 million when all cash flows were discounted at the expected 20 per cent long-term cost of capital for such projects. Following the announcement of such a project, a fully informed market should reasonably have revalued stock in the corporation upward by $250 million.

Nevertheless, the project was not proceeded with – at least in this first-round evaluation. The difficulty in such a decision is that the 'market' is not fully informed. Indeed, for this style of decision the market could never be fully informed since the existence of such an opportunity offering above-market returns is itself predicated on less-than-full market knowledge. Without some non-replicable proprietary input, opportunities for such returns would be competed away by a fully informed market until the internal rate of return did equate to the long-term cost of capital.

In this particular project, unique mining reserves were available within a limited time frame under option but the take-up of the option was contingent on commitment to develop. Even after take-up of the option, when property rights to the resource become the unique input that provides protection from competition, full information cannot be made available. The faithful disclosure of expected profitability itself risks undermining the soundness of the property rights. In a country with no history of respect for such rights the spectrum of value associated with potential expedient redefinition of property rights translates into substantial uncertainty in the overall project return. In a corporate (public company) environment there is no mechanism to inform the owners of the corporation without also informing competitors and others, and the risk by so doing constitutes a potential loss in value exceeding the loss in value associated with a higher short-term cost of capital.

Decision-makers faithfully acting on behalf of shareholders in this style of decision therefore have an incentive for strategic misinformation, until such time as the actual profitability of the project becomes known through performance alone. Thus feedback from third-party sources (stock market analysts, and changes in stock price following progressive announcements to the market) did not and could not form a useful foil to test the correctness of choices.

The decision to proceed had (has) to be made on the strength of privately held valuation alone. In this case, the announcement of such a project with no prior warning would probably have resulted in a *decrease* in the stock price rather than an increase. Of course, once the commitment is made and the property rights secured, there is scope for bringing in joint-venture parties to reduce the firm's exposure, but this can only be done *ex post*. The initial decision has to incorporate the director's own subjective judgement as to the likely terms of such risk sharing.

This illustrates one of the key differences between choices typically analysed in the subjective expected utility model, and the large decision choice problem. Arrow (1958) draws the major line of distinction (between what he sees as the two schools of thought) by the applicability of the law of large numbers. Choice in the former is between alternatives that are part of a large set whose uncertainty characteristics can be defined and can be understood in aggregate terms. Alternatively, the '[second school of thought] stresses the sequential nature of many choice situations; choices are frequently extended in time, with a choice at one stage having an effect on choices at a later stage', and 'a choice at period 1 should rationally take account of the possibility that a second decision will be made in period 2. Thus the proper policy within a firm must consist of a *strategy* rather than a single decision' (Arrow, 1958, 61). The recognition that the value of such choices is dependent, at least in part, on future decisions whose input conditions are influenced by the path chosen is the basis of Knight's original characterization of 'uncertainty' as being non-definable in probabilistic terms, and also in the work of Shackle for similar reasons.

Ultimately, such decisions to proceed or not to proceed are rationally arrived at through:

• judgement of what the 'true' long-term value will be in the market place when the market *is* relatively well informed, how this value compares to the private value held now, and the expectation of how such private value too is likely to change with new information; and

• the opportunity cost; alternative ways to proceed with the same physical project, as well as other physical projects, and how these alternatives compare to the project as currently presented in terms of market value, private value and expected changes in value.

These criteria, though always derived in part from quantitative analysis, are subjective judgements based on anticipated future value.

In the case under study, the decision to proceed is a commitment to direct $100 million of the corporation's resources into a project that will probably then be valued at perhaps negative $50 million. Alternative investments are possible that will yield short-term increases in the market value substantially greater than this. The expected negative shareholder value in the short term is the most evident undesirable attribute of the proposed course of action. Offsetting this undesirable attribute is the potential for long-term shareholder value of $250 million, achievable after market-measurable proof that the expected future events have or will materialize in accordance with the plan.

Shareholder Value and Individual Utility

The example in the previous section illustrates that:

- at the moment of choice, entrepreneurial gains or potentially high profits cannot be used for risk minimization or to minimize the scope for losses except in an expectational sense. 'Value' in the mind of the actor cannot abstract from the full impact of the scope for low utility results;

- even in a corporate environment so-called objective rules provide only limited assistance to individual decision-makers involved in capital investment choice. The most important elements that influence risk – the decisions *ex post* that allow risk to be minimized yet still allow entrepreneurial profits to be sustained – cannot be quantified *ex ante*.

The value of the project under consideration – the balance of desirable and undesirable attributes of the choice – must ultimately be judged in a utility dimension, in the mind of the decision-maker. This value must then be compared to the cost, that is, the value, again assessed by this balance of desirable and undesirable attributes, of the most attractive alternative foregone.[2]

How then do decision-makers rationally assess these desirable and undesirable attributes that are the foundation of value in their minds?

This assessment is not done, and arguably *cannot* be done, independently of choice. For choice, the assessment of value only has to include elements that differ between choice alternatives, whereas any assessment independent of choice must include *anything* that contributes to an actor's envisaged future utility or disutility.

The expected utility model makes the assumption that value (utility) is arrived at by a *simultaneous* process of weighting the utilities associated with the spectrum of attributes (from undesirable to desirable) of the choice alternatives. This model was discussed in Chapter 4. Because utility in this model is independent of choice it has the above-mentioned failing that, to be meaningful, it has to include the totality of anything that makes up a person's utility for the time being. The Shackelian model, also discussed in Chapter 4, explicitly separates attributes that might lead to surprise from those that would not lead to surprise, but likewise assumes a process where the undesirable attributes are *simultaneously* balanced against the desirable.

For human action any assessment of value is only meaningful within a choice context, because only within such a context will 'change' – the value of which is the object of assessment – ensue. Further, in this context elements common to (and therefore unnecessary for differentiation between) the alternatives under consideration can be excluded. Any assessment of value independent of choice is inconsistent with the model of man as *Homo economicus*. Man as *Homo economicus* has no rational reason to deploy resources (time spent thinking) on anything that is irrelevant to action.

How then might an actor following the *Homo economicus* model come to conceive of value? In simple situations the attributes that constitute value in any intended course of action are clear. This is also the case where repetition and continual learning takes place. Such a situation characterizes most consumer choice. The value of more complicated alternatives is much harder to appreciate. The less frequently that relevant attributes receive consideration, the less evident will be the value attaching to them. It takes time and energy to engage in the valuation process. Before embarking upon any valuation process actors must conceive that resources directed into this process will return value to them that exceeds the value they can obtain by directing their time and energy resources elsewhere. Thus any valuation process must start with this conception of self cost: the value an actor can obtain by directing his or her time and energy elsewhere – presumably into some routine or already-understood activity. It follows that:

1. Potential situations will receive scant contemplation unless and until there is scope for change that results in the implied changes in value. 'Value' is a vacuous concept outside of change, and in the realm of human *action* change means choice.[3]

2. In choice alternatives the most important characteristics can rarely be assimilated easily or costlessly. This implies a ranking mechanism for those characteristics which, in the mind of the actor, most influence choice. Choice must be based on the *difference* in value between available alternatives. Actors will consider *first* those attributes which constitute value in some higher level rank ordering sense and continue until the expected difference in value from further consideration is less than the cost of assimilation.

3. Saying that an actor will choose to assess value between alternatives in accordance with a value-based rank ordering rule is bordering on a tautology. The contradiction is avoided because the process is a

sequential one, with the starting point being some decision-independent higher order concept of value. This 'higher order' value derives from the *class* of alternatives of which all those under study are a part.[4]

4. If some element of uncertainty (such as the probability of a meteorite strike) has an effect on the value of all alternatives equally, including status quo alternatives, then no matter how important or how likely such an occurrence is, it does not influence choice and its value remains essentially unassessed.

5. Comparative utility maximization is a term for this process. It proceeds until the utility *differences* between choices are insufficiently great that the expected change (gain) in utility from further consideration is less than the self cost. But it is a sequential, not a simultaneous process. Desirable attributes (such as the potential to make super-profits) will not come into the actor's consideration until after more important requirements (for example, minimum risk to life and limb) are satisfied, at least in an expectational sense.

Under conditions of uncertainty, alternatives that have an attractive *expected* outcome – if all potential outcomes could somehow be *simultaneously* considered – may fail to pass the conceptual filter associated with the satisfaction of more important requirements. In the presence of perfect markets, the potential to make super-profits may well be exchangeable to offset the risk of sub-par outcomes, but the decision environment in this model is one where such markets do not and cannot exist at the time of decision. In the absence of these market mechanisms or some other alternative that allows internal offsetting of outcomes on either tail of the subjective distribution, the 'value' of outcomes that conceptually offer high utility will be excluded from the subjective assessment of value.

Comparative Examples

Before proceeding to extend this value-formation model to intertemporal choice, it is useful to highlight some similarities between the conclusions and characteristics set out above and models of choice drawn from diverse sources in the literature.

Keynesians, or Post-Keynesians (Davidson, 1991), following Keynes, have developed tools for comprehending real world behaviour under uncertainty separate from the probability distributions commonly used by neoclassical economists. From this Post-Keynesian perspective, 'decision makers either avoid choosing between "real" alternatives [retreat to liquidity] because they "haven't got a clue" about the future, or follow their "animal spirits" for positive investment action in a "damn the torpedoes, full speed ahead" approach' (ibid., 130). Such observed demands for liquidity and/or blind promotion of investment are features of the Keynesian macroeconomic world, yet are 'irrational' from the standpoint of the expected utility model.

If investments are to have some 'utility' independent of choice as presupposed by the expected utility model, then a charge of irrationality is the logical conclusion from this perspective. But from the choice-centred or opportunity cost perspective of the temporal utility model, this Post-Keynesian characterization is entirely rational. From this perspective, actors can readily proceed with capital investment choice given *dramatic* shortcomings in knowledge so long as they are convinced that the change in value associated with the missing knowledge impacts all alternatives equally.

A similar argument can apply to the much-touted Keynesian 'animal spirits' concept.[5] 'Animal spirits' are synonymous with survival. Survival as the primary motivating force for action is inconsistent with the neoclassical 'utility maximizing' man. On the other hand, the model set out in this and subsequent chapters provides for rank ordering of preferences, and 'survival' (in advanced Western societies, synonymous with 'job security' for most people) is arguably ranked very highly on this scale. Satisfaction of at least some minimal level of survival in this model is thus a precursor to utility *maximization*. Utility maximization – the resolution or satisfaction in an expectational sense of a set of preferences representing lower marginal utility – may not enter the equation if the 'survival' precursor step remains unsatisfied. Given substantial uncertainty in investment choice, and much less or *no* uncertainty associated with investment in cash, then the temporal utility model can readily accommodate such a result. Cash is a viable investment so long as the actor values the expected returns from delayed projects (offering lesser expected uncertainty) more highly than the same project proceeded with sooner. The return on cash in the intervening period is not predicated on the interest earned – at least, not solely – but on the increased value of the (more certain) delayed project.

The procedural rationality issue raised by Simon (1986) and introduced in Chapter 4 may be resolved similarly. Whilst on the surface the limited knowledge and computational power that Simon assigns to his decision-maker *does* severely check his or her ability to comprehend uncertainty, when framed within the temporal utility model, much of the uncertainty disappears. Even *dramatic* shortcomings in knowledge do not need to be assimilated so long as the actor is convinced that the value or loss in value associated with the missing knowledge affects all alternatives equally. Hence the process of *decision* under this model is potentially a far easier task than the process (as thought necessary) of first assigning 'utilities' to uncertain choices *and then* comparing them.[6]

Finally, the notion that value deriving from both undesirable and desirable attributes (subjective risk, expected return) might be arrived at in some sequential or non-contemporaneous way rather than via some *simultaneous* transformation function as implied by the von Neumann and Morgenstern model receives considerable support in cross-disciplinary literature. Hayek (1967) examined rule-guided action in this context. Actors in Hayek's model are not considering all factors simultaneously, but are first considering just 'certain classes of facts': these facts *alone* eliminating whole classes of activity from the choice set.

Hayek in this and other works (for example, Hayek, 1952) also invokes psychological support for a number of propositions, including the difficulty in discerning the logical order of processes taking place in the human mind. What is important here is whether the factors constituting utility are evaluated *simultaneously* within the mind, or whether the factors are considered in some sequential way. He notes: '[as] K.S. Lashley has pointed out, "spacial and temporal order thus appear to be almost completely interchangeable in cerebral action".' (Hayek, 1967, 49). This suggests that value formulation following some sequential process may be completely consistent with human behaviour without the subject being aware of it, or with the subject even incorrectly perceiving the process to be a simultaneous one.

Drawing from prospect theory, Tversky and Kahneman (1986) highlight a choice process in two phases, where the preliminary analysis in the first phase frames the decision for the second (evaluation) phase. This first phase aims to eliminate certain choices from consideration, and is primarily controlled by the 'norms, habits, and expectancies of the decision maker' (ibid., 73). Of relevance here is the sequential nature of the process, that only certain characteristics of the choice are considered in the earlier phases of the process, and that the benchmark for such comparison is grounded in pre-existing 'norms, habits, and expectancies' of the actor.

Ainslie (1992, 199) also contrasts economic models of choice with models that incorporate strategic influences:

> Utilitarian theories heretofore have depicted choice-making organisms as analog computers, weighing the values of alternative rewards against each other and reaching a quantitative solution. However, ... the more important tasks facing at least some organisms are digital tasks: People must construct sets of categorical requirements that will permit some kinds of weightings but not others. Furthermore, a person must use a combination of these two somewhat incompatible modes of analyzing his options. A simple weighing of preferences will leave a person open to temporary changes of preference. On the other hand, a decision-making process that does not respond to weights, but only to categories, will have difficulty in distinguishing between trivial and vital incentives.

Individual solutions to the awkward problem of mixing these modes may constitute a large component of people's character styles.

DEFINING CHARACTERISTICS OF ENTREPRENEURIAL CHOICE

Chapter 3 introduced entrepreneurship and expounded the view that *the* defining characteristic of entrepreneurial choice is imagination and, derived from this, the (superior) ability to envisage the future. This section analyses how value in an intertemporal sense follows from this entrepreneurial vision. Under this model entrepreneurial vision affects choice in four ways:

1. to recognize differences between private valuation of future events and likely market valuation of such events;

2. to translate value attaching to things that are readily valued in the market (consumer goods and the like) faithfully, or *more* faithfully, into value associated with capital goods earlier in the chain of production in the absence of market mechanisms;

3. to envisage alternative futures, or a larger range of alternative futures; and

4. to recognize and develop mechanisms for the management of obstacles, both internal and external, that might inhibit fulfilment of rationally determined choices.

Any of these characteristics can lead to changes in the value of capital beyond evident market-determined values. Figure 6.1 shows a model, similar to Ainslie (1992), that illustrates changes in value over time. It shows value (or 'utility') on the vertical axis, and time on the horizontal axis. With an observer positioned at any point in time (say, T_0) the value attaching to two events, labelled A and B occurring at T_1 and T_2 respectively is shown by the lines.

The upper two lines illustrate exponential discount functions associated with well-developed markets under the assumption of widespread knowledge of these events. The lower two lines illustrate discount functions following a hyperbolic form which, according to Ainslie (1992) and others,[7] are associated with human (and *animal)* preference behaviour when only private knowledge of the events is considered. This hyperbolic form of time-based preference is referred to as the *matching law.*

Whilst Ainslie's model was based almost entirely on empirical work of a *psychological* nature there are grounds for support for this, or a model which yields similar results, using *economically* based behavioural assumptions. The development of this economic model is set out below (p. 72). Whilst the

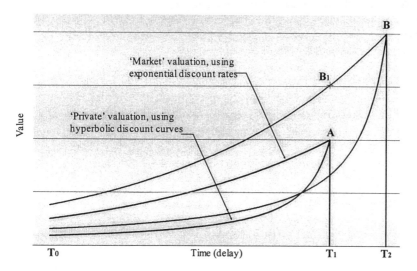

Figure 6.1: Private and 'market' value through time

economic model differs from the Ainslie model, the outcomes are not materially different, hence for simplicity the balance of this section follows a functional form similar to the one used by Ainslie.

In this model private valuation functions, prior to the event coming to fruition, are uninfluenced by and independent of the market valuation. The assumption is that there are no external market valuations of A or B until T_1 and T_2 respectively. Actors form their assessments of value only on some intrinsic characteristic or on their expectation of what the market price will be when the event comes to fruition.

Using *exponential* discount functions, the lines extending in time towards T_0 from the two temporally separated events (event B at time T_2 and event A at time T_1) do not cross. Relative valuations in a rank-order sense remain unchanged through time. With no additional information preferences do not change as the events get closer. If the exponential valuation line from B is rated more highly than the exponential value from A at time T_1, then it remains more highly rated throughout.

Using *hyperbolic* discount functions for private valuation, the relative valuation of the two temporally separated events changes through time. Preferences change to favour the earlier alternative as it looms nearer, even in the absence of additional information.

This model provides insight into the choice problem. At time T_0 an actor may have to make an irrevocable commitment towards alternative A or alternative B. If three choices are available, perhaps one will be abandoned.

Even without irrevocable commitments, the actor's valuation of each alternative at time T_0 is still important, because it forms part of a path-dependent decision process. For example, perhaps more information on both alternatives is required in order to make a subsequent choice, and this early valuation determines how much and what prioritization should be put on the resources necessary to obtain this additional information. Either way, the *privately held* valuation influences choice.

If perfect market conditions applied, alternative B would be favoured over alternative A. How can an actor rationally make a choice in favour of alternative B at a time (prior to T_1) when there are no external market valuations? The Ainslie model highlights three of the difficulties:

1. *Change in preference order* Lines representing exponentially derived valuations never cross. Lines representing hyperbolic functions do not *necessarily* cross, but if they do they give rise to changes in preference and to strategic behaviour. This property was analysed by Ainslie and is also evident in the economic model. It provides important explanatory support for stability or instability of choice and for the association between entrepreneurship and risk-taking.

2. *Consistency in preference* As long as the time delay is sufficient, rank ordering of two alternatives in the Ainslie model will be consistent with rank ordering in the exponential model. Thus private valuations, at least in a rank-ordering sense, are consistent with market valuations. This characteristic also applies to the economic model.

3. *Private valuations undervalue all alternatives* compared to market-based values. This is certainly the case for small values of the time delay in the Ainslie model, and can always be guaranteed in the economic model. The importance of this property is in providing incentives for entrepreneurship – to nurture otherwise undervalued projects and capture the change in value as they are brought into the domain of market-based valuation.

The model will now be used to examine the four characteristics of entrepreneurship noted on page 62. For ease of illustration the choice will be characterized thus: Event A represents a potentially higher dividend with more immediate beneficial results (valued V_A at time T_1). Event B is the potential return from investment of the money otherwise payable out via the dividend. A decision to make the investment is a decision to forego the immediate benefits of the dividend in favour of the expected future benefits.

Difference Between Private and Likely Market Value

In the presence of full and complete markets, the two exponential discount lines extending back from times T_2 and T_1 to T_0 exist. Decisions in such a market are easy at any time. At time T_1 the value of the capital investment V_{B_1} exceeds the value of the highest-ranked alternative foregone V_A.

Similarly, where there are no other alternatives the decision to pursue the proposed capital investment choice at time T_0 is relatively unambiguous. At time T_0 the private value of either alternative may be low, but the choice unambiguously favours alternative B. The present value of the return from the investment (based on Ainslie's hyperbolic rates) exceeds the present value of the next best use of the investment funds.

In this model actors with such temporal preferences would not normally *commit* to alternative B at time T_0. Given its availability in a suitable form, a *market-based* alternative coming to fruition at time T_1 is valued in the mind of the actor higher than the non-market-based alternatives under consideration.

This illustrates the first entrepreneurial characteristic from page 62: an entrepreneur's ability to reconcile the private valuation of future events and the likely market valuation of such events. Figure 6.2 demonstrates this problem.

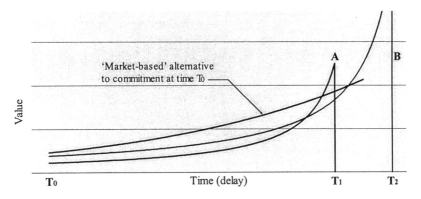

Figure 6.2: Initial choice: Difference between private and market value

Assume for a start that there is a market-based alternative which also comes to fruition at T_1 but that has a value of just three-quarters of V_A at T_1. At time T_0 this alternative may be valued much higher than either alternative A or B. To decide at T_0 to follow the path of private value an actor requires more than just some instantaneously held concept of value. He or she must consider, *inter alia*, that:

- The future value of market-based events is, for all practical purposes, established by its current market value. Conversely, a non-market event valued in a private way is not so constrained. The fact that a decision regarding the non-market path is *not* required is to guarantee such an outcome, because any internally held value will be lacking many characteristics that only have to be understood nearer the moment of choice. To paraphrase Arrow (1958, 61) an actor's private formulation of value must consider 'the relation between the action taken at any time point in the future and the information available *at that time*, though not available at the time at which the initial decision is made' (emphasis added).

- Future events privately conceived, imagined, and understood more vividly and more thoroughly will be valued in the mind of the actor more highly than events that are less thoroughly envisaged. In contrast, market-based events have 'value' that is underpinned by external factors and that is less subject to this visionary constraint. More strongly held entrepreneurial vision means higher private value. Thus an entrepreneur with this visionary attribute is less subject to distraction from obvious market-based alternatives than is an actor with less developed capabilities in this area.

- Choosing the private value path at T_0 is not the same as choosing alternative B over alternative A at T_0. It is a decision regarding expenditure of resources on information in anticipation of such a (subsequent) choice. However, in multiple choice it may be an actual decision to *exclude* one or more alternatives. If a binding decision were necessary at T_0, neither alternative B nor alternative A would rank ahead of the market-based alternative since choice is based on private values held at the moment of choice.

Value Within the Structure of Production

The second entrepreneurial characteristic – to translate value attaching to market goods (consumer products and the like) faithfully, or *more* faithfully, into value associated with capital goods earlier in the chain of production – is subject to the same or similar discounting and 'comparison to market' as the intertemporal valuation described in the previous section.

The value of a copper mine, at least as it is dependent on the value of copper, can be readily understood in an established market because the lengthy chain of production from copper concentrate, blister copper, copper wire-bar and so on to consumer goods made of copper is also well understood. In such a well understood industry, each link in the chain of production supplies a market associated directly with that product, but the value of these intermediate markets is a derivative of the end market satisfying consumption demand. Even thinly traded intermediate markets can be relied upon for consistent valuation because the well understood structure of production facilitates arbitrage across intermediate markets in the chain.

The situation is different for capital investments whose value is dependent on outputs directed into less well understood lengthy chains of production. Capital investments of this nature – extending the market-based structure of production – are an important class of new capital investment activity.

An example drawn from Smith (1776) illustrates the importance of this for understanding capital value in a modern context. Attributing the 'Wealth of Nations' to the division of labour, Smith explained the higher productivity of such a system as stemming from, *inter alia*, the 'improvement of the dexterity of the workman' and 'how much labour is facilitated and abridged by the application of proper machinery' (Smith, [1776] 1976, 17–19). New capital (physical, and human) in the Smithian model increasing the division of labour takes over the role hitherto undertaken within some less-distinct process within the firm.

If the physical capital that brings about these productivity improvements already exists in some other application, then the value of it in this new application presents no difficulty. But a market-based mechanism to value capital associated with increasing specialization would be the exception rather than the norm. Stigler (1951) also uses this example from Smith and partitions a firm 'not among the markets in which it buys inputs but among the functions or processes which constitute the scope of its activity', that is, activities that are internal to the firm and for which no separate market pricing currently exists.

Assume that this is the case, and that a particular function or process engages a firms resources for, say, just one-fifth of the time. Despite poor capital utilization this particular function or process is performed within the firm because there is no alternative mechanism for its fulfilment. Now assume that there are five such firms similarly engaged. An entrepreneurial opportunity exists to make a new capital investment aimed at outsourcing this particular process or function on behalf of all five firms and extending the structure of production.

The recognition of such a situation is the precursor to what Buchanan (1994) highlights as the primary determinant of this productivity gain in an economy: the extension in input specialization. An entrepreneur who understands the process has an opportunity to specialize in the production of only this factor, turning it from an internally produced good into a market good. The productivity gains associated with a five-fold increase in production rate, replacing a production activity hitherto undertaken in five separate environments, provide the economic incentives to invest in the resources necessary to bring it about. In an extension of the example shown in Chapter 9, a five-fold increase in production yields a potential 37 per cent decline in cost. Prior to such an increase in specialization coming about there is no market price for the good being produced.

An ill-informed market can only infer the contribution of this particular input to the cost of production of the overall product of which it is a part. To be sure, the price or expected market price is bounded on one side by the existing cost of production, and on the other by the competitive price that would just bring forth the new investment. In the example quoted, a five-fold output change suggests a market price anywhere from the existing cost of production to a figure 37 per cent less than this. Even this range may be understated since it does not consider increases in demand in the end product if *its* price changes following reduction in input cost.

The differential assessment of how these gains are distributed leaves scope for large discrepancies between an entrepreneur's *ex ante* assessment and the market's assessment of capital value *ex post*. Indeed, even the existing (internal) cost of production is unlikely to be known with much precision, as is the cost of production for the new process.

The entrepreneurial elements associated with such capital investments are overlooked by many authors. Arrow (1979) also comments on the same example and draws attention to Smith's third characteristic: that 'a worker concentrating on a limited set of tasks may see a way of developing machines for handling them'. Arrow plays down the importance of individual actors reconciling private value with expected market value as a precursor to this style of choice, noting that '[for modern society] we depend today for our new machines on the "speculators and philosophers" of whom Smith thought little'. Arrow's observation is only a partial escape from the problem. In the absence of an established market, much of the knowledge that 'speculators and philosophers' rely upon for extending the structure of production and judging the value of the end product must come from 'workers' currently engaged in this existing activity. Human capital is integrally linked to entrepreneurial decision-making.

From a capital value viewpoint Arrow also overlooks the contribution that 'workers' make towards what Romer (1990) calls the defining characteristic of technology: the instructions, or the *recipe*, for turning the raw materials into other economic goods. The quintessential 'recipe' is simply the *recognition of the idea* – an input that is easily replicable and non-rivalrous. Investments capitalizing on this input are very sensitive to how quickly a competitor can enter the market, and returns are sensitive to the length of time that (high) profits can be sustained. Thus the present value of any capital investment cannot (initially, at least) be built on any reliable market measure, and value is dependent on human characteristics subject to huge differences between private and market valuation.

Further, it is the human capital of existing workers that is most at risk with the introduction of new technology. A new business aiming to sell its product to the five competitor firms has to convince these firms to stop doing something that they now do internally. It has to convince them to rely thereafter on market-based supply. *Individuals* within these firms who have to be convinced are likely to be the same ones whose human capital investment in these same processes will henceforth be written off. The defence of this human capital is itself a significant factor in the success or otherwise of dislodging internal production processes in favour of externally supplied products. None of this can be understood *ex ante* except in a subjective way.

Value Within the Emerging Market Order

The third characteristic of entrepreneurship has to do with assimilation of completely new ideas. It has to do with the ability, or superior ability, of entrepreneurs to envisage alternative futures, or a larger range of alternative futures. This sub-section takes up the uncertainty aspects first introduced in Chapter 5 (pp. 46–50) and extends the steps set out in that section.

Any new investment whose value in a market-based sense is to materialize in the future will be valued in the present according to how consistently it fits into or can adapt to the environment at the time. Five elements of entrepreneurship in how this envisaged future may be understood or accommodated have been identified:

1. The influence that is likely to have an impact upon future value has to be understood (discerned) as either a random event independent of human influences, or dependent in some way on human influences.
2. Random influences may be beyond human control but must still be understood both in terms of their stochastic characteristics and whether these characteristics are changing through time.
3. Random influences do not affect each alternative equally. The differential impact must be assessed. Alternatives which are less sensitive to such influences must be envisaged, and the increased value of the reduced sensitivity must be compared to value changes elsewhere.

Influences that affect future value from conceptually knowable sources, that is, derived from action by *other* market participants, must be recognized. These influences fall into two categories – detached and strategic:

4. Other market participants introduce pecuniary externalities. They unwittingly impose costs, and their actions confer unsought benefits. As with the random influences, these detached influences do not affect each alternative equally. The differential impact must be assessed. Alternatives which are less sensitive to such influences must be envisaged, and the increased value of the reduced sensitivity must be compared to any value changes elsewhere.

5. Value is also influenced through strategic action – by other market participants adapting their own actions and deliberately enhancing or undermining the likely success of the venture. Strategic influences are also associated with the fulfilment of choices by an actor him- or herself (or, in the corporate environment, the institutions). These strategic influences do not affect each alternative equally. The differential impact must be assessed. Alternatives which are less sensitive to such influences must be envisaged, and the increased value of the reduced sensitivity must be compared to any value changes elsewhere.

The scope for *loss in value* – that is, the entrepreneurial or risk element of capital – was foreshadowed in Chapter 2 as being the primary determinant complicating capital investment choice. Nowhere is this characteristic more evident than in the five items above.

If, in the event of failure, there is scope for resources to be redirected elsewhere in a way that yields almost as much value, then the value that is 'at risk' is reduced even if the 'cost' (in the accounting sense) is increased. This ability to envisage alternatives that result in lower costs in an economic sense but superficially similar or even higher costs in an accounting sense is arguably the primary distinguishing characteristic of entrepreneurship.[8]

Recognition of Strategic Influences

The fourth characteristic of entrepreneurship – mechanisms for the management of obstacles that might inhibit fulfilment of rationally determined choices – is the one that gains most elucidation from the Ainslie model. This model explicitly recognizes that there is scope for actors to change their minds independent of choice-specific information. Entrepreneurs are more alert to this possibility.

The first of these issues relating to internal strategic behaviour was introduced though not highlighted on page 66 and illustrated in Figure 6.2. Given the availability of a *market-based* alternative with less (expected) value but less uncertainty than either of the *private* alternatives, decisions under the pure 'private value' model favour the market-based alternative. Only when alternative A is impending (near to time T_1) does its private value exceed the value attaching to the market-based alternative. A delay – hesitation in commitment, procrastination (so called) – serves to give the private valued alternatives the greatest chance of success against the obvious (less uncertain) but fundamentally lower value market options. Unfortunately, if the private valued alternatives are temporally distinct, then the hesitancy does not necessarily guarantee that the correct private valued alternative is chosen. Figure 6.3 demonstrates the problem.

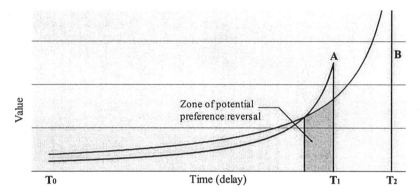

Figure 6.3: Private value preference reversal

Using the private discount functions, alternative B is preferred over alternative A when both alternatives are some time into the future (at T_0, say). Close to T_1 the relative valuation changes. By this time there is almost no uncertainty associated with alternative A, whereas alternative B, yet to materialize in the future, is still subject to considerable uncertainty. The clarity with which alternative A is viewed obscures the less clear but fundamentally greater value of the other option.

There is a parallel in capital investment choice having to do with risk and return. For any given project, the fundamental characteristics that underpin the expected return are typically well understood and the addition of more information rarely changes these fundamentals. In Figure 6.3 the height of the lines at time T_1 and T_2 represents this expected return which can be estimated quite well a long time in advance. Detailed planning of large capital projects changes the expected return on investment very little. Its major impact is on the understanding of uncertainties.

Assessed in advance, when little knowledge is available, *both* alternatives exhibit lots of uncertainty. Therefore the characteristic that most differentiates alternatives when assessed a long time in advance is the expected return. When one alternative is much better understood (alternative

A immediately prior to T_1) the characteristic that most differentiates alternatives is no longer the expected return, but the uncertainty.

The bias in intertemporal choice comes from this uncertainty. Temporally distinct choices cannot be compared in some unbiased way, because the alternative whose value materializes sooner will *ceteris paribus* always be less uncertain. A compensating mechanism must allow for some expectation of what the uncertainty associated with the temporally more distant choice will be when it materializes.

An alternative approach is the strategic issue sketched by Ainslie. Actors who recognize the phenomenon may develop mechanisms to overlook certain signals that might lead to preference reversal if they know from past experience that it has led to choices which they have later regretted. Such a situation is explored by Hayek (1967), who postulates rule-guided action that excludes certain classes of facts as being one of the primary elements of choice.

This strategic behaviour is also a primary characteristic of entrepreneurship, and comes from an entrepreneurial capacity to envisage likely changes in value, independent of information. The scope to recognize such likely changes in value is a precursor to mechanisms to counter it.

ECONOMIC MODEL OF INTERTEMPORAL VALUATION

On page 63 a model of intertemporal valuation drawn from Ainslie (1992) was introduced and reference was made to *economically* based behavioural assumptions to support this model. This section sets out some characteristics drawn from the temporal utility model that suggest intertemporal valuation consistent with the Ainslie model.

Any event planned to come to fruition in the future is subject to more uncertainty than the same event not so temporally distant. In the case of capital investment choice, additional information as it becomes available through time will guarantee such a result, but the result must also be true even with no additional information (the case put forth by Ainslie).

With value defined in utility space, even *certain* outcomes result in uncertain utility perceived from a distance if the actor has other opportunities in the intervening period that also offer utility. The certainty or uncertainty in utilities attaching to future events is a function of these other opportunities, and *ceteris paribus* these other opportunities reduce as the event in question emerges. Economic support for the Ainslie model is founded on the way that uncertainty reduces through time.

Consider again Figure 6.1, which shows the private value at any time associated with events expected to occur at some future time. These 'values,' are derived from the amalgam of desirable and undesirable attributes that an actor perceives at that time. If a choice were actually made, revealed preference suggests that representation of value as a single line as shown in Figure 6.1 is the correct one. Without the benefit of revealed preference, a single-line representation is problematic: a distribution of potential values is a more meaningful characterization. Figure 6.4 suggests a distribution of utilities for alternatives A and B as conceptually viewed from time T_0.

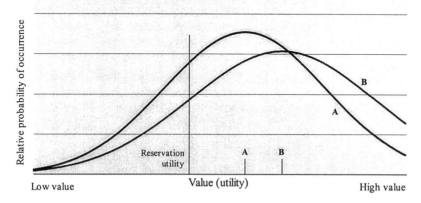

Figure 6.4: Value for grossly uncertain future choices

At T_0, both alternatives are subject to substantial uncertainty – with alternative B having fundamentally higher value (in some 'average' expected sense) but exhibiting greater variance due to it being temporally further away.

Consider now the choice situation in the event that there was available a 'do nothing' option or a market-based alternative with effectively no uncertainty (a choice defined at the reservation line). This is the 'rule' or benchmark against which choices are valued. Against this benchmark a risk-averse actor would not choose either alternative. Yet at T_0 the actor is not being called upon to choose between alternatives – he or she is simply being called upon to make a decision regarding expenditure of resources (more thinking time, more information) in anticipation of such a (subsequent) choice.

In one sense, the value that an individual places on options that he or she would not actually choose is outside of the realm of economic analysis. In another sense it is fundamental to the problem at hand because the subjectively held value determines what alternatives are *rejected* from further analysis and in the direction and extent of future learning for non-rejected alternatives. In this respect subjectively held values *are* relevant.

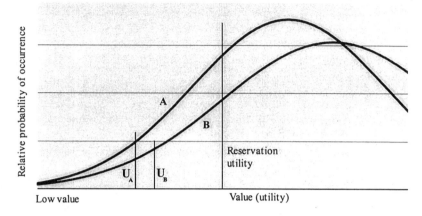

Figure 6.5: Private value based only on 'risk' preferences

The value can be determined by phrasing the question in another way. For any given characteristic aversion to risk, at what non-risk market value (in utility terms) is an actor indifferent to choosing any of these uncertain alternatives? This is illustrated in Figure 6.5.

Figure 6.5 assumes that the actor's risk preferences are such that he or she could accept an uncertain alternative so long as there is less than a 5 per cent chance of utility being less than the 'non-risk' alternative. 'Value' (represented by U_A and U_B in Figure 6.5) based on only this criteria is low, but is in the same rank order as 'value' based on some *expected* utility. As with the model in Figure 6.2, when value has to be assessed a long time into the future it is substantially lower than any market-based alternative, but the rank order of value for the non-market alternatives is consistent with market-based rank ordering. Thus the utility represented by U_A, U_B and the reservation line in Figure 6.5 corresponds at T_0 to the privately held of alternatives A and B, and the market-based alternative in Figure 6.2 respectively.

Consider now the case where the assessment is made closer to the time when alternative A comes to fruition. Uncertainties in the utility associated with alternative A have been substantially removed, but alternative B still exhibits considerable uncertainty. Figure 6.6 shows such a case. In this figure, the mean values of the distributions are unchanged from Figure 6.5 – only the variability is changed.

In this example, outcomes associated with alternative A have less than a 5 per cent chance of a result less than the reservation utility, whereas the residual uncertainty associated with alternative B means that there is still an 8

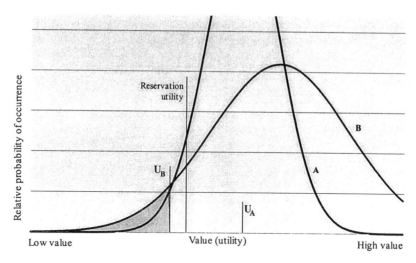

Figure 6.6: Emerging (future) value with uncertainty resolution

per cent chance of failure under this option. A risk-averse actor can now be satisfied with alternative A on this basis, but not with alternative B.

Thus alternative A is valued according to some other criterion (the *expected* value, U_A) whereas alternative B is valued as before at U_B. An actor would now choose the uncertain alternative A over some market-based option. As with the Ainslie model, preferences have changed. Alternative A is now valued more highly than alternative B.

If choice must be made at this time, and without the influence of strategy as suggested by Arrow (see the discussion, p. 66) the temporally closer option (alternative A) will be chosen over the more highly valued (in some absolute sense) but temporally further removed option (alternative B).

The primary difference between the construction described above and the Ainslie model is that in this economically based opportunity cost model, once the reservation threshold has been passed, 'value' is likely to change very little. Since alternatives now satisfy the risk-based threshold, actors can value them on a more market-based criterion. This suggests an *exponential* style of discounting, though not necessarily at rates which are the same as the market-based exponential discount rate.

If a decision can be delayed, or limited just to tentative acceptance of alternative A pending further progress of time, then the value of alternative B will probably increase proportionally more than the value of alternative A, potentially allowing this option to be chosen before the deadline for acceptance of alternative A passes. Figure 6.7 shows the situation according to this model, with a risk-averse actor seeking a high level of certainty before valuing alternatives thereafter on a market-based model.

Figure 6.7 shows the characteristic reversal of preferences (private valuation lines cross over) similar to the Ainslie model. In this economic model, private valuations do not necessarily change according to a hyperbolic rule (or even according to an exponential rule) – all that is necessary for the model to hold is that value increases as time advances.

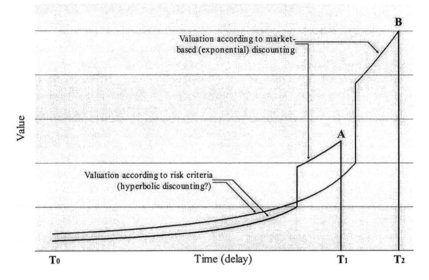

Figure 6.7: Changing private value through time with preference reversal

The key elements providing economic support for the Ainslie model are: (a) the possibility of preference reversal, and (b) private valuations that are much lower than (expected) market valuations under conditions of uncertainty when events are temporally distant. In the economic model the risk-based precondition for private valuation provides low valuations for temporally distant events, and the distinct step (increase) in valuation once this is satisfied gives rise to preference reversal.

This model reinforces the behavioural characteristics that are essential to the strategic interaction described by Ainslie. Assuming private valuation characteristics similar to Figure 6.7, risk-averse actors who procrastinate can rationally choose alternative A over the (inferior) market-based alternative shown in Figures 6.2 and 6.4. But without strategic thinking these actors have no obvious rational mechanism (via further procrastination, for example) to choose alternative B over alternative A.

Thus, the model provides support for Arrows assertion (discussed on p. 66) that, to rationally choose alternative B over alternative A, an actor must consider 'the relation between the action taken at any time point in the future and the information available *at that time*, though not available at the time at which the initial decision is made'.

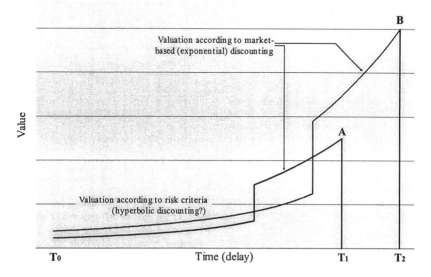

Figure 6.8: Changing private value, limited preference reversal

Figure 6.8 shows a similar situation to Figure 6.7, except in this case the actor is assumed to have a lesser aversion to risk or a greater ability to faithfully envisage the future. The risk criterion is satisfied sooner. In this model, which represents a more entrepreneurial choice than the model above, valuations consistent with market value are arrived at sooner, and the kinds of strategic interaction necessary to yield a choice in favour of alternative B in the Ainslie model do not need to be as strong or as well developed. Alternatively, with well-developed internal strategic capability, actors who can reach valuations like Figure 6.8 can rationally make choices between alternatives much more temporally separated, thereby increasing the range of exploitable options that will ultimately prove profitable once they can be valued by an (external) market mechanism.

NOTES

1. Because the venture was not proceeded with, estimates of present value, cost of capital and internal rate of return were not developed in any reliable way. Figures presented in this example have been rounded and modified for ease of illustration. This example also suggests an explanation grounded in probable changes in share market valuation. Since the author was only indirectly involved in the decision-making described in the example, the possibility that other factors may have played a part, or even the major part, in arriving at the decision cannot be ruled out.

2. The conception of cost as the value of the foregone alternative in this sense exactly follows Buchanan (1969, 43) wherein six implications of a choice-bound conception of cost emerge:
   1. Cost must be borne exclusively by the decision-maker.
   2. Cost is subjective; it exists in the mind of the decision-maker and nowhere else.
   3. Cost is based on anticipations; it is necessarily a forward-looking or *ex ante* concept.
   4. Cost cannot be realized, because that which is given up cannot be enjoyed.
   5. Cost cannot be measured by someone other than the decision-maker because there is no way that subjective (expected) experience can be directly observed.
   6. Cost can be dated at the moment of decision.

3. 'Value' is a meaningful concept given change due to influences *beyond human control*, and beyond human ability to influence or adapt to it. Nevertheless, '[man] must yield to the inevitable. He must submit to destiny' (Mises, 1966, 14). Analysis of this type of situation is outside the scope of this book.

4. A company will recognize (and incorporate into some strategic plan) those elements of each *class* of activity which most impact value. For example, the *selling price of copper* may be the factor to which value is most sensitive in all styles of copper mining. When assessing two alternative copper projects, the starting point to differentiate between them would therefore be whether one or other project is more or less sensitive to the price of copper. If projects cannot be differentiated by these more important (in some 'relatively absolute' sense) attributes, then evaluation must proceed to achieve such differentiation via attributes that are less important. Thus power stations are frequently sited on the basis of coal supply costs. Even though coal supply costs are usually much less important for the economics of power generation than (say) the capital cost of the plant, the capital cost *differences* between plants are less important than the coal supply cost differences between plants.

   A similar ranking mechanism applies for assessing value in the sense of private decisions, or the private impact of decisions in the corporate environment. The starting point for comparative value will be some 'relatively absolute absolute' (as Knight would probably term it) that for the decision at hand represents the most important element of value. Thus, for example, an individual actor assessing corporate alternatives may focus first on his own job security. If projects cannot be differentiated by this more important (in some relatively absolute sense) attribute, then evaluation will attempt such differentiation via attributes that are of lesser importance.

5. 'Most, probably, of our decisions to do something positive, the full consequences of which will be drawn out over many days to come, can only be taken as a result of animal spirits – of a spontaneous urge to action rather than inaction, and not as a weighted average of quantitative benefits multiplied by quantitative probabilities' (Keynes, 1936, 161).

6. Of course, actors in this or any other model must still come to understand whether or not common uncertainties do in fact affect the value associated with all choices equally. In many cases such a conclusion may be readily deduced, and is borne out by experience in developing mineral projects, where the selling price of the mineral is subject to gross and unresolvable variability – but still is given scant regard in financial evaluations. If all alternatives have the same output and are selling into the same market, then the change in value due to this uncertainty is likely to be quite similar across all alternatives. And for most non-diversified companies within any one market segment, the rise and fall of the

product price has already been internalized by the corporation's owners and is therefore a characteristic whose variability in this absolute sense is outside of the choice problem. (See further discussion on this issue in Chapter 7, note 3.)

7. As quoted by Ainslie (1992), the original work by Herrnstein (1961) described preference as simply proportional to reward rate and amount (the non-delayed total *value*) and inversely proportional to delay (hence the hyperbolic form of the function). Subsequent work by Ainslie and by Mazur (1986) has refined the general form of the function to be:

$$V = \frac{A}{Z + \beta\,(T-t)}$$

where:

V   is value at time $(T - t)$
A   is non-delayed value
Z   is a constant (notionally = 1)
β   is the delay constant
$T - t$ is the time interval between assessment and occurrence.

8. In the experience of the author, most entrepreneurs, though popularly labelled 'risk-takers', actually consider themselves to take *fewer* risks than others who are quite risk averse. With limited ability to envisage alternatives outside the market environment, non-entrepreneurial actors choose from a spectrum of activity where higher returns *are* synonymous with higher risk. Applying this benchmark to entrepreneurial action logically results in the popular label. In the non-market setting of entrepreneurial valuation, the alternatives that an entrepreneur has open, in the event of failure of his or her primary plan as it were, are unobservable. Yet frequently these unobservable alternatives represent a much lower proportion of capital (value) at risk than would be suggested on the assumption that the alternatives are merely market-based ones.

This position is well supported, at least by anecdotal evidence. For example, Packard (1995, 64) chronicles one large decision early in the life of the Hewlett-Packard Company, one of the most successful entrepreneurial companies in American history: 'we built a more permanent plant adjacent to our existing facilities. We designed it as a general-purpose building, and I remember thinking that if we couldn't keep the company going, we could lease out the building as a supermarket.'

In another example, that has strong parallels in the market environment to issues of liberty analysed by Buchanan (1993) in a political environment, Packard quotes a further instance of strongly risk-averse entrepreneurial behaviour in refusing to take on debt: 'firms that did not borrow money had a difficult time, but they ended up with their assets intact and survived during the depression years that followed. From this experience I decided our company should not incur any long-term debt' (ibid., 84). These two examples, in my view much more representative of entrepreneurial behaviour, are the antithesis of risk-taking entrepreneurial behaviour as commonly portrayed.

7.   Choice under uncertainty

This chapter sets out the second part of the theoretical development in the book: a model of individual choice under uncertainty.

The chapter is arranged in three sections. The first formally sets out and develops the model, called the *temporal utility model*. It extends the theory of economic behaviour expounded by Buchanan (1969) and explicitly considers uncertainty using the notion of opportunity cost as the analytical coupling device. The second section (p. 87) examines results that are consistent or inconsistent with the standard models of choice, and highlights those areas of decision-making that might gain from the insights brought out in the model. The third section (p. 97) considers empirical support for the model, examining the link between uncertainty and investment.

The efficacy of the model can be judged from the robustness of its predictions on capital investment choice. Three criteria, following Kuhn (1970), and Popper (1934) have been established:

1. *Risk versus uncertainty* The model provides a mechanism for understanding and differentiating risk from uncertainty and the influence of each on capital investment choice. It allows for risk aversion and for the empirically supported tendency towards indecisiveness and delay in decision[1] given uncertainty, even in the case of apparently obvious expected value. These elements have already been introduced in previous chapters and are expanded upon in this and succeeding chapters.

2. *Consistency with neoclassical models where uncertainty is absent* Many elements of choice in the neoclassical framework assume *no* uncertainty even when it is evident, yet yield results that are well supported by empirical work. The temporal utility model, if applied to similar cases, must yield results that are at least consistent with the standard neoclassical construct. Further, the standard neoclassical subjective expected utility model of von Neumann and Morgenstern, which does set out to address these uncertainty issues, has proven remarkably robust. If this standard model is to be shown as incorrect, any new model (the temporal utility model), if applied to similar cases, must at least suggest plausible explanations of why such an (incorrect) model might still yield apparently robust results. This aspect is covered in pp. 87–95.

3. *Conceptually falsifiable* The model must define a set of circumstances and demonstrate results under these circumstances that are at least conceptually falsifiable in a way that differentiates it from the standard neoclassical model. These issues are taken up in part in pp. 87–95 and 97–106.

In a corporate decision environment, use of the model for capital investment choice requires an extended process of decision-making. This extended process involves successive procedures that iteratively evaluate alternatives within a set of corporate institutions. This institutional environment and decision process are set out in Chapter 8.

TEMPORAL UTILITY MODEL

The temporal utility model focuses on subjectively valued unique choices characterized by some distribution of values. It is concerned with just one, or a very narrow set of, interdependent choices (strategies) whose value *ex ante* cannot be appraised by reference to market-related characteristics.

In Chapter 6 the formation of value in the mind of the actor was characterized only in terms of *comparative* value between choices. Nevertheless, this formal illustration of the model is usefully started with a conception of this distribution of value in Bayesian terms pertaining to one alternative alone, and this is set out in the following sub-section. The extension of the model to represent comparative value between choices follows in the subsequent sub-section.

Valuing Uncertain Events Independent of Choice

In a theory of choice, cost must be reckoned in a utility dimension (Buchanan, 1969). Alternatives involving uncertain outcomes must similarly be valued in a utility dimension. Figure 7.1 shows a model of a single alternative.

In Figure 7.1 the subjective distribution of anticipated value is shown by the curve, where the height of the curve represents some relative probability of occurrence. There is a range of envisaged possible outcomes that translate into utility on a scale on the horizontal axis. On the adverse (left) side of the horizontal axis are outcomes that leave the actor worse off (with lower utility than he or she might otherwise enjoy) than if a different course of action were taken. On the advantageous (right) side of the horizontal axis are outcomes yielding high utility.

The model does not presuppose any particular scale of value, or that such a scale is even stable through time. It simply requires that such a scale exists.

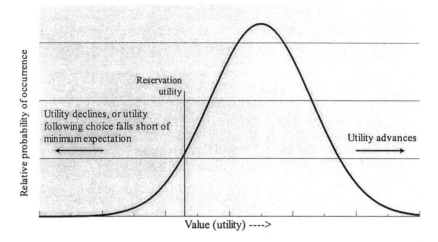

Figure 7.1: Subjective distribution of value under uncertainty

In this first construct the model uses a simplified manifestation of such a scale. It assumes the actor's attention is first focused on satisfaction of some *reservation* utility (shown in Figure 7.1) as a precondition, and then, after this is satisfied in the expectational sense, focused on the utility represented by the maxima or some utility greater than the reservation utility.

For this initial model it is convenient to think of the reservation line as the utility that leaves the actor no worse after choice than before choice.[2] In this respect, the reservation line is akin to the 'neutral point' or the point of indifference used in Shackle's model described in Chapter 4. Outcomes that fall short of this reservation line represent risk. In a corporate environment, it is convenient to think of the reservation line as the cost of capital. Outcomes that result in a return to capital less than the cost of capital represent risk.

The initial focus is on reservation utility. In cases of uncertainty, 100 per cent success is an acknowledged impossibility. For each individual actor, the 'allowable' proportion and style of outcomes that fall short of this reservation line is a function of the actors aversion to risk.[3] Actors who are very risk averse will seek out alternatives that have, say, less than 1 per cent chance that the outcome will fall short of the reservation line. Less risk-averse actors will be satisfied with alternatives that have no more than, say, 10 per cent chance of the outcome not satisfying this reservation minimum.

If this reservation criterion is satisfied in an expectational sense, then other preferences become the criteria that represent 'value'. In this case the value attaching to these other preferences is what underpins choice. If this reservation criterion is *not* met, then the antecedent risk-related preferences remain the focus of attention, the basis of value and the underpinning of choice.

The initial focus on reservation utility serves to satisfy risk aversion independent of the value (utility) at the mean or median of the subjective distribution. Risk aversion has to do with the left side of the distribution only.

In a market setting (as opposed to an entrepreneurial choice situation) actors typically choose only from alternatives whose attributes and market value are widely recognized. In this setting arbitrage ensures a strong correlation between variability and expected return. The opportunity cost for actors to indulge their aversion to risk is the return foregone on some other *market-determined* alternative. Consumer choice fits this characterization in all but a few cases. In many other areas of economic activity, value attaching to potential courses of action is also unambiguously greater than any typical reservation line. Thus in these circumstances 'value' focused only on the left side of the distribution (based on the risk elements only) rarely influences choice. The neoclassical model of 'value' holds.

Outside the market setting there is nothing to suggest any correlation between variability – which determines the proportion of the expected outcomes whose value falls short of the reservation utility – and expected return. Thus uncertain alternatives exhibiting high notional value (in the neoclassical sense) do not necessarily represent higher risk in the sense of this model, because there is no mechanism outside the market for alternatives to be arbitraged into the risk-return spectrum.

Choice Characterization

Consider now a more faithful representation of the model, where objects of choice are represented by distributions and where the elements making up the distribution exclude components that are common to all such alternatives. Such a model is illustrated in Figure 7.2.

The distributions in Figure 7.2 are incomplete and would ordinarily be so. Actors will seek to differentiate choices starting from the low-utility end of the set of potential outcomes; hence potential outcomes offering high utility will only be assimilated if there is no prior mechanism of differentiation.

Valuation preparatory to choice starts again with the initial focus on reservation utility. Above (p. 82) the reservation line was defined as the utility that left the actor indifferent to proceeding or not proceeding. This benchmark made the tacit assumption that such an alternative choice was actually available and that such a choice itself had no uncertainty.

In consumer choice, or choice not involving large decisions, this style of benchmark is realistic. The 'do nothing' alternative usually fits this characterization. If the choice is between buying apples of uncertain quality

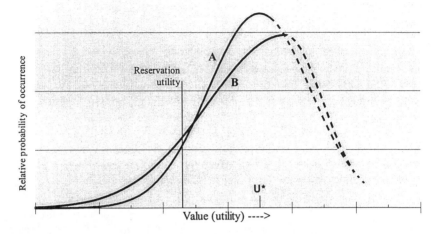

Figure 7.2: Differentiation of choices focusing on low utility outcomes

and buying oranges of uncertain quality, the third choice – to buy neither – is a reasonable foil against which the value characteristics of the two 'primary' choices can be compared.

In large decision choice, the 'do nothing' case is itself one of the alternatives, is itself subject to uncertainty, and cannot necessarily fill the role assigned to the reservation utility in the simpler choice problem. In the end, actors must choose from the best alternatives available to them. But this does not necessarily mean that the alternative with the least risk should then be redefined as having *no* risk.

The dilemma is resolved by recognizing that, even though the choice situation under study is a large decision choice pertaining to the actor's complete future opportunity set, it is still but one segment of a more complete temporal experience, including history-to-come, that defines an actor's scale of preferences at some higher level than the immediate decision problem at hand.

In such a problem, therefore, an actor's perception of the utility representing indifference (the reservation utility) does not necessarily have to represent an actual choice available to him or her. Rather it represents an amalgam of past value and an expectation of future value that can change through time. Used in this way it is a relatively absolute[4] benchmark (a rule of assessment) which may be considered stable for the immediate problem at hand.

The example in Figure 7.2 shows the choice alternative A with 7 per cent of envisaged outcomes falling short of the reservation line. Alternative B has 12 per cent of envisaged outcomes falling short of the line.

If these alternatives were the only ones available, a very risk-averse actor would choose alternative A over alternative B, regardless of the set of high-utility outcomes potentially available with alternative B. The median or mean utility (in the neoclassical sense, applying the subjective expected utility model) will not influence choice.

Actors with a greater tolerance for risk may be indifferent to the two choice alternatives from this (risk) perspective. In this case the focus of attention changes to some other criterion.

In this simplified representation, the temporal utility model does not specify what this second criterion is. (The neoclassical 'utility' from the subjective expected utility model is an appropriate second criterion.) For this example, consider some higher utility U^* – the maxima of alternative A – as the criterion that represents 'value'. The symmetry of the distribution representing alternative A means that there is a 50 per cent chance of achieving outcomes that will result in utility greater than U^*. Alternative B, on the other hand has a 'most likely' outcome with higher utility, but still offers only a 50 per cent chance of a result that exceeds U^*. Thus an actor may still not be able to differentiate between the two choices. The focus of attention must change to some other criterion.

This step-wise approach is continued sequentially until some utility that is the focus of the actor's attention for the time being allows differentiation between alternatives. Potential high-utility outcomes do not directly influence choice whilst alternatives can be differentiated using some lower utility criterion.

This is not to say that potential high utility outcomes cannot *indirectly* influence choice – even at the early stages of this valuation process. If actors can envisage a way (using market mechanisms, for instance) whereby potentially high utility results can be used to offset risks (that is, low-utility results), then they *can* be considered, but only by way of a changed alternative, not by way of offsetting *utilities*.

Risk and Uncertainty in the Temporal Utility Model

Several criteria for judging the model were set out at the start of this chapter. The first of these had to do with a mechanism for understanding and differentiating risk from uncertainty, and the influence of each on capital investment choice. This component can now be addressed, along with the accompanying treatment of risk aversion.

Before proceeding, it is useful to reiterate and expand on the comments introduced previously (see note 3) concerning the definition of risk aversion in this model and the definition more commonly applied in the neoclassical literature. An actor is risk averse according to most models in the neoclassical world if he or she exhibits a diminishing marginal utility with *wealth*.

For capital investment choice, *uncertainty* is portrayed by the distribution of value such as illustrated in Figure 7.1. Reckoned in the utility dimension, 'uncertainty' means any set of potential outcomes whose utility cannot be defined by a unique point on the horizontal axis.

Risk is the utility associated with outcomes that fall short of some minimum expectation defined by the reservation line.

Alternatives subject to uncertainty do not necessarily represent risk. If the entire subjective distribution of potential outcomes has utility to the right of the reservation line, then uncertainty does not mean risk. Moreover, under this utility-based model of choice, all actors are assumed to be risk averse and there are only degrees of risk aversion characterized by the relative tolerance for potential outcomes to the left of the reservation line.

Decision-making at the level of the firm is still undertaken by individuals. Nevertheless, utility in the mind of these individuals follows, at least in part, from shareholder value. Where agency issues are excluded (the basis of the proposition in the final chapters of this book), 'shareholder value' or 'return on investment' becomes the proxy for utility on the horizontal axis.

Using this proxy, 'uncertainty' is the variability in the likely return to shareholders associated with the set of possible outcomes following the investment. The reservation line is the expected marginal cost of capital associated with the extension of a firm's business into the investment under study, but figured in some long-term sense consistent with the life of the investment and the long-term structure of the firm. It is *inter alia* a function of shareholder expectations concerning the individual investment as if shareholders were fully informed about the investment. Alternatives do not necessarily have the same cost of capital. 'Risk' is the loss in shareholder value associated with outcomes that fail to achieve a return that exceeds the marginal cost of capital.

One further comparison between the temporal utility model and the subjective expected utility model having to do with risk aversion is in order. In Chapter 6 it was pointed out that utility of each alternative in the subjective expected utility model, being independent of choice, had to include the totality of anything that makes up a person's utility for the time being. From the *Homo economicus* viewpoint, a 'total' valuation was seen to be unnecessary since choice is based only on the *differences* between alternatives.

The temporal utility model looks only at utility differences. Nevertheless, 'utilities' that only incorporate elements that *differ* between choice alternatives must still be compared according to some rule, and to incorporate risk aversion that rule has to account for utility in some 'total' sense. The 'rule' enters the temporal utility model by way of the reservation line and subsequent foci of evaluation.

The difference is significant. In the subjective expected utility model actors simultaneously assess both the rule that underpins the way they act (their propensity for risk) *and* the decision at hand. In the temporal utility model the actor's propensity for risk is logically separated from and temporally antecedent to his or her assessment of the range of utilities associated with the choice at hand. This is not to say that the rules for choice are not influenced by an existing choice problem, but the effects in this model are second order.

MODEL INTERPRETATION

The temporal utility model, as it applies in a general sense, is sketched out in the preceding section. This section aims to demonstrate and interpret use of the model in an individual sense as it applies to capital investment choice within firms. The objective is to examine a series of cases using the model, to compare and contrast the use of the model in these cases against other models in the neoclassical literature, and to define a set of circumstances wherein the model could be conceptually falsified.

Valuation under Uncertainty: Classic Case

Here we examine the simplest case, where there is full information, uncertainty (using the definition in Chapter 3) but effectively no risk. Both choice alternatives have a range of potential outcomes, but the entire range of utilities attaching to these outcomes offers utility exceeding the reservation utility (ignoring a small part of curve A to the left of the reservation line). Figure 7.3 shows this case. All models value Alternative B over Alternative A.

Consider first the neoclassical subjective expected utility model. This model arrives at the distributions by transforming the 'wealth' associated with each outcome into individual utility according to the person's utility function in wealth. The distribution of utilities does not necessarily follow the pattern of the normal distribution as shown.

The subjective expected utility model then uses the assumption of transitivity of preferences to reduce each distribution to a single utility. Since both distributions are the same shape, after reduction the rank ordering will place alternative B higher on the utility scale than alternative A. Given full information and the assumption that subjective probabilities can indeed be assigned to the elements making up value (including the states of nature

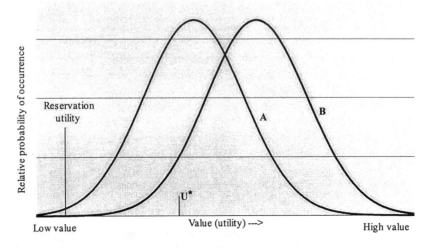

Figure 7.3: No-risk choices: Alternatives with the same uncertainty

consistent with each outcome), then there can be little to object to in this construct.

The temporal utility model arrives at the same result as the subjective expected utility model, but via a different route:

1. It starts with the distribution of potential outcomes defined in utility space. The distribution is independent of and does not presuppose any risk-aversion characteristics of the actor. It merely defines the utility that the actor would enjoy given the particular outcomes translated into utility terms.

2. The temporal utility model assumes that actors will seek first to satisfy the reservation utility, and then seek to satisfy progressive benchmarks representing higher utilities, and so on until choices can be sufficiently differentiated.

3. In the case shown in Figure 7.3, both cases completely satisfy the reservation utility requirement. The actor is then assumed to focus on some other objective, say U*, as the criterion of choice. In this case, alternative B has more than 85 per cent chance that final utility will exceed U*, whereas alternative A only has about a 50 per cent chance that final utility will exceed U*. This is significant. Alternative B is chosen.

The vast majority of economic activity surely fits the characterization illustrated in Figure 7.3. It does not preclude a dispersion of possible outcomes. It fits the 'law of large numbers' that Arrow (1958) suggests is the major line of distinction between neoclassical models.

Where all envisaged outcomes for alternatives under consideration exceed the reservation line, the subjective expected utility model yields the same results as the temporal utility model.

Uncertainty Equivalent Choice

This sub-section is usefully started by foreshadowing the conclusion: when the distribution of potential outcomes associated with two alternatives is defined in utility space, with both alternatives *exhibiting the same uncertainty*, then the temporal utility model yields the same outcome as the subjective expected utility model, *regardless of risk*.

Consider first the case shown in Figure 7.4 with two distributions of outcomes that have minimal overlap. The distributions may be located *anywhere* throughout utility space. It is clear from the figure that any weighting of utilities or use of the transitive preference ordering assumption in the subjective expected utility model will yield an expected utility for alternative B always higher than alternative A.

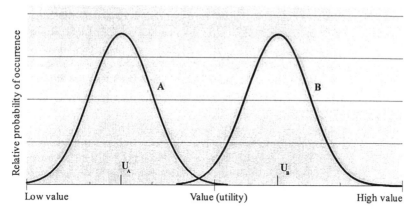

Figure 7.4: Choices between alternatives with the same uncertainty

The process in the temporal utility model arrives at the same result. For *any* level of utility which is the actor's focus of attention for the time being, stepping sequentially from low to high utility, there is a higher probability of exceeding it if alternative B is followed rather than alternative A.

Expand this now to the case in Figure 7.3 with no risk, Figure 7.5 with substantial risk, or *any* case where the subjective distribution is the same across choices.

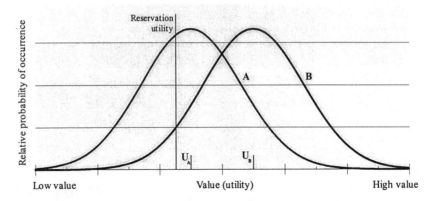

Figure 7.5: Risky choices: Alternatives with the same uncertainty

In *any* case where the characteristic shape of the distribution is the same across choices, the subjective expected utility model favours alternative B, since the reduction of the set of outcomes to one expected utility, applied to both cases, will always yield U_B higher than U_A.

The temporal utility model does not apply this reduction, but proceeds in a step-wise fashion starting from assessment of alternatives against the reservation utility. Nevertheless, as shown in Figure 7.5, alternative B *always* wins on this criteria:

- If there is risk – both cases fail on this reservation criterion – then alternative B will still be favoured on the basis of least risk;
- If there is no risk (the case in Figure 7.3) then alternative B will be favoured on the basis of return;
- If only *one* alternative satisfies the reservation criterion it will be alternative B.

Hence, using the temporal utility model, even for overlapping distributions, rank ordering (and therefore choice) is identical to rank ordering using the subjective expected utility model.

Rank ordering does not mean value. Where there is no risk, value under the temporal utility model is arguably the same as value under the subjective expected utility model. Where there is risk, the temporal utility model will assign a lower value, but between choices the rank ordering will not change with this value change. Using the logic of the temporal utility model, the subjective expected utility model obtains the right answer using the wrong method.

Observations on how individuals actually choose can only be based on revealed preference, and on this basis there is nothing to differentiate choice under the subjective expected utility model and choice under the temporal utility model. Choices made on the basis of utilities represented deterministically (after reduction, by their subjective expected utility) would be indistinguishable from choices made on the basis of the temporal utility model. This result will be true regardless of where the reservation utility line is positioned.

Whilst the rank ordering leading to choice is the same regardless of the model used, the subjectively held value is not necessarily as consistent throughout. Assume, for example, that there is a third completely certain choice available with utility the same as the reservation line. In other words, there is *also* the scope for a 'do nothing' alternative that leaves the actor indifferent to change. Then whilst alternative B will always be valued more than alternative A, only if alternative B also satisfies this reservation criterion will it be preferred to the 'do nothing' alternative. Such a result has important implications for understanding preference reversal, hesitancy in choice (procrastination), and liquidity preference.

Most consumer choice where there is uncertainty is likely to be characterized by one or other of the models in Figures 7.3 and 7.5. Market processes can bring this about in a number of ways:

1. For purchases at relatively small cost, value becomes well understood through repeated purchase and use. Most common commodities purchased on a repetitive basis have just a narrow range of expected outcomes (utility). Even where there is a wide range of possible outcomes, people learn and adapt their patterns of behaviour to accommodate the uncertainty – through guarantees and warranties, trial and error on small samples before commitment to larger samples, and extensive product information. Further, learning-by-doing allows high-utility outcomes to be understood, so the completeness of distributions required in the subjective expected utility model can quite correctly be assumed in place.

2. One-off purchases (such as the purchase of a new car) are also likely to fit this model. Even though value may be difficult to assess and learning-by-doing may be problematic, alternative choices will not necessarily have *different* degrees of uncertainty.

3. Competing products available in the market place share many characteristics. Information that reduces the uncertainty associated with one product also reduces uncertainty with competitive products. Competition is likely to lead to relative consistency in the degree of uncertainty across choices at any one time, reducing over time as markets become better informed.

In cases where new products are being introduced or where there *is* residual risk, guarantees and consumer protection provisions ensure that (at least in the mind of the actor making the choice) there is very little scope for an outcome on the adverse side of the reservation line.

Where uncertainty is the same across choices, revealed preference is unlikely to yield any more explanatory power or any different results using the temporal utility model than it is using the neoclassical model. If there is uncertainty, but still substantial risk, perhaps neither choice is made (that is, a third, non-risk alternative is chosen), or if a choice amongst the two *is* made – the only choices observable – the one with the least risk also has the highest expected utility.

Conceptually falsifiable results for the model are unlikely to be obtainable where uncertainty is the same across choices.

Uncertainty Different Across Choices

This sub-section considers the case where uncertainty is different across choices. It is discussed under the assumption that there is no 'do nothing' case. The 'do nothing' case is just an extreme form of one alternative with zero uncertainty and low expected return, and is therefore automatically subsumed within the more general case as described.

Again foreshadowing the result, this time the temporal utility model yields results that are different to the subjective expected utility model. Three conditions are necessary for this to occur:

1. Uncertainty is different across choices.

2. The distribution of values for alternatives overlap.

3. There is risk.

Figure 7.6 shows the typical choice situation addressed by the model. In this figure alternative B has less risk but also has the lower expected return. Valuations derive from conflicting objectives.

The subjective expected utility model arrives at U_A or U_B through balancing high-utility outcomes with low-utility outcomes; hence, assuming the complete distribution is known, alternative A will be chosen.

The temporal utility model eschews a weighting mechanism, and only considers high-utility outcomes if there is no other method of differentiation between choices. The focus starts with the reservation utility:

- If there is substantial risk – both cases fail on this reservation criterion – then rank ordering will favour alternative B over alternative A on the basis of least risk. This result is different to the result from the subjective expected utility model.

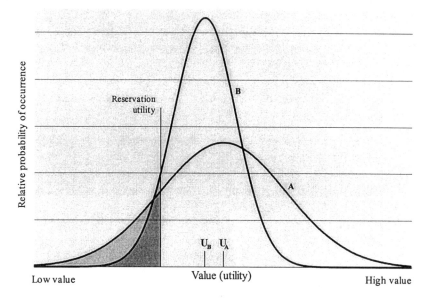

Figure 7.6: Risky choices: Alternatives with different uncertainty

- If only *one* alternative satisfies the reservation criterion it will be alternative B. This result is also different to the result from the subjective expected utility model.

- If there is no risk (both alternatives satisfy the reservation criterion) then rank ordering will favour alternative A over alternative B on the basis of return. This result is the same as the result from the subjective expected utility model.

In how much of the economy, then, is such a model likely to apply?

All competitive, fully informed markets for investments (stock markets and the like) whose value is derived on an intertemporal basis fit the model in Figure 7.6. In these markets, alternatives with higher returns always have greater variance because arbitrage ranks them in such a spectrum.

Such a situation is probably not as widely applicable to potential choices that are based on non-market knowledge. Nevertheless, *every* case ultimately passes through the stage characterized by Figure 7.6 at least once prior to commitment.

Consider the case of any large capital investment project within a firm. Assume that, on initial examination, the risk associated with the project is similar to other alternatives, and that the expected return appears to be substantially better. This simplifies decision-making in one sense because it effectively rules out any other alternative in the physical sense. But it does not resolve the choice dilemma. Large decision choice is a process, and the elimination of physically distinct alternatives does not mean that the final choice is fully defined. It merely establishes a more refined *sub-set* of alternatives having to do with the same physical project. For example, the choice may shift to:

1. proceed now (the case now represented by line A in Figure 7.6); *or*

2. invest in more information and then proceed (line B in Figure 7.6).

Such a choice acknowledges a level of commitment to proceed at some time in the future, but aims to establish the timing for such a move. Nevertheless, until the irrevocable commitment the 'choice' is reversible so it only constitutes a choice in the sense of elimination of options no longer to be pursued.

Because this case (uncertainty different across choices) offers the greatest scope for testing of the temporal utility model, it is useful to pursue the most common application by way of highlighting the difference with other models in the literature. How does the temporal utility model handle reduction in uncertainty associated with information? The situation is modelled in Figure 7.7.

Investment in information reduces uncertainty. Nevertheless, *ex ante* at least, investment in information also results in a downward shift in the expected return due to the cost of the information. The decision to 'proceed' or 'study some more, and then proceed' is a choice that exactly pits these two competing aims against each other.

Figure 7.7 illustrates such an evaluation process, assuming no change in the cost of capital (no change in the reservation line during the evaluation process). New potential investments enter the evaluation phase with uncertainty similar to curve A. Assuming new information has no *a priori* effect on the expected return, the phases of evaluation (labelled A to D) reduce uncertainty *and* reduce the expected return.

In Figure 7.7, if the physical project is proceeded with after Phase A of the evaluation there is a 20 per cent probability that the outcome will yield an unsatisfactory return. After extensive and costly evaluation, the same project after Phase D of evaluation yields a lower expected return, but only a 7.5 per cent chance of failure. A decision to 'proceed now' or to 'invest in information with a view to proceeding later' characterizes choice throughout the complete process.

This type of choice situation is quite different to models which examine the economics of information elsewhere in the neoclassical world in which some *a priori* fixed distribution is assumed to exist independent of the observer. In these models (for example, Stigler, 1961) new information

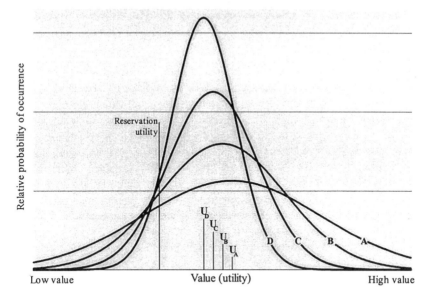

Figure 7.7: Information reduces uncertainty

serves to *increase* the actor's expected return through discovery of events on the high-value end of the spectrum.

In the model above, new information always lowers the expected return (*ex ante*, at least) but increases *value* when such value is predicated on the utility of outcomes falling short of the reservation line.

Summary

These are the conditions under which the temporal utility model yields results that are different to the standard model:

1. Uncertainty has to be different across choices. Above (p. 89) we set out the case where uncertainty was the same across choices and demonstrated no difference in result between the models.

2. The distribution of values for alternatives must overlap. If distributions do not overlap, the same argument applies. For *any* level of utility that is the actor's focus of attention for the time being, stepping sequentially from low to high utility, there is an unambiguously higher probability of exceeding it for one alternative (the alternative with the higher subjective expected utility) than the other alternative.

3. There is risk. If there is no risk, the reservation criterion is automatically satisfied, and value under the temporal utility model is arguably the same

as value under the subjective expected utility model. Only when one or both alternatives are subject to risk will the results differ under the two models.

The third and final criterion for judging the model can now be addressed. This criterion relates to circumstances whereby results can be conceptually falsified in a way that differentiates the model from other models in the neoclassical literature.

The most evident environment for such differentiation is where there is a change or reduction in uncertainty, but where there is no meaningful change (or perhaps even an increase) in the *expected* return. Under these circumstances, the temporal utility model predicts a change in investment activity (an immediate increase where uncertainty decreases, or an immediate hiatus where uncertainty increases) whereas the subjective expected utility model suggests little or no change.

Consider first a proposed corporate acquisition that has a lot of uncertainty and whose status towards proceeding is part-way through the evaluation process (the process illustrated by the four phases in Figure 7.7). Perhaps this process is proceeding without the knowledge of the stock market and therefore based primarily on privately arrived-at value. Now introduce an externality that significantly changes the uncertainty, but does not necessarily change the expected return. A typical externality is the action of another company in the industry announcing a similar acquisition. What impact is there on choice?

Capital investment decisions are easier to make if feedback from a fully informed market can be meaningfully compared against privately assessed value. The absence of this feedback contributes to hesitation. Such an announcement (of another firm in the industry doing the same thing) independently reinforces the logic of the valuation process – in effect, immediately reducing the uncertainty – even if the same announcement makes no observable difference or even reduces the expected returns from the project.

Under the temporal utility model externalities that result in instantaneous reductions in uncertainty can trigger outbursts of investment activity even with no discernible change in expected return (or interest rate).

Consider now a second case where externalities cause a change in value under the temporal utility model – a case where the externality is likely to *increase* the expected return whilst also increasing uncertainty. The temporal utility model suggests that this would trigger a temporary hiatus in investment. In contrast the subjective expected utility model posits an expected *increase* in investment.

The case is best understood in terms of a change in the reservation line. Recall that the reservation line represents the marginal cost of capital in a long-term sense. In effect it represents the 'rules of the game'. After any period of stability in these rules, projects or potential projects under continual assessment will be ranked according to marginal returns. Under the subjective expected utility model, projects with a return on investment exceeding the marginal cost of capital are commenced, and projects with an expected return less than the marginal cost of capital remain 'on the drawing board'. Under the temporal utility model projects on the drawing board fall into two categories:

1. those that have a high expected return on investment but which currently fail to satisfy the reservation condition (these projects will be actively under investigation aiming to satisfy this condition); and

2. those that satisfy the reservation condition but which remain undeveloped because of the (opportunity) cost – perhaps the 'project' proceeded with today has a present value less than the present value of the same project proceeded with tomorrow.

Any major shock in the world economy (such as the 1987 stock market crash, or the outbreak of Gulf War) will trigger an increase in the cost of capital, a rethink in the rules of the game. This will be represented by an *increase* in the reservation utility for the time being. Of course, such a shock may also change the fundamental economics of investment itself.

If the cost of capital increases, investment will decrease *ceteris paribus*. But any shock of this nature influences more than just the cost of capital. What is the situation with someone whose wealth is intact, whose projects are insensitive to interest rates, and who stands to *gain* from the shock? Oil and coal producers were in this situation upon announcement of the Gulf War. Under the subjective expected utility model, firms in this situation have an unambiguous incentive to proceed. Under the temporal utility model, an increase in the reservation line would suggest the opposite. A change in the rules of the game would require an immediate reassessment to ensure that projects on the drawing board still satisfy the reservation condition, even if the *expected* return is improved as a result of the shock.

Thus under the temporal utility model a shock would trigger an hiatus of investment, and only after assimilation of this new information and adjustment in the style of project would the expected return influence choice.

EMPIRICAL SUPPORT

Support for the temporal utility model hinges on the link between uncertainty and investment. Whilst there is strong anecdotal support for the propositions outlined, few empirical studies have been completed on the relationship between investment and uncertainty, and what work exists is far from conclusive (Leahy and Whited, 1995).

This section examines some of this work and is set out in three parts. In the first sub-section some of the approaches adopted by various researchers are examined and some of the literature is reviewed. There appears to be no support from this work for the proposition that increasing uncertainty leads to *increased* investment. Almost all studies show results that are supportive of the propositions in the book (that increasing uncertainty leads to *reduced* investment), though they arrive at this result from approaches different to the one adopted here.

The link between flexibility of labour and the character of investments is examined in the next sub-section (p. 101), which looks at the concept that, under uncertainty, more flexible production technologies (technologies that have a higher labour/capital ratio) might be favoured.

In the final sub-section (p. 103), investment characteristics in capital intensive industry are subjected to scrutiny, and the basis of future empirical work to support or contradict the model is set out.

Whilst the basic account of the temporal utility model has been set out in the first sections of this chapter, a translation mechanism is still necessary between 'value' in the mind of an individual actor and the capital investment choice process within a firm. This translation mechanism is examined in Chapter 8. For convenience, empirical support for the model set out in the balance of this chapter may be overlooked with no loss in comprehension or continuity.

Empirical Studies

Empirical studies link changes in some variable (the 'shock') with changes in the return on investment. Some studies, rather than examine the (average) return on investment, attempt to draw out the threshold return necessary to trigger investment.

If the marginal revenue product of capital is a convex function of the shock, then increased variability leads to an increase in the expected return on investment (and therefore increased investment). The reverse is true if the function is concave.

Convex functions are posited to derive from several sources, including the greater flexibility of labour relative to capital and the fact that bankruptcy limits the downside risk. Concave functions derive from competition coupled with the irreversibility of capital. In these models (with concave functions), low returns cannot be avoided because of sunk costs, but the counterbalancing high returns cannot be fully captured because of competition and further investment.

In standard economic theory, firms invest up to the point where the present value of a marginal unit of capital equals its cost. Nevertheless, empirical work does not easily yield this simple result. Summers (1987b) surveyed 200 major US corporations; meaningful results were obtained from 95 companies, and the use of 'very high' discount rates[5] – ranging from 8 to 30 per cent were found when the real cost of capital for these companies was only from one-quarter to one-fifth of this rate. The mean discount rate found for depreciation allowances – near riskless elements of the cash flow – was 17 per cent when, according to Summers, the after-tax cost of funds associated with these allowances is near zero in inflation-adjusted terms.

The Summers result is consistent with experience in worldwide mining developments, where companies typically apply hurdle rates of at least 15 per cent in after-tax, inflation-adjusted returns even for projects that are well known and situated in developed first-world countries. The average cost of capital for these companies is in the order of one-third of this rate. Echoing Dixit and Pindyck (1994, 7), standard economic theory suggests that 'the hurdle rate appropriate for investments with systematic risk will exceed the riskless rate, but [according to this theory] not by enough to justify the numbers used by many companies'.

If risk or uncertainty are to be the prime contributors to understanding this difference, then empirical studies must start with two definitional items: the measure of investment; and the indicator of variability (or volatility, or confidence) that is to be used.

The measure of investment

Most studies of investment under uncertainty use Tobin's q, or a variation of Tobin's q, as the indicator of investment return. Tobin's q is the ratio of the market value of a firm's assets (as measured by the market value of its outstanding stock and debt) to the replacement cost of the firm's assets (Tobin, 1969).

According to Carlton and Perloff (1994) the advantage of using Tobin's q as an indicator of investment return, is that the difficult problem of estimating either rates of return or marginal costs is avoided. The disadvantage is that, although the market value of a firm's securities can usually be readily obtained, the replacement costs of assets is much more difficult to estimate. Indeed, intangible assets such as research and development and the importance of the brand name are typically ignored, and this results in values of q greater than 1. (A value exceeding 1 suggests some market power).[6]

The implication of using Tobin's q is that firms have an incentive to invest when q is greater than 1 because this means that capital investment is worth more than it costs to replace. If q is less than 1, then assets can be more economically purchased via the stock market. Changes in Tobin's q represent marginal returns.

Whilst the use of Tobin's q is widespread in the literature and has proved most useful, it is a measure of the value of *recognized* investments; new capital investments cannot necessarily be judged using this benchmark since there will be no recognition of them until after commitment.

The options approach to capital investment analysis suggests that new investments require a return *exceeding* that implied by this measure, since committing to an investment means exercising the option to wait, and this implies a cost. Literature following this approach aims to discern the return on investment that is necessary to *trigger* investment – that is, *including* this options premium.

Pindyck and Solimano (1993) and Caballero and Pindyck (1992) use the maximum observed value of the marginal revenue product of capital within a country or an industry as a proxy for the investment trigger.

Uncertainty indicator

Uncertainty can be due to many characteristics, and many of these are unobservable in empirical work. Nevertheless, uncertainty is only meaningful to the extent that the variability that is the source of the uncertainty is associated with an element that impacts the return. Within any one industry, the achieved return on investment is sensitive to only a few such variables. Since most production processes involve a large number of diverse inputs but only a small number of outputs directed into a narrower market, the marginal unit revenue and volume associated with these narrow output markets are the primary sources of return-on-investment sensitivity.

Hurn and Wright (1994) follow an approach that is closest to the objectives in this book, aiming to separate out idiosyncratic uncertainty elements. In their case, they looked at the level and variance of oil prices on decision-making for oil field developments. Hurn and Wright use the assumption that prices themselves follow a random walk and their results show that variances in the price of oil do *not* impact the delay in investment. Unfortunately, these results are open to question because of the difficulty of separating the changes in the price with changes in uncertainty about the price.

Most researchers use a measure of risk (or variability) derived from the Capital Asset Pricing Model (CAPM). Brainard *et al.* (1980) use a sample of 187 firms from the years 1958–77 to assess the affects of a CAPM-based measure of risk on investment via average q (see Leahy and Whited, 1995, 3). Pindyck and Solimano (1993) use the volatility (variance) of the marginal profitability of capital as a proxy for uncertainty. Leahy and Whited (1995) use both the variance in individual stock returns and the covariance of the return with the market return, where the latter is calculated as the value-weighted returns on the NYSE, AMEX and NASDAQ.

Investments are founded upon expectations, particularly of those characteristics that impact most strongly on the return on investment – price and offtake volumes, for instance. Forward-looking measures are the only relevant ones in this decision. Yet it is not clear that stock-market-derived indicators of volatility are necessarily forward-looking measures in the same way as, say, indicators of demand derived from commodity futures markets.

Market-derived indicators of demand reflect the valuations of a large number of buyers and sellers, and this represents *more* information than any one firm or group of firms within an industry has available on its own. The reverse is true with indicators of volatility. Private knowledge within a firm may be well anticipated *internally* and well understood – and therefore represent a minimal source of uncertainty. Yet the same knowledge may translate into substantial volatility in the stock market (when private information is formally announced, for example). In these cases, 'uncertainty' amongst individual actors stems from unanticipated stock market reaction (including unanticipated increases in volatility in stock price) rather than volatility *per se*. Volatility in stock prices might be a direct influence on investor's decisions to purchase or not to purchase the stock of a particular company, but may be only a very indirect influence on decisions by actors within those companies to engage in capital investments in real producing assets.

An Example: Flexibility of Labour versus Capital

If a firm has the flexibility to adapt to unanticipated change, then *ceteris paribus* returns will not be as sensitive to uncertainty as they would be with less scope to adapt. This freedom to change is a fundamental consideration in any investment choice and will be discussed at length in Chapter 11.

A number of models of investment behaviour (for example; Oi, 1961; Hartman, 1972, 1976; Abel, 1983: all quoted in Leahy and Whited, 1995) postulate that because labour is more flexible than capital, firms with higher labour/capital ratios can benefit (achieve higher returns to capital) under uncertainty. If labour can adjust to price shocks, for example, then the presence of price fluctuations will lead firms to change their capital/labour ratio, thus causing the marginal revenue product of capital to change by more than the movement in price.[7] Abel (1983) discusses such a model. Pindyck and Solimano (1993) also describe a model using fixed proportions of labour and capital, whereby flexibility is introduced through underutilization of capital.[8]

Figure 7.8 illustrates this 'flexible labour' model. Assume first a project with no uncertainty that has a return of U_A. Now introduce some uncertainty as shown by curve A. Curve A has an *expected* return of U_A, and as long as the source of the uncertainty is mean preserving and there is a linear relationship between this variable and the return, then the expected return is unchanged. With sufficient ability to adapt, some of the negative outcomes can be avoided, and some of the positive outcomes can be exploited. The *expected* return on this now-asymmetric distribution improves to U_B.

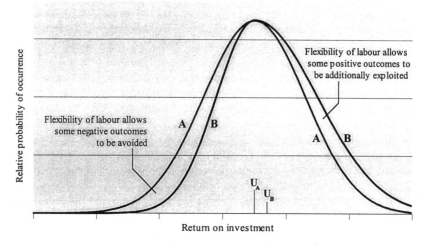

Figure 7.8: Flexibility leading to increasing returns under uncertainty

The asymmetric change is a characteristic of *anything* that facilitates adaptation, not only labour flexibility. Following Abel (1983), Leahy and Whited have attempted to capture the impact of this through examination of labour/capital ratios within their data set.

The results from this work show no evidence to support the theory that flexibility of labour can induce convexity in the marginal revenue product of capital leading to increased investment under uncertainty.

One of the difficulties in meaningful interpretation of these results is differentiating 'uncertainty' from *unanticipated* variability. Since stock prices reflect all that is generally known about some stock, changes in price are appropriate proxies for unanticipated events. Following this logic, the *variability* of stock prices is assumed to reflect variability in the input or output factors that a firm faces.[9] Yet changes in a stock's price are frequently just noise. Decision-makers within a firm have difficulty separating stock price changes that are valid signals of market value from changes that are due to this noise. Anything that is not understood in some fundamental way is frequently regarded as noise and will not necessarily impact decisions in the manner suggested in these models.

If an industry is faced with some unanticipated shock, then *ceteris paribus* the more flexible firms will suffer least. If there is general recognition that the future will be more variable than the past, then firms will adopt different technologies that allow increased adaptability.[10] But even if these changes mean technologies with higher labour/capital ratios, this does not imply any *a priori* direction in the sign of capital investment to provide for less sensitivity to increases in variability.

Investment in Capital-intensive Industry

As was suggested on page 101 the indicators of volatility in a private intra-firm sense may be quite different to the indicators of volatility suggested by changes in stock price. This result is supported by the work of Leahy and Whited. Managers appear to take little cognizance of the uncertainties facing other market participants, but base their decisions on their own uncertainty characteristics. Moreover, industry-wide uncertainty (such as uncertainty about the price of copper for a copper producer) still subjects producers to the concave relation between return-on-investment and price, but this uncertainty may be sufficiently idiosyncratic that it is not reflected in the stock returns of producers.

The temporal utility model suggests that uncertainty influences individual investment choices in two ways:

1. The stock market value is an indicator of the cost of capital (the reservation line in the temporal utility model) and is the *rule* by which individual projects come to be assessed. More volatility in stock price *ceteris paribus* means a lower stock price, and a lower stock price means a higher cost of capital. Yet, as set out in Chapter 6, for particular projects the relevant indicator is the marginal cost of capital and at the time of decision-making this is only understood in an expectational sense. A mining company suffering under stock market pressure due to its investments in uranium and asbestos production may have a low marginal cost of capital for a new venture into copper production, but this will not be reflected in stock market returns.

2. The *rule* by which individual projects come to be assessed is only the hurdle that has to be jumped, and variability (or uncertainty) in the height of this hurdle is different to variability (or uncertainty) in the project's ability to jump. Project uncertainty is much more volatile than is the cost of capital, since cost-of-capital issues pertain to the whole company, which might involve dozens of such projects. It is this *project* uncertainty that is the prime focus of decision-makers' attention.

Figure 7.9 shows the situation portrayed in terms of the temporal utility model. Assume from this figure that a project (Case A) satisfies a firm's criteria for acceptance: the *expected* return is U_A, and, as subjectively understood, there is less than a 5 per cent chance that outcomes will result in a return less than the cost of capital. Now consider some unanticipated exogenous shock that increases the variability of returns.

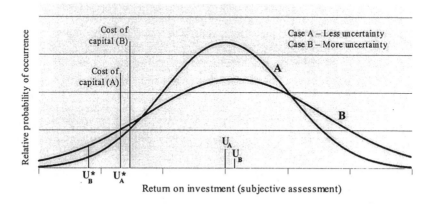

Figure 7.9: Uncertainty impact on individual investment decision

Even with no change in *expected* return the attractiveness of the project is relatively worse than prior to the shock. The return on investment is reduced relative to the cost of capital, and there is a higher probability of outcomes yielding returns that are less than the cost of capital. This is the case that is effectively being examined in the empirical work described in the first section of this chapter.

Now consider the case where the exogenous shock is also *advantageous* to the project in question (Case B in Figure 7.9). Stock market reaction increases the cost of capital, but the *expected* return still exceeds the cost of capital by the same amount as before. From an aggregate perspective, the new situation is neutral with respect to the shock. From an individual project perspective, the result is not neutral. Idiosyncratic uncertainty means that the project now fails to satisfy the reservation precondition.

As drawn in Figure 7.9, the reservation precondition, formerly at U^*_A, is now at U^*_B – a change that is substantially greater than the change in *expected* return. Where the uncertainty measure is derived only from changes in the cost of capital – by the use of stock market volatility indicators – this change in reservation condition remains unrecognized.

Several implications flow from this representation. To understand these implications, the style of investment must be identified, and it is the style of investment that also offers scope for differentiation of these effects empirically. For ease of explanation, assume that the shock is a demand shock, implying increased uncertainty about *price* (the price of copper, for a copper producer). Further, assume that the firm has a portfolio of potential projects in various stages of evaluation, including some projects for which commitment was immediately pending. What is the impact of this shock?

1. The immediate effect of any shock is a fall in share price of producing firms – signalling a relative preference for investment away from the industry subject to the shock. The cost of capital for all new investment in that industry increases. Until the (changed) uncertainty is understood, all commitments are put on hold, suggesting an immediate hiatus of investment activity, pending a change in rank ordering as described in 2–5 below.

2. The shock may result in an increased *expected* return for some projects (like Case B in Figure 7.9). These projects are potentially as viable as before, but now fail the reservation precondition. Additional knowledge and/or modifications to the project to balance the (increased) upside potential with the now-increased downside risk must be developed to again satisfy the reservation precondition[11] following which the project can be re-ranked.

3. If the expected return does not change, or if it decreases, then there is an unambiguous negative effect on investment. The negative effect is due to the twin effects of the higher cost of capital and the higher probability of outcomes with returns less than the cost of capital. In the copper industry, for example, this would be the case for all copper-based projects whose return on investment *and* cost of capital is sensitive to the price of copper.

4. Not all projects within an industry have a return on investment that is sensitive to the price of the product. Capital investments aimed at reducing the cost of production have a revenue source (the saved operating costs) that is independent of the price of the product. Thus, even with no change in *expected* return, this style of project is relatively advantaged compared to projects in 3 above.

5. Capital investments can also be directed into projects aimed at reducing the sensitivity of the whole project to the shocks. The marginal cost of capital for this style of project derives from the expected reduction in average cost of capital for the project as a whole. Investments into product diversification, 'tied' offtake arrangements (even agreed to at below-market price), and vertical integration fit this style of investment.

The examination of these elements suggests a number of ways that the model can be tested empirically, some of which have been examined in more detail in Runge (1996) showing further support for the model.

NOTES

1. Indecisiveness or procrastination, frequently viewed as a failing, is a commonly observed phenomena in large decisions. This phenomenon, and its counterpart: institutionalized mechanisms for the correction of recognized or possible indecisiveness, are essential elements of any theory of capital investment choice. The procrastination problem was examined (and labelled the 'bad news principle of irreversible investments') by Bernanke (1983), and also studied in other contexts by Baldwin and Meyer (1979).
2. The existence of a reservation line that leaves the actor no worse after choice than before choice is to suggest that there is such an option available against which alternatives may be compared. Clearly this may not be the case. The issue of what constitutes the benchmark against which uncertain outcomes can be compared is addressed more fully on pp. 83–5.
3. In this model, risk aversion is defined differently to the definition in the neoclassical literature. With most neoclassical models actors are risk averse if they exhibit a diminishing marginal utility with *wealth*. In the model used in this book, risk aversion is figured in the *utility* dimension – it has to do with the tolerance for an outcome that results in reduced utility. See additional discussion on this topic on p. 85.
4. The dilemma with the 'large decision' problem is that, since it is assumed to encompass the complete future opportunity set, the choice itself subsumes the guidelines usually available for decision-making of a 'lower' order. This problem is analogous to the problem of post-constitutional and constitutional levels of political interaction studied by Buchanan. Following Knight, Buchanan applies the principle of the *relatively absolute absolute*, which requires adherence to and acceptance of established patterns of authority, behaviour and values while at the same time and at still another (and 'higher') level of consciousness calling all such patterns and values into question (see, for example, Buchanan, 1992, 78–9). A simplified but more formalized application of this principle to the corporate decision environment is set out in Chapter 8.
5. The survey by Summers (1987b) was focused on the discount rates applying to *depreciation allowances*, not capital investment as a whole; however, 94 per cent of respondents used the same rate to discount depreciation allowances as all other project cash flows.
6. Lindberg and Ross (1981) examine a large number of US companies and find the highest values of q for firms with a strong competitive advantage, very strong brand images, and/or patent protection. Those with the lowest values are generally in highly competitive, often shrinking industries with limited barriers to entry.
7. There is some anecdotal evidence for this proposition. The RioTinto Group – the world's largest mining company – analyses projects using country-specific tax rates *as well as* (amongst other analytical techniques) tax rates substantially less than the standard rate. The impact of applying a lower tax rate on a standard discounted cash flow analysis is to bias the technology in favour of more capital intensive mining schemes: increasing the average revenue product of labour, reducing the project sensitivity to labour costs, but, in the event of *ex post* variability being greater than expected, facilitating expansion with increasing marginal revenue product of capital. Nevertheless, techniques also employed in this and most other mining companies, following the model in Chapter 7, limit investment choices at least initially to outputs less than the long-term average cost minima. Thus *observed* investments may follow the model suggested by Abel (1983), but this does not necessarily imply that total investment increases under such a model. Projects that are viable for outputs at the long-term average cost minima may be non-viable at the lesser outputs that this strategy implies. It is not known what relative importance is placed on these analytical

techniques within RioTinto or other mining companies compared to the 'standard' discounted cash flow analysis.

8. '[E]ven with fixed proportions, this convexity can result from the ability of the firm to vary output, so that the marginal unit of capital need not be utilized at times when the output price is low or input costs are high' (Pindyck and Solimano, 1993, 268). This approach is similar to the example in note 7. Following the model in Chapter 9, non-utilization of marginal capital is unlikely to be viable based on *price* being low, but if the producer faces a downward-sloping demand curve, then non-utilization of marginal capital may be justifiable based on *marginal revenue* being low.

9. I can find no empirical support for this proposition. The brief discussion on p. 101 suggests that this might not be the case, or that it has only a very weak connection with volatility or confidence for decision-making within the firm itself.

10. Following deregulation of electricity generation in the UK, Australia and (to a lesser extent) USA, there is a distinct trend toward more flexible electricity generating plant, with gas turbines and co-generation facilities being favoured over the (previous) focus on large generating stations. Thus increased uncertainty following deregulation *does* favour technologies with higher labour/capital ratios, but *reduced* investment.

11. In the late 1980s a situation similar to this occurred in the world copper industry. Rebels on the New Guinea island of Bougainville unexpectedly forced the closure of the massive Bougainville Copper Mine, and forced the re-evaluation of political uncertainties everywhere in the less-developed world. The cost of capital for mining projects throughout the less-developed world increased. At the same time, the reduction in supply of copper to the world market implied an increase in *expected* return on copper projects elsewhere. The higher expected return implied for copper projects in Chile (for example) allowed easier negotiation and stronger guarantees between copper producers and the Chilean government to prevent a similar problem in that country, and, after this uncertainty had been assimilated, triggered a major boom in Chilean copper investments.

8. Capital investment choice process

This chapter describes the process leading to capital investment choice within a firm. It postulates and develops the theory for rational investment in information even without changes in expected return. It examines the institutions for uncertainty reduction and highlights important limitations on these institutions that lead to results substantially different from the profit maximization ideal.

The chapter is in four sections. The first examines the capital investment choice process, assuming an individual (an entrepreneur) to be the single decision-making entity. Each iteration in this process involves confirmation and refinement of rules as well as identification of the opportunity cost associated with choice alternatives.

The second section (p. 121) introduces the institutions influencing capital investment choice and their impact on uncertainty reduction. Institutions that reduce uncertainty but do not necessarily affect the *expected* value are important in the temporal utility model in ways that are not evident in the standard models. Such institutions play a pivotal role in overcoming the limited knowledge and computational power problems that observers such as Simon (1986) see as the primary barriers to acceptance of many of the neoclassical postulates.

The third section (p. 128) drops the assumption of the firm acting as a single, coordinating entity and examines how the iterative choice process is played out within the corporate institutions typically charged with this decision authority. This section compares 'value' as it influences investment in information with value as it influences actual large-scale capital investment. In addition, it examines the role of institutions and individuals who have agenda control within those institutions. It suggests that limitations on achieving efficient outcomes (in the narrow neoclassical sense) stem from the way projects are presented and in the way that the evaluation rules themselves are selected or rejected.

From the time when actions offering potential entrepreneurial profits are identified to when they are acted upon, the market place is characterized by unexploited gains from trade. Given the lengthy delay involved in any capital investment decision process, such a state of affairs is the norm in this sector of the economy. In the final section (p. 133) uncertainty-based criteria are developed to correspond to the marginal revenue/marginal cost criterion that defines the limit of choice in a world of no uncertainty.

CHOICE AS AN ITERATIVE PROCEDURE

The choice process begins with uneasiness and an imagined set of conditions that, if acted upon, potentially offer higher utility than some default option likely to transpire in the absence of such (redirected) action. This section traces the process from when such alternatives or sets of alternatives are first conceived and understood in only the broadest way, to when action to bring about the envisaged alternative ensues.

Choice Environment

Chapter 3 characterized uncertainty and went on to describe the steps whereby this uncertainty came to be understood in the capital investment choice process.

The first step in understanding uncertainty requires distinguishing the factors influencing the choice that are due to pure chance from the factors which are the result of human action.

Pure chance events

Uncertainty deriving from true chance has no impact upon capital investment choice once its characteristics are known, but the *process* of choice must still discover these characteristics and take the following points into account:

- Of the pure chance factors, what *are* the uncertainty characteristics? Are the uncertainty characteristics (the variance, or β value, for example) the same across alternatives, or are there differential variations across sectors or across time?
- In discovering these uncertainty characteristics, the cost of search must be balanced against the expected increase in value following the search.

Events that are the result of human action

Many events or elements of uncertainty which are outcomes of human action are at least conceptually discoverable.[1] Included in this category are the actor's *own* action or expected action both *now* (at the time of the initial decision) and in the future, when there is likely to be a changed environment, only parts of which can be rationally predicted in advance. This style of uncertainty can be conceptually divided into two categories:

- strategic action, whereby the capital investment choice itself is likely to generate behaviour by the actor him- or herself or by other market participants explicitly influencing the choice decision. *For example, choice decisions part-way through a phased development should logically ignore sunk capital, and may therefore be different to the decision that the same actor might predict he or she would make from the vantage point prior to any investment taking place*;
- action by other market participants as passive participants (price-takers) consistent with the typical assumptions in neoclassical consumer choice theory.

Even allowing that these influences are conceptually discoverable, the marginal cost to do so outweighs the marginal benefit of much information. Choice must ultimately be subject to residual uncertainty. Resolution of these uncertainties requires investment in information. Yet only some of this additional information can be balanced against an *ex ante* expected return.

By way of a counter-example, Stigler (1961) examined the economics of information, assuming a distribution of prices independent of human factors and whose dispersion was known. In this case, the marginal cost in additional search could be balanced against the *ex ante* marginal value. There was a *determinate* result that the actor had a certain probability of discovering.

Stigler recognized that this did not encompass the full gamut of the search process:

> If a buyer enters a wholly new market, he will have no idea of the dispersion of prices and hence no idea of the rational amount of search he should make. In such cases the dispersion will presumably be estimated by some sort of sequential process, and this approach would open up a set of problems I must leave for others to explore. (Stigler, 1961, 219)

The difficulty, recognized but not followed up by Stigler, is that in this style of search, that is, aiming to discover the dispersion of values, additional search does not result in any change in expected value *ex ante*. If the 'true' dispersion prior to search was thought to be, say, β_1 there is no *a priori* expectation that, after search, it will be any different to β_1. The value of search at the margin aimed at discovering dispersion characteristics – even for events that stem from pure chance – cannot be rationally balanced against *ex ante* changes in expected utility (at least, expected utility as traditionally defined).

The same difficulty applies where information relates to events that are the result of human action. Here there is no given dispersion of potential outcomes to be 'discovered', but rather, the search process is one of generating alternatives and selecting and modifying one's own actions such that the final result is subject to less dispersion (less uncertainty). The value of search at the margin cannot be rationally balanced against *ex ante* changes in expected utility as traditionally defined. *Ex ante,* only the dispersion of potential outcomes will be less, not the *expected utility* (as traditionally defined).

This is the choice environment examined in this sub-section. The results presented by Stigler (1961) are accepted within the sub-set of uncertain choices examined by him. We aim to complete the analysis by examining cases where additional search, or investment in additional information does not change the *expected* value *ex ante*, but *does* result in a reduction in uncertainty *ex ante*.

Shackelian Choice Model

Shackle (1983) examined the process whereby individuals face decisions leading them into the unknowable future: 'A question faces everyone at almost every hour: what will the sequel be, if I do this, or if I do this?' The question is identical to the capital investment choice problem.

The process which leads to acceptance (implementation) or rejection of particular courses of action can be thought of as comprising five primary components understood according to the flowchart in Figure 8.1:

1. The first component, deriving from the institutional setting, defines the *constraints* on the available choice set: 'The individual has a conception of the technology of nature and of the capacities and propensities of human nature. Thus he has notions of the sort of thing that can take place' (Shackle, 1983, 60).

2. The second component represents the initial entrepreneurial element in the process – envisaging choice alternatives: '[This phase] is *imaginative*, the origination of various inceptive modes of use of the chooser's array of means of action, and the conceiving, for each such mode, a skein of rival imagined sequels' (ibid., 64).

3. The next phase is that of critical *examination*. The 'sequels which, in such time as his deadline or some exterior signal allows him, the chooser has invented for any one mode, must be tested for possibility. The path of each must be scanned for obstacles. Those sequels which emerge unscathed are the basis of the claim of the particular course of action or mode of inceptive use of resources to be the chosen one' (ibid.).

4. The next phase is that of *valuation*. In Shackle's construct, each sequel 'imagined and deemed possible for some course of action must be assigned a representative point on an axis of desiredness – counter-desiredness' (ibid.).

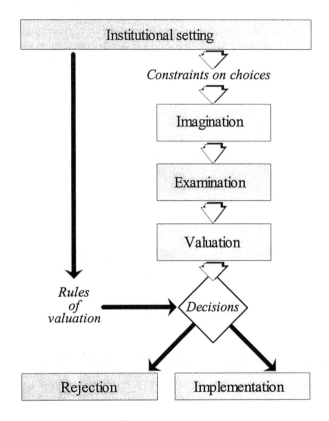

Figure 8.1: Shackelian choice model

5. The final component, defined more narrowly by Shackle, but nevertheless an essential element in the process, again derives from the institutional setting and involves the *rules of valuation*: '[C]omparisons of one sequel with another in the performance of this task cannot be made directly by means of such a technological description, for when two sequels are compared, one may be more desired than the other in one respect but less desired in another' (ibid., 62).

There are two primary difficulties with this monosequential approach:

1. If 'each choosable course of action must be linked with some imagined sequels, or some combination of imagined sequels, which belong to this course alone', it follows that elements of the future that are common to all alternatives do not need to enter the evaluation. Yet the process set out by Shackle assumes that prior to valuation, the scanning for obstacles and testing for possibility is constrained only by 'such time as [the actor's]

deadline or some exterior signal' allows. Such scanning and testing is logically constrained by the expected value returned from such effort, and 'signals' or deadlines are *not* external to the decision process.

2. Shackle postulates a certain rule of valuation. Whilst it is assuredly true that the process *starts* with some initial rule, to suggest that all rules are external to the decision process is to imply that all of the elements that differentiate between choices are known beforehand. Such a situation is unlikely. Actors will consider *first* those attributes which constitute value in some higher-level rank-ordering sense and will continue revision and extension of the rules until the expected difference in value according to these extended rules is less than the cost of assimilation.

The modification of the Shackelian model to address these difficulties is set out in the next sub-section.

Iterative Choice Model

The assessment of choice alternatives proceeds from the Shackelian model but is instead conceived as an iterative one. Each iteration consists of all five steps, with choices and rules of valuation being determined in part from preceding iterations.

In each step (except the final step) choice alternatives are assessed only to the point where differences in value allow rejection of alternatives. Choice under this model is not one of selecting any particular course of action, but is rather one of *rejecting* a course of action that can be demonstrated to offer lesser value. Only in the final step can any one alternative be thought of as being comprehensively understood (accepted for implementation).

This iterative process is introduced using the example of Stigler (1961) regarding the purchase of a used car – a process better understood but nevertheless conceptually no different from the capital investment decision process within a firm.

At the start of the Stigler example, the car-buyer is already positioned in a used car lot. The model starts at the point where he *has already decided to buy a used car.* It sets out a decision-making mechanism as an optimization problem given a known dispersion of prices of used cars. This is actually just the penultimate step in a more comprehensive decision process, since some prior step in this decision process must have addressed the question: What about buying a new car, or, for that matter, keeping the old car longer? The answer is that these alternatives have already been eliminated *during some prior iteration* of the decision-making process.[2]

If in the Stigler example *new* cars are not in the choice set, then presumably the value associated with the *set* of potential new cars (the rejected set of alternatives) is less than for the *set* of used cars. Within the precision of the information, the attributes that differentiate between the set of new cars and the set of used cars must have been such that lesser-ranked attributes (for example, the attributes that differentiate one new car from another new car, or one used car from another used car) could be ignored on a comparative basis.

How then does the iterative process advance *ab initio*? How does an actor learn which attribute is important or unimportant so that alternatives can be rationally compared?

The process is assumed to start with an institutional setting and an established paradigm[3] under which business within the firm is conducted. Such a paradigm is not immutable, but for the purposes of this example includes only such elements as can be assumed to be so. This paradigm defines at the highest level the rules to be applied for choice within the corporate context. It includes codes of moral behaviour (for example, that the firm will not engage in bribery in pursuit of corporate objectives) as well as implicit rules forming part of the corporate culture. Thus choice alternatives which have attributes that fail to satisfy these most highly ranked value requirements are immediately rejected, regardless of any notions of 'expected return' or 'uncertainty' expressed in more formal (less subjective) ways.

Following Choi (1993, 7), 'every human action presupposes an associated paradigm; its identification is the crux of decision making under uncertainty', and 'individuals will continue searching for a paradigm until they find one'.[4] Whilst the identification of this paradigm is vital, it is the crux of the problem only in the sense that it is the starting point from which all subsequent rules for decision-making under uncertainty are ultimately derived. Actors cannot make choices without first having a rule that allows choices to be compared. The paradigm is the first such rule, however primitive.

For any established firm the paradigm will include such things as its moral codes of conduct but it will also *exclude* certain activities. For example, capital investments into, say, baby foods would be excluded from a mining company's choice set because the corporate institutions have no mechanism to comprehend such choices. The institutional setting is not just defined by actions or choice sets included or excluded. Indeed, the ability or inability to comprehend changed or different situations is also part of this paradigm.

Starting from this initial guideline, Figure 8.2 illustrates the process extended from Figure 8.1 to incorporate progressive revision, rejection of non-viable options and extension to the rules of valuation. The first iteration is concerned only with *classes* of investments, not individual investments, since the detail of an individual case is not required just to differentiate it from other whole classes of investment. Perhaps in practice an *individual* investment will be used as an exemplar of this class, but at this early stage in the decision process the focus of evaluation is on the class, not the individual investment.

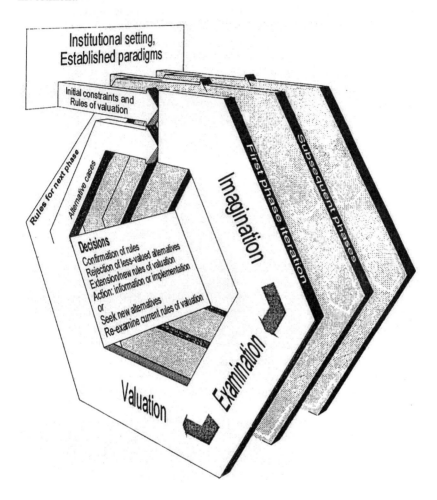

Figure 8.2: Iterative choice model

'Choice' in any early iterations does not mean implementation, hence the *feasibility* of any class does not have to be proven: the actor must merely be satisfied that following additional search, research and information such an outcome is likely. It is not necessary to *design* a conveyor system, for example, to be satisfied that such a system will work and to know what a properly designed conveyor system will cost.

Information is prioritized on a class basis. Thus, as a class, the value of copper industry investments is most sensitive to the selling price of copper. There is little value (that is to say, the marginal value is less than the marginal cost) in seeking out information about one particular copper mine until actors can be sure that copper mines in general will not be excluded because of some overarching negative perception about copper that affects all such alternatives. Many mining companies face this dilemma with politically sensitive minerals such as asbestos, uranium, lead and mercury.

The difference between a rule and the application of a rule may be difficult to discern. 'Selling price' itself is not a rule, but knowledge that 'copper mines are most sensitive to the selling price' *is* such a rule. It is an understanding amongst corporate decision-makers that is institutionalized in a near-paradigmatic way. People engaged in certain industries carry with them perceptions of what is important and what is not important, and these perceptions form the initial rules that underpin subsequent valuation: 'Rules which we cannot state thus do not govern only our actions. They also govern our perceptions, and particularly our perceptions of other people's actions' (Hayek, 1967, 45).

Institutionalized mechanisms that allow actors to make valuations under uncertainty carry with them a danger. The danger is that the set of alternatives brought forward for consideration are *selected* on the basis of the institutionalized value scale and then (initially, at least) *valued* according to the same ranking mechanism. Entirely different sets of alternatives may be equally valid when selected and ranked on a different scale. The following example dramatically illustrates this danger:

In the late 1980s, Johannesburg Consolidated Investments Limited (JCI), then a large South African mining house, was engaged in the evaluation of the Potgeitersrus Platinum deposit in the northern part of South Africa. Reserves were sufficient for many decades of production, and the majority of these were at depths appropriate only for *underground mining* – a technology that constituted JCI's primary area of expertise. A large and potentially profitable underground mine was planned. Approval for implementation was imminent.

Due to circumstances which would not normally have arisen at such a late stage in the evaluation process (in this case, the availability of certain taxation advantages) the company had occasion to re-examine the deposit from an entirely different perspective as an *open cut mining* proposition. This re-examination was undertaken using different personnel (Runge Pty Ltd – an Australian consulting firm) who focused on not only *planning* a new open-cut mine but also on re-examining the *rules* by which the deposit came to be understood.

Dramatic changes followed. Reserves under these new rules *increased* because much of the material previously considered to be waste contained lower grades of platinum, and this material was viable to mine in an open pit environment. The marginal cost of recovering the contained metal from these lower grades of material was easily covered by the value of the contained platinum when only the extra costs of delivery to a processing plant rather than dumping to waste were considered.

The result was that the mine commenced profitable operation in 1991 as one of the world's largest *open pit* platinum mines. Further, the development of the underground mine was not precluded since the reserve depletion associated with the open pit mine involved only minimal impact on the economic viability of any underground development.

Two lessons can be drawn from this example:

1. Rules at a high level need not be fixed in a strict sense of the word (for example, as in the *legal* system) yet may still be treated as such in the decision framework of an actor. Changes to *these* rules can lead to dramatic changes in action (what some observers refer to as a paradigm shift).

2. If *all* alternatives fail some acceptance criteria, then other alternatives will naturally be considered. Yet, provided *one* alternative satisfies the acceptance criteria, there is not necessarily any mechanism to alert the actor that other *even more* valuable options are potentially available. There is clear economic value in pursuing alternatives already shown to be viable, but there is no such incentive in expending effort to seek out alternatives that may not exist when these alternatives *ex ante* have no expected value beyond existing options.

These two aspects highlight the contribution of entrepreneurial alertness and its role at this stage in the process.

Following Shackle's 'imagination' and 'examination' steps, the valuation or decision mechanism can now be defined. This mechanism always involves a comparison between one alternative and some other alternative, and decisions following each iteration are the same:

1. *Confirmation* of the valuation criteria used in the current iteration. The relative value of the alternatives (both the rejected alternative and the one brought forward for further consideration) must confirm the importance of the ranking criteria adopted for their acceptance or rejection.

2. *Rejection* of alternatives that are of less value based on this criteria.

3. Development of an *extended valuation criterion* for the next iteration, using characteristics of the set of alternatives that have been tentatively accepted. If the iterative process is now to proceed looking at just one

class of alternatives, say copper projects, then the first criterion, the copper selling price, may be insufficient to differentiate between them.

4. *Advancement (action)* – expenditure on information – to allow more detailed examination of the tentatively accepted class of alternatives; that is, to examine and compare one or more sub-sets of this class based on a now wide-ranging set of attributes.

If the currently established valuation criterion is not met by any of the options, then the process offers two additional possibilities:

1. other alternatives are considered, and/or

2. guidelines for valuation used to arrive at the current iteration should be re-visited and questioned.

The choice process cannot proceed past any one iteration until the extended rules applying to the next iteration are defined.

Two additional aspects flow from this model:

1. Action in the early stages of the process is only concerned with increasing the subjective value of alternatives that, until a very advanced stage, cannot be valued via any market-based mechanism. Even final implementation (the go-ahead) of major projects is rarely a *carte blanche* approval on the irreversible conversion of corporate cash into physical assets, but instead represents just a more pronounced commitment to expenditure on physical assets over information. Frequently, the initial phased development of large capital projects is predicated on the reduction in uncertainty (information) achieved through actual production, rather than production *per se*. It is not uncommon for the early phases of production associated with major capital projects to offer poor returns when only production aspects are considered, yet this is still a viable strategy for project developers who can then proceed to later stages of project development with increased confidence and efficiency.[5]

2. The process does not provide for any abandonment, since even continuing with a status quo option is still action in this model. If all alternatives fail to fulfil corporate guidelines, then the only retreat is a revision of those guidelines. In the ultimate case, even the institutional setting and established paradigms can be brought into question.[6]

Early stages of the evaluation involve uncertainty that will prohibit commitment based on typical corporate risk-aversion profiles. How then does the assessment of value proceed? Using a copper versus coal mine example, and assuming that corporate actors have risk aversion defined as 'less than 5 per cent chance of losing money', decision-makers face the situation portrayed in Figure 8.3.

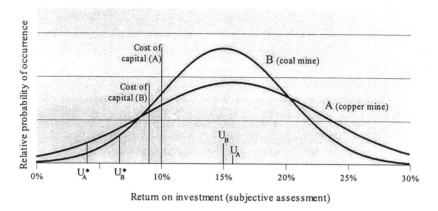

Figure 8.3: Private value of uncertain alternatives

Under the model in this figure, additional resources on 'search' reduce the dispersion *ex ante* but there is no *ex ante* change in expected return (the values of U_A and U_B in Figure 8.3 do not change *ex ante* with additional information).

The procedure leading to choice or interim choice proceeds thus:

1. Both alternatives indicate an expected return which exceeds the cost of capital; and assuming that new information has the potential to reduce the uncertainty without influencing the expected return, then neither project can be eliminated from consideration on these grounds. The information may well change the expected return, but the direction of this change is not known *ex ante*. Expenditure on search is warranted and may be rationally pursued.

2. The choice alternatives are each shown with a different cost of capital. This is the norm. Status quo alternatives and extensions to existing operations would ordinarily have lower costs of capital due to better market understanding. Also, status quo alternatives commonly have less uncertainty because knowledge is better. Nevertheless, *neither* project can proceed because neither project satisfies the reservation criterion of 'less than 5 per cent chance that the return will be less than the cost of capital'.

3. Whilst neither project can be rejected, can one project be shown to be inferior to the other? Using the representation in Figure 8.3, a determinate outcome cannot be made. If a forced determination had to be made, alternative B would be favoured since at the '5 per cent probability of loss' line it has a higher subjective valuation (U^*_B) than alternative A. Expenditure on information is warranted for alternative A. The limit of this expenditure is determined by the point when one or other alternative

can be rejected. Within this narrowly defined choice set, two criteria apply:

(a) if the cost of information to bring the subjective valuation of A (U^*_A) up to the same level as alternative B is more than the difference between these two on an expected value basis (that is, $U_A - U_B$) alternative B would be favoured on both criteria;

(b) if the cost of information to bring the subjective valuation of A (U^*_A) up to the same level as alternative B is more than the difference between these two on a reservation utility basis (that is, $U^*_B - U^*_A$) then a stalemate situation applies. Value foregone (elsewhere in the actors' opportunity set) is more than the expected increase in value[7] resulting from the new information. This situation is examined below.

4. Since neither alternative can be eliminated in this round, the first-level iteration must be undertaken again after alternative A has been re-evaluated.

5. If after this round both alternatives are equal on the reservation criterion (the U* valuations), then the expected value criteria (NPV of the *expected* outcome) should become the basis of valuation.

The *size* of project doesn't influence choice under this model. Larger projects are already discounted by the higher relative cost of capital that their size implies.

Even for projects which are not mutually exclusive, the model provides a valid ranking criterion for claims on the next increment of the firm's capital. Projects rejected in any round may still be re-examined in subsequent rounds (against further alternatives) although the higher marginal cost of capital, coming as it does after fulfilment of earlier round commitments, means that stricter criteria for acceptance apply. Thus projects that are extensions to existing activities of the firm can be accepted even with lower returns than other projects: because the lesser uncertainty of these extensions allows the reservation criterion to be satisfied even with higher costs of capital.

Iterations and information search continue until either of two events happens (from an *ex ante* perspective):

1. The uncertainty reduces to the point where there is less than 5 per cent chance of the outcome falling short of the reservation line (cost of capital line). The project can proceed; or

2. The expected cost of information necessary to bring the project to the point where it satisfies the reservation criterion exceeds the increase in notional value under this criterion (a stalemate).

A stalemate means that the project is potentially viable (the expected return exceeds the cost of capital), but the cost of proving it so, given the risk-aversion characteristics of the existing owners, will probably render it uneconomical. In this case, several devices are usually employed to break the stalemate:

1. Parts or all of the project are sold to an actor with lower aversion to risk or with lower costs of capital.

2. The project is put on hold. Again, this is just 'another' alternative – an alternative that provides for reduction in uncertainty through reduced information costs derived from pecuniary externalities in the market.

3. A self-interested agent who can convince the firm to commit to the uncertainty-reducing expenditure on information can *then* present the firm with a viable project investment, given that such costs are then sunk costs and do not affect the decision to proceed.

At least two further outcomes flow from option 2: (a) under this temporal utility model, it is rational for the owners of such a project to wait, despite the project being notionally viable (under standard neoclassical constructs); (b) the increased value derived from waiting exceeds the cost (that is, the deferred present value).

A strategy of project advancement whereby actors *plan* to wait may not be viable except at the very start. If actors knew *ex ante* that they were likely to be in such a situation they would be unlikely to start. Nevertheless, such a strategy still makes economic sense *after* commencement because information costs are usually sunk costs. This situation is not uncommon in many jurisdictions. For example, the non-transferability of tax credits associated with past information costs effectively imposes a transaction cost on the transfer of the project to other parties.

INSTITUTIONS FOR REDUCING UNCERTAINTY

The focus of this section is on the role of institutions in reducing uncertainty and the implications for economic activity.

If the uncertainty is actuarially determinable, then institutions addressing this can function even outside a market environment: pooling of resources among actors with identical utility functions can achieve satisfactory results. Such institutions, though important in market economies, are of only minor interest in this book. If the uncertainty is *not* actuarially determinable, then institutions addressing this are not so easily defined. The primary area of interest in this section involves such institutions. Two styles of institutions are considered:

1. where the uncertainty is independent of the actor. Institutions servicing uncertainty-reducing functions in this area provide the mechanism to

distribute risk and, via market prices, to align expectations and thereby reduce 'real' risk. They free individual actors to focus on only those characteristics that are unique to the task at hand;

2. where risk reduction is a strongly subjective phenomenon. Institutions also play a role in subjective risk reduction independent of identifiable changes in real market phenomena.

The role of institutions for uncertainty reduction was addressed by Lachmann (1971), who focused on the 'plan[s] which guide the observable acts' of human action and the uncertainty associated with such plans. Contrasting the truly random influences that give rise to this uncertainty and the influences that derive from human action, Lachmann notes that '*formally* for the actor there is no difference between the action of others and any other circumstances affecting the constraints bounding his freedom of action' but that '*materially* a significant difference lies in the fact that, since human action is more volatile than the conditions of nature, it is far less easy to predict. In a complex society such as our own, in which the success of our plans indirectly depends on the actions of millions of other people, how can our orientation scheme provide us with firm guidance? The answer has to be sought in the existence, nature, and functions of *institutions*' (Lachmann, 1971, 49; original emphasis).

In this construct, Lachmann suggests that '[i]f the plan is a mental scheme in which the conditions of action are coordinated, we may regard institutions, as it were, as orientation schemes of the second order, to which planners orientate their plans as actors orientate their actions to a plan'. This construct is analogous to the iterative planning cycle described above.

Institutions form the guidelines for the preparation of plans and the mechanism (rules) within which such plans are valued and choices compared. Institutions cover a spectrum of formality: from the more rigid structure of the legal system through to informal codes of conduct. Later phases of the process are characterized by less formal institutions. Rules deriving from actual plans are the orientation points or guidelines for action (or *plan implementation*), as Lachmann suggests – this being just the last step in any such planning process.

Institutions for Actuarial Uncertainty

In Chapter 3, the neoclassical position deriving from Knight (1921) was mentioned, wherein Knight refers to the conversion of uncertainty to 'effective certainty'. The Knightian model sees this as 'simply a matter of an elementary development of business organization to combine a sufficient number of cases to reduce the uncertainty to any desired limits'. Where uncertainty can be defined in some actuarially assessable way, such an institution or business organization does indeed fulfil this purpose. Insurance is the quintessential example of such an institution.

Whilst such modern organizations themselves are hardly 'elementary' or 'simple', the conception of them in a market economy does qualify for these terms. Markets are normally thought of as requiring *differences* in valuation between buyers and sellers. Insurance-type institutions do not even require these differences since the mere pooling of interests of a group of identical risk-averse actors will accomplish this task. Gains from trade (capitalizing on the increased value through pooling) provide the incentive structure for the establishment of the pool, but otherwise such institutions are among the most rudimentary elements of a market-based economy.

Market Institutions

The focus in this and the following sub-section is on institutions which accomplish their task of uncertainty reduction when there is no actuarially assessable way of defining the uncertainty. These institutions are styled 'market' institutions because they exist only through actors with different knowledge and risk characteristics interacting in a market setting. The stock market is the quintessential example of such an institution.

Whilst nature also introduces uncertainties that may be hard to quantify in actuarial terms, it is from the results of *human* action that this style of uncertainty is usually derived.

In the standard neoclassical models, the role of institutions in the choice process is a minor one. The reason is that 'utility' or 'value' in these models incorporates the full impact of all uncertainties associated with *each* choice. This is not the case with the temporal utility model.

On page 112 and throughout the development of the temporal utility model, the important fact has been noted that elements of the future common to all alternatives enter the evaluation only by way of the *rules* used for valuation. It is the institutional setting that defines these rules.

How such institutions undertake this task and how this is understood within the temporal utility model is best illustrated from a starting point from which this institutional support is missing. An example is during the early stages of a privately funded business built on some idea that is unknown in the market.

In the early stages of such a business, there is no mechanism to separate out uncertainties associated with the business proper from uncertainties that pertain to whole classes of businesses. The new business cannot be slotted into any particular class. Without these mechanisms the profitability and adaptability *of the business itself* must be sufficiently high that even with such uncertainties the reservation criterion is satisfied. If the business is to survive in times of poor economic conditions, then this presupposes either:

- a very high *expected* return during 'normal' times; and/or
- an actor whose tolerance for risk can accept a high proportion of potential outcomes falling short of the reservation value.

These are the conditions associated with entrepreneurial activity: superior vision to imagine opportunities and/or less aversion to risk. These conditions are the antithesis of the institutionalized world.

Yet the lack of market mechanisms to address these uncertainty problems is not all bad. Less market interaction means fewer constraints on early-stage businesses. The maximum adaptability that this implies offers scope for the minimization of potential losses. Business owners must be alert to many more factors influencing their success or failure, but are aided in this by more flexibility in adapting to them.

When the business has been operating for some time there is scope for greater market knowledge and interaction in all phases of the business. Enter the financial institutions. Finance can be obtained consistent with rates and conditions applied to sectors of the market that the business is associated with. In effect, the *rule* by which the business is now valued becomes better defined (and more restrictive) but the uncertainties related to this factor are now assumed by this market institution and do not have to be borne by the project itself.

The underlying assumption is that the cost of addressing uncertainty elements common to wide sectors of the economy will be less in an institutionalized setting than in a project-only setting. Whilst this is almost universally true, it is not the only consideration. To take advantage of this reduced cost, the project itself must accept constraints that keep it within the institutionalized setting. These restrictions themselves limit the adaptability of the individual project and therefore introduce new uncertainty.

This highlights a third characteristic of entrepreneurship relevant whenever there is scope for capital value change. It is the reluctance on the part of entrepreneurs to sacrifice adaptability – even in return for supposed increases in expected value.

The argument is analogous to Buchanan (1993) in an efficiency – liberty context: 'Individuals want to be "free to choose" among alternatives, and they do not want their choice sets constrained by the actions of other persons', and 'Liberty, rather than efficiency, assumes critical importance, although these two objectives are complementary in most applications' (Buchanan, 1993, 1). Efficiency in the capital investment choice context means the *expected return*. Acceptance of institutional constraints on business activity is normally predicated on its scope for increases in this return, and this is usually the only consideration in neoclassical constructs. The temporal utility model also offers a counterpart to 'liberty' in Buchanan's context. In this model, outcomes that do not satisfy the reservation criterion represent the scope for failure – the commercial equivalent to (loss of) liberty.

This two-pronged objective is frequently overlooked. An increase in expected return *will* normally reduce the risk (outcomes on the adverse side of the reservation line), but the satisfaction of the (risk) criterion is the *precondition*. Businesses that sacrifice adaptability in pursuit of *expected* returns must ensure that the institutional constraints do not also increase the scope for failure.

If we accept that institutional constraints can lead to efficiency without increasing the scope for outcomes that do not satisfy the reservation criterion, how can these institutional constraints be made to apply only to the institutionalized parts of a firm's activities?

Institutional constraints may be set out in some formal way (such as a loan covenant), but it is the less formal but no less valid constraints that frequently have the earliest effect on corporate conduct. Firms that have an established record in one line of business and have capital structures consistent with this line of business are severely punished if they venture too far outside this line of business. The immediate punishment takes the form of declining share price – an institutional reaction that has minimal impact on existing operations but signals to the firm: 'we have no mechanism to understand what you are *about* to do.' The cost of capital at the margin – the capital to fund the proposed new ventures – has increased dramatically. Thus the uncertainty-reducing value of the stock market effectively applies only to those activities that this institution truly understands. Many *new* business activities, even within large established firms, cannot be entered into on the assumption that existing low costs of capital will apply to them, and at the time of decision only the *expectation* of market reaction fulfils any uncertainty-reducing role (if at all).

Institutions are the embodiment of the rules and characteristics of activities that are understood in a market setting. Nevertheless, less-formal institutions also serve the same vital role in uncertainty mitigation *within* a firm. They form what has become popularly known as the 'corporate culture'. These less-formal institutions are typically the result of a set of rules which, over time, have exhibited sufficient consistency that modes of behaviour have come to follow predictable patterns throughout the organization. The origin and role of these less-formal institutions can be seen by extending the previous copper mine example and stepping through several phases of the choice process shown in Figure 8.2.

The starting point is a firm engaged in the copper mining business. Assuming a well understood history and scope of this business, the variability of the copper price will be institutionalized into the cost of capital (share price, terms of debt finance) for this firm. Investors can accommodate variability in returns due to variability in copper price more readily than individual mines can accommodate this.

At the level of the firm, the variability in the copper price does not have to be considered, except that any project, to satisfy the reservation criterion, has to show sufficient scope for returns to exceed the (marginal) cost of capital. It is this marginal cost of capital that represents the institutionalized impact of copper price variability. New copper projects can be triggered when the cost of capital reduces (even with no change in expected return) or when exceptionally good deposits are found.

The variability in the copper price *is* institutionalized, so managers can give such a factor scant consideration. Nevertheless, this does not relieve them from considering such variability since valuations are still based on the differences between individual projects, and the 'scope for adaptability' is one of these key differences. Adaptability is *not* institutionalized. All copper projects may lose money when the price of copper is low: that is acceptable, since the market has already incorporated this possibility into the cost of capital; but managers must still consider whether one project is better than another at adapting to such circumstances.

In succeeding phases, even these characteristics may be fixed and outside the control of the personnel involved. The sunk costs associated with fixed elements may effectively rule out change within the range of adaptability needed to make a difference.

The impact of the market institution is to allow a manager to ignore very important attributes (for example, variability in the copper price) outside of his or her control and allow him or her to concentrate on lesser attributes (such as adaptability) that *are* under the manager's control.

'Action' or 'management' is meaningful only in respect of factors that the actor has the scope to change. Hence, the rule or 'basis of valuation' for the implementation of alternatives will exclude higher-level institutionalized factors already in place. The rule for production operations frequently simplifies to: 'Meet production targets'. Where business activity involves low marginal costs and high capital (sunk) costs, this rule is even extended to read 'regardless of cost'. Thus, over time capital-intensive industries such as mining, airlines and electricity generation institutionalize lower-level rules *not because they are the fundamental characteristic influencing success,* but because they are the only characteristics that operators in subsequent phases of the decision process have control over. Success for these actors is synonymous with meeting production targets (mining), on-time and reliable aircraft (airline industry) and maximum utilization (electricity industry).

In a market setting, if institutionalized rules are inconsistent with the success of the underlying activity that they are seeking to simplify, competition (and losses) soon make this evident. Within a firm these competitive checking mechanisms may be quite underdeveloped.[8] They can remain masked for a considerable time and frequently only become apparent when the profitability or lack thereof becomes evident in the competitive market setting.

The institutions for decision-making within the firm are set out in more detail below.

Institutions for Subjective Risk Reduction

The institutional environment set out in the previous sub-section involved spreading risk widely among market participants and the mechanisms for promoting consistency in expectations. Both these functions result in real change in risk and real efficiency enhancement – although at a cost of less adaptability.

This sub-section recognizes that decisions are made on a subjective basis and that these assessments only indirectly mirror what might take place in the real world. Institutions also serve to facilitate uncertainty reduction in a purely subjective sense – where there is no discernible real impact on choice (except perhaps easier, faster decisions).

Institutions that serve this function are best understood through their impact on the 'low utility' end of the distribution of possible value (see Figure 8.3). Note that many of the institutions previously discussed do not eliminate or even reduce the probability of failure; they merely transfer the pecuniary impact of this to other market participants who can accommodate such events at lower cost.

Assume now that a project has failed, or that the assessment process is focused on such a possibility prior to commitment. Assume further that market-based institutions are available to accommodate this possibility. Even so, only the *pecuniary* losses have been accounted for through the market institutions. Participants in the project are also subject to non-pecuniary losses, and the likelihood of this represents a low-utility outcome that influences choice at the level of the individual. Failed projects have an effect on the people involved in them even if they are in no way responsible for the failure.

Since choice is always undertaken at the level of the individual, and cost is borne by the individual alone, these subjective influences cannot be overlooked. What institutions exist for risk-reduction in this regard?

Most such mechanisms are informal rather than formal, and constitute codes of conduct that are generally accepted in the community of like persons with which the actor identifies. Thus Niehans (1948, 445, quoted in Arrow, 1951) argues that the businessman is 'only responsible for doing as well as he can under the hypothesis which actually prevails'. If the community (institution) of businessmen comes to have some consistency in their world-view, then even if individual businessmen hold differing views, the world-view represents an escape (subjectively understood) from 'real' risk acceptance. The uncertainty that the world-view excludes had been institutionalized and is exploitable by self-interested agents.

Thus, to the extent that market discipline can be excluded, institutions also facilitate self-interested behaviour and *private* risk reduction, even to the detriment of corporate objectives. Whilst these agency issues are outside the scope of this book, one such issue involving the devolution of decision authority is relevant to the discussion at hand and is taken up below (p. 132).

INSTITUTIONS FOR CAPITAL DECISION-MAKING WITHIN A FIRM

Firms do not make capital investment decisions. People (individual actors) within the firm make the decisions – and they do so within some institutional framework. This framework does not necessarily guarantee that the result is a faithful amalgam of the subjective valuations of the individual actors who participate. Nor is such an amalgam necessarily a desirable objective.

This section examines how the iterative choice process plays out within the corporate institutions typically charged with this decision authority. It examines two distinct concepts within this theme as examples of how the decisions flowing from this process may, but often do not, yield outcomes that are profit maximizing at the level of the firm.

Process-induced Decision Structure

The iterative decision process set out at the start of this chapter has two outstanding characteristics that differentiate it from choice in standard neoclassical models: choice involves multiple sequential steps; and the information and rules of valuation change from step to step. Decisions later in the process are path dependent.

The difficulties raised by following this process are best illustrated by an example. This example assumes that the decision-making entity (the company board) arrives at decisions via a consensus or near-unanimity rule, but that there is agenda control in the way that choices are brought to its attention. Moreover, individuals who are party to the collective decision have significant influence over the rule of valuation in each round.

Consider, for example, a firm proposing to invest in a production facility for some new micro-processor technology. The production could involve one of two possible technologies; plants could be located in either, say, California, Texas or Singapore; and within each location up to three potential sites are available. These three attributes are the primary economic factors that differentiate choices. Table 8.1 sets out the matrix of possibilities. Index numbers in the right column of Table 8.1 assume all 18 sites were evaluated in detail by some omniscient actor remote from the choice process, but these numbers are never available to the actors themselves.

Table 8.1: Base data, process-induced decision

Location	Technology	Site	'Value' ranking [a]
California	A - High volume, low cost	Site C_1	24 / 4
		Site C_2	20 / 8
		Site C_3	16 / 15
	B - Flexible/scaleable	Site C_1	14 / 7
		Site C_2	12 / 15
		Site C_3	10 / 20
Texas	A - High volume, low cost	Site T_1	21 / 10
		Site T_2	20 / 10
		Site T_3	19 / 10
	B - Flexible/scaleable	Site T_1	11 / 15
		Site T_2	10 / 15
		Site T_3	9 / 15
Singapore	A - High volume, low cost	Site S_1	19 / 12
		Site S_2	17 / 12
		Site S_3	15 / 12
	B - Flexible/scaleable	Site S_1	11 / 15
		Site S_2	11 / 15
		Site S_3	11 / 15

Note: [a] Numbers in the right column adjacent to each site are an index representing 'value' in accordance with the expected return and 'value' according to a risk-based criterion. Higher numbers represent a more preferred case.

The *detailed* comparison of these alternatives is not normally possible in real-world circumstances. The number of options is usually unmanageable; nor is such an evaluation warranted. The majority of options will differ in value from other options by an amount that is less than the cost of the information necessary to differentiate them. Further, the optimum choice from the perspective of an omniscient actor is not necessarily the benchmark upon which to judge the efficacy of the choice process – the numbers are presented to illustrate the difference between results achievable in a sequential decision environment and results potentially achievable using alternate sequences of choices and rules.

The process of decision-making proceeds by looking at *classes* of projects taken to be representative. The end result is a function of the order in which these classes are decided upon and the criteria used in each stage of valuation. Table 8.2 sets out two such preference orderings.

Table 8.2: Preference ordering according to focus of valuation

Criterion	Focus of valuation	Preference order
By location	Return on investment	California > Texas > Singapore
	Risk	Singapore > Texas > California
By technology	Return on investment	Technology A > Technology B
	Risk	Technology B > Technology A

At the very early stages of any evaluation, the focus of valuation is usually on *expected return on investment*. This seems reasonable given that:

• actors are not deciding on *implementation* of the project, hence they are not actually taking a *project* risk. The risk only pertains to the likely increase in value associated with the additional information cost and this is not necessarily correlated with the project risk;

• *ex ante* the return on investment will not change with additional information. If new information is directed towards alternatives that are rank ordered on this criteria then *ex ante* the actor has the greatest probability *ex post* of demonstrating that these resources were well spent;

• The 'value' or rank ordering on the basis of risk in Table 8.2 assumes completed evaluations. Yet decisions in the early stages of the evaluation, if focused on this criterion, must be made either on risk as then understood or on the *expectation* of risk as it will apply in some final analysis. As demonstrated in Chapter 6, when viewed from a temporally distant vantage point, even risk-based valuations are likely to be ordered similarly to valuations focused only on the expected value.

The 'return on investment' valuation criterion favours California over the other locations, and Technology A over Technology B.

On this criterion, sites in Texas and Singapore are rejected, despite the fact that the high 'typical' return for the class of sites in California is at least partially derived from sites that have risk characteristics that can never be accommodated. Unfortunately, this information is not known at the time the decision (to reject the other locations) is made.

In subsequent phases of the evaluation the nature of the decision changes. Early phases are decisions to reject alternatives and to invest in information. In due course, the alternatives that are rejected are not physical projects, but logical projects – the same physical project styled differently (started sooner, or higher/lower production, for example); also the investment in not small amounts of funds directed towards information gathering, but large amounts of money in actual investment. With this shift comes a shift in focus. Actors know that a final decision to proceed cannot be made until the reservation criterion is satisfied, and the focus is therefore on alternatives offering the greatest scope for such risk reduction. Within the sub-set of options now under study (that is, California only), Technology B is favoured over Technology A.

Finally, site by site alternatives are evaluated. Under the temporal utility model, only options that satisfy the reservation criterion can be proceeded with; if more than one option satisfies this criterion, the one with the highest return on investment is selected.

Assuming, for example, that the value 10 represents the minimum acceptable risk value, then after three phases of valuation, Californian site C_2 using technology B will be selected (expected return index 12, risk index 15).

An entirely different result follows if the agenda for the first-round evaluation is focused on the technology to be used. Technology A is favoured and, within this sub-set of options, sites in Singapore are ranked highest on the reservation (risk) criterion. The final selection, site S_1 using Technology A yields an expected return (index) of 19 with risk (index) of 12.

The result in this context is similar to results in a social choice context examined by Arrow (1951). Given full information, the selected option in the first instance is actually inferior to almost half of the other alternatives available. The seemingly inefficient outcome is the result of the order of valuation and rules for valuation – both of which can only be understood *ex ante* through *prior* experience of the actors, not by derivation from the choice set itself. Indeed, confirmation of the rule *ex post* is also problematic, since the 'confirmation' can only be based on the selected set of alternatives. The opportunity cost (the value of foregone alternatives) is not available in this final choice set.

Incentive-incompatible Structure

On page 127 (and in note 8) mention was made of institutionalized rules and the importance of consistency in these rules to the underlying activity to which they are applied. Such issues are readily addressed once they are recognized. Yet recognition of such a situation in a corporate environment is a non-trivial task. Many such 'rules' are tacit and hardly understood in any conscious way, even by actors themselves.

Institutions also fill a role in facilitating incentive compatibility. Assume, for example, that all participants in a firm – management, agents, stockholders – have identical preferences with respect to risk. Following Fama (1980), firms achieve more efficiency when agents have incentives that are compatible with the firm's objectives. Such a firm would appear to be near-ideal from this perspective. Yet the absence of private agendas inconsistent with the firm's objective does not necessarily guarantee the efficient result.

The example involves a large corporation investing in projects that have high information costs in comparison to the change in expected value necessary to understand them. This is the stalemate described on page 120.

If a firm has a project in stalemate and the project is large in comparison to the firm size, then indeed one or other of the actions set out on page 120 will be necessary. Alternatively, individual small projects may be amalgamated – not literally, but in a corporate decision context – such that sub-par returns or losses from one may be accepted because of above-par returns on other projects. The lack of information merely means that *ex ante* it is unknown which projects will actually turn out to be sub-par and which will turn out above-par.

Such a decision strategy is valid at the level of the firm, and, taken in aggregate, satisfies the reservation criterion. It is indeed an argument favouring larger sized firms. The difficulty arises when actual projects are made the responsibility of individual managers and incentive-compatible remuneration structures are employed. The firm has a risk tolerance for 'no more than 5 per cent probability of loss', the manager has the same tolerance, yet the individual project for which he is responsible is accepted by the firm, based on a degree of knowledge that does not allow this requirement to be satisfied.

Through aggregation, the firm is prepared to accept a higher probability of failure amongst individual projects, yet to the extent that the agent is remunerated consistently with the firms incentive-compatibility model the agent will be more risk-averse than necessary. In these circumstances, the temporal utility model suggests that the manager's actions will be focused on uncertainty minimization and risk reduction rather than profit maximization, constrained only by actual returns exceeding the cost of capital. Despite apparent incentive compatibility, such a focus is actually inconsistent with the firms objectives. Three mechanisms are available to address this issue:

1. Agents of the firm who are (were) responsible for the initial aggregated investment decision can accept some of the shared responsibility for the individual projects within this set.[9]

2. Agents in charge of individual projects can be chosen with risk tolerance substantially greater than the firm as a whole. And/or

3. The mechanisms (institutions) of subjective risk minimization mentioned briefly above (see page 127) can be invoked, consciously aiming to mitigate private risk behaviour.

LIMITS OF UNCERTAIN CHOICE IN A MARKET ECONOMY

Actors who pursue choice in a world of no uncertainty adjust their deployment of resources to equate marginal costs with marginal returns. In a world where uncertainty prevails, this equality at the margin is problematic, since marginal costs are typically subject to less uncertainty than are marginal returns. If a firm has a large portfolio of potential investments at its disposal, all of which have expected returns exceeding the cost of capital but all of which exhibit uncertainty, where does it rationally allocate its resources?

Consider a situation where a firm has a spectrum of investments and potential investments. Three styles of investments can be identified within this spectrum:

1. *Committed but not yet complete projects* These projects involve sunk capital, but the limited external knowledge about the project means that there are substantial differences between the firm's private valuation and the external market valuation. Resources deployed in this style of project are aimed at *market-based* value changes. Such value changes may have only minimal direct impact on the project in question but may significantly influence market-based constraints (such as: the cost of capital) on future projects, including extensions to the project in question.

2. *Investments pending implementation* Such investments may be understood to the point where the probability of loss is within acceptable limits, but may be stalled because the present value of the same project *delayed* for some time may exceed the present value of the project proceeded with immediately. The higher present value of the delayed project may be a function of the expected future lower cost of capital, or

the expected arrival of further information over time enhancing the expected return. Resources deployed in this style of project are aimed at *private* value changes.

3. *Investments with an expected return exceeding the cost of capital, but which currently do not satisfy the reservation criterion* Projects of this nature may be in stalemate or may offer scope for *private value* enhancement through investment in information.

Value maximization implies that resources should be prioritized into activities offering the highest expected increase in value. This issue was alluded to in Chapter 7, where expected returns being sought from new capital investments were shown to be four to five times the real cost of capital for these same activities. Such an outcome is consistent with the temporal utility model, where the cost of capital being referred to is the average cost of capital for *existing* projects. *New* investments must be judged on the (expected) marginal cost of capital that applies to that project alone. This marginal cost of capital must be higher than the average cost of capital even for the same style of project because of less information about new projects. To satisfy the reservation criterion with a marginal cost of capital higher than the 'average', the *expected* return for new investments would clearly need to be substantially more than the observed *average* cost of capital.

Table 8.3 sets out some simple data for a ten-year life project, using an after-tax cost of capital of 5 per cent, and an expected after-tax internal rate of return of 14.4 per cent. In this example, numbers have been deliberately selected to be consistent with the findings in Summers (1987b) such that the present value of the expected returns is 50 per cent greater than the initial capital outlay when calculated using the cost of capital as the discount factor.

Consider this project first using traditional evaluation criteria similar to Summers (1987b). The project can clearly proceed because the *expected* present value of future in-flows ($150 million) exceeds the value of out-flows ($100 million). The traditional criteria suggest that like projects can proceed to the point where marginal revenues (discounted at the risk-adjusted rate) equate to marginal costs, yet the Summers findings suggest that this is *not* the case in practice. The marginal-revenue–marginal-cost limit occurs with discount rates for the marginal revenues much higher than the average cost of capital for this style of project. Higher discount rates are an outcome of non-diversifiable risk associated with the project not being captured in the cost-of-capital calculation.

This result is consistent with the temporal utility model. In the temporal utility model it is not the *expected* annual cash flows that are discounted at the cost of capital rate, it is the cash flows representing a 95 per cent chance

Table 8.3: Cash flow data and return on investment at the margin

Year	Undiscounted cash flows ($ m.)	Returns, discounted at 14.4% ($ m.)	Returns, discounted at 5% ($ m.)
	−100.00 [a]		
1	19.43	16.99	18.50
2	19.43	14.86	17.62
3	19.43	13.00	16.78
4	19.43	11.37	15.98
5	19.43	9.94	15.22
6	19.43	8.69	14.50
7	19.43	7.60	13.81
8	19.43	6.65	13.15
9	19.43	5.82	12.52
10	19.43	5.09	11.93
		100.00	150.00

Note: [a] Initial capital investment (cash *outflow* $100 m.) occurs in the year prior to project commencement. Undiscounted cash flows in years 1–10 of project are cash *inflows*.

of betterment. The 14.4 per cent return is an *outcome* of this process. Given time-proven understandings of uncertainty within firms, it is simply more convenient to define hurdle rates using an expected value criterion as a proxy for the reservation criterion, but the hurdle rate is not in itself a datum.

Nevertheless, any similar commitments should logically follow a similar relationship. Investment of $1 into activities with similar uncertainty anywhere within the company should yield an expected $1.50 increase in value. Investment in information is subject to similar uncertainty, so a similar ratio of investment to expected increase in value should apply at the margin. This was the situation alluded to in note 7.

The limits of uncertain choice in a market economy, assuming that a firm aims to maximize both the privately held and the market-determined value, means equating at the margin the changes in value according to the reservation criterion. Under this criterion, firms can rationally invest in information even where such investments themselves are subject to uncertainty, and even where *ex ante* they imply no change in expected value in the choice alternative itself. When assessed using just the expected return rather than the reservation criterion, the limits at the margin will always be established with expected returns exceeding the cost of capital because the cost of capital only institutionalizes uncertainties that are already well understood. Only in a world of no uncertainty does the reservation criterion converge to the expected value criterion.

NOTES

1. Shackle (1983) considered that '[if a person's] act of choice is in some respects an *absolute origination*, something not wholly implicit in antecedents, he may deem his thoughts to be not entirely determinate, but able to come in part *ex nihilo*. If a choice can be of this kind ... [then we] cannot know them by inference from causal circumstances operating in the present, for the power to do this would contradict [their essential character].' For our purposes, even many conceptually discoverable elements must remain unknown at the time of decision, and the uncertainty introduced thereby can be thought of in the same manner as this (Shackelian) uncertainty due to human action that is never discoverable.
2. In some prior step in the process the actor must also have established that the dispersion of prices was a random set, and he or she must also have established what the stochastic characteristics of this set were.
3. As originally developed, Kuhn (1970) applied the term only to scientists. However, it is used here analogously to apply to human action in general but otherwise following the Kuhnian model.
4. Choi (1993) uses the term 'paradigm' to apply to the complete set of overarching values or rules governing choice under uncertainty, including those derived or researched during the decision process. In this book, I restrict use of the term to the narrower one applied by Kuhn, wherein derived 'values' or rules consciously adopted during the choice process are excluded on the grounds that the process also allows for their revision in the event that results or tentative results fail to confirm their appropriateness.
5. Such a case, analysed from an 'options value' perspective, has been examined by Dixit and Pindyck (1994, 48, 319).
6. This, I submit, is precisely the case when corporations become bankrupt or, in the extreme case, resort to criminal activities in an apparent attempt at face saving: face saving presumably being a more highly ranked objective in the mind of some corporate office-bearers than conformance with generally accepted standards of corporate morality.
7. This implies that actors will invest in information up to the point where the marginal value of the information equals the marginal cost. Yet this decision to invest in information is itself subject to uncertainty. Thus actors are again constrained by the reservation criterion. Investment in information will fall short of the MC = MV ideal, and will actually be limited to the point where, in this example, actors are 95 per cent confident that the change in subjective value ΔU^*_A will exceed the cost.
8. For example: a senior manager for a large international mining company who had worked his entire career in production was promoted to a corporate management role in charge of ten major mines. His experience (the 'rule' he had followed to achieve success in a production role) was that: 'When prices are low, you expand production to improve the mine economics. When prices are high you expand production to improve the mine economics'. Not surprisingly, in his new role he set about an expansion strategy.

   Within a 'production' framework such a seemingly unambiguous rule *may* be correct because in a production situation capital is sunk, and in such highly capital-intensive industries marginal costs are usually much lower than average costs (and lower than market prices) even during periods of cyclical low prices. Yet the same rule is unlikely to be correct in the corporate environment when new capital *is not sunk* and is within the manager's ability to change. At this (senior) level of decision-making, the focus must be on productive activity that can achieve returns *despite* the (quite correct) decisions from production managers who ignore sunk costs.
9. The examples set out in Peters and Waterman (1982) could be interpreted through this explanation.

9. Capital investment models

Within a production process, capital is organized in a definite way. It consists of heterogeneous elements which complement each other. Capital is applied in discrete steps. Much of this capital is idiosyncratic, with value that is strongly linked to other elements in the process. Value in other uses may be much less than value in the intended use (assuming that expectations come to fruition). The loss in value implied with irreversibility means that decisions to invest are categorically different from decisions associated with continuous production functions.[1]

This chapter is the first of three setting out a model of entrepreneurial capital investment decision-making aimed at drawing out these differences. The model highlights the composition of the capital structure at a microeconomic level and it focuses on the impact of entrepreneurial expectations on decision-making.

In a contestable market (what Shepherd, 1984, terms an 'ultra-free entry' market) participants can enter and leave with no loss in value. This defines one end of the capital investment decision spectrum, at the other end of which is the world of irreversible choices and totally sunk costs.

The chapter starts with a review of the meaning of capital and capital decisions from a change-in-value perspective. It draws on the insights from contestable market theory as a foil for understanding the capital investment decision environment.

A simple case study is set out.[2] Results from this case study are first presented in a form consistent with standard neoclassical models of production. This standard form treats capital and labour as the primary arguments in a production function which has the following constraints:

- that the function is continuous and differentiable;
- that capital is represented as capital *services* – as an implicit rental rate rather than as a specific item requiring decision;
- that uncertainty can be ignored or is consistent across choices; and
- that expectations are constant and consistent with current prices and costs of production.

The introduction and case study within this chapter limits the scope to choices whose characteristics can be explicitly understood *ex ante*, and constrains discussion to the first two of these four constraints.

Chapters 10 and 11 extend this case study by explicitly examining the non-continuous character of the production function and examining the heterogeneity, complementarity, expectations formulation and uncertainty characteristics of the capital choice problem.

CAPITAL-INTENSIVE PROCESSES

Capital Value and Decisions

This section is usefully started by revisiting what is meant by capital and capital value. In Chapter 2, capital was defined as the *value*, assessed in the present, attaching to something envisaged in the future. Chapter 7 further highlighted that, since actors must always choose *only* between the best alternatives available to them (doing nothing is still a choice), there is no absolute benchmark, only relative benchmarks, for defining value. Nevertheless, whilst 'value' arguably *does* include everything that might be a part of these envisaged alternative paths leading to the future, choice has only to consider the *differences* in value between envisaged alternatives.

Under the definition, liquid or circulating capital (capital in a 'free' form: that is, as money) is clearly 'capital'. Persons holding money value it because they can envisage some real future that it might contribute towards bringing to fruition. 'Value' as it is relevant to the *decision* to invest is distinguished from 'capital' thus:

The decision to invest is a decision concerning the potential *changes in value* associated with changes that might take place between the time when the entrepreneur 'invests' (or dehomogenizes) his or her money capital until the time when he or she is in a position to recover that capital in a 'free' form (that is, as money) and how these changes in value compare to the next best alternative open to him or her.

This distinction, focusing on when an entrepreneur is 'in a position to recover his capital in a "free" form' is expanded upon below, and plays an important role in the expectational constraints on the capital decision problem.

Market Setting for Entrepreneurial Choice

One of the difficulties in describing the entrepreneurial choice situation is that it is a dynamic one and it lacks the easy explanation and computational elegance of the static, perfectly competitive neoclassical model. The primary attributes of the market setting used for this study and considered broadly applicable to most entrepreneurial choice are as follows:

1. Where entrepreneurial profits exist there are economic forces working to erode them. Markets will change. The rate of change is in part a function of the magnitude of the expected entrepreneurial profits. Decisions to invest in capital to fulfil entrepreneurial opportunities are built upon an actor's expectation of the shape of this profit profile extending into the future.

2. Changes in the market order being addressed by new entrepreneurial opportunities are also characterized by choices of a capital nature on the demand side. Customers or potential customers have to adjust their way of doing things to take advantage of new opportunities. Capital investment and divestment decisions are necessary on the demand side. Expectations of the rate of adjustment on the demand side influences supply-side choices.

3. Changes always involve uncertainty. New products and new ways of conducting business are always less well understood than existing ways. Change implies that the expected value of the new is sufficiently greater than the well-understood value of the old to offset this uncertainty. *Ceteris paribus*, the size of the market for a new product increases as knowledge of the product increases.

4. Processes using capital involve sunk costs. Where there are sunk costs there is scope for loss in value – an outcome on the adverse side of the reservation line in the temporal utility model. Reconciling what this scope for loss in value means is a precondition to 'value' assessed in the efficiency dimension and forms a critical role in any such choice.

There are two market settings that are the focus of attention in the example that follows (and in Chapters 10 and 11):

1. The first is the 'new' product market that the entrepreneurial capital investment opportunity is aiming to address. An entrepreneur envisages an unfulfilled opportunity to supply the world with widgets and sets about exploiting this opportunity. This is the product market.

2. The second is the market associated with the capital inputs. This is the market for the machinery that makes the widgets. Some elements of this market may be very well developed (the factory building, for example). Other elements may be quite ill-developed (the custom-made or custom-adapted lathes, for example).

The choice problem being addressed involves the investment in the machinery that make the widgets. The choice is grounded in expectations of demand in the product market and underpinned by the sunk costs and other characteristics associated with the capital inputs market.

If the machinery is of a general-purpose nature and can be effectively deployed to make many other goods, then the decision has a substantially different character than if it is purpose-built and valueless in any other application. The nature and extent of these entry and exit costs are significant factors in this capital investment choice.

Contestable Markets or Competitive Markets?

This section examines the characteristics of the capital inputs market. This market is assumed to be a broadly *competitive* market, but not a *contestable* market. New and used machines can be readily bought and sold, but not costlessly.

The uniqueness of most machines and the direct costs of purchase and sale mean that losses in capital value (true sunk costs) are the norm rather than the exception in the real economy. Nevertheless, even without these costs, sunk costs are inherent in the capital decision borne out of entrepreneurial expectations. The difference between market-based value subject to information asymmetries and internal-to-the-firm value derived from longer-term expectations provides an inherent sunk cost.[3] Observers such as Tirole (1993) have examined such sunk costs for their commitment value supporting short-term monopoly power and concomitant entrepreneurial profit. An example illustrates the normal case.

In this example an entrepreneur invests in an item of capital costing $100 with the intent to make its services available over its expected (and actual) six-year life. Labour and other operating costs are nil, and the market value declines at 25 per cent per year. At the end of the six-year term the machine is sold for scrap at its market value. Taxes are payable at an assumed 35 per cent rate, and depreciation allowances for tax purposes reflect market-based valuations. The cash flow for such a case is set out in Table 9.1. It uses a discount rate of 15 per cent which is assumed to be consistent with uncertainties surrounding the project.

If a constant rental rate is to apply for use of the capital over its full expected life, then a calculated annual 'rental' charge of $29.32 applies (the first line of the table). The internal-to-the-firm value (the last line of the table) has been calculated year-on-year by discounting the expected future cash flows from that year on.

Using the constant annual rental rate, the market value and the internal-to-the-firm value coincide at the start and end of the machine life, but there is no equality in the intervening period. The internal-to-the-firm value during the life of the machine, when valued according to the present value of

Table 9.1: Cash flow for market or internal-to-the-firm value

	Start	Year 1	Year 2	Year 3	Year 4	Year 5	Year 6
Annual 'rental' charge		**$29.32**	**$29.32**	**$29.32**	**$29.32**	**$29.32**	**$29.32**
Initial capital cost	$100.00						
Tax-dep'n, at 25% (decl. bal.)		$25.00	$18.75	$14.06	$10.55	$7.91	$5.93
End-of-year 'market' value		**$75.00**	**$56.25**	**$42.19**	**$31.64**	**$23.73**	**$17.80**
Salvage value / resid. value							$17.80
'Profit' for tax purposes		$4.32	$10.57	$15.25	$18.77	$21.41	$23.38
Tax payable at 35% rate		$1.51	$3.70	$5.34	$6.57	$7.49	$8.18
Cash flow	($100.00)	$27.81	$25.62	$23.98	$22.75	$21.82	$38.93
Discount factor at 15% rate	1.0000	0.8696	0.7561	0.6575	0.5718	0.4972	0.4323
Present value of cash flow	($100.00)	$24.18	$19.37	$15.77	$13.01	$10.85	$16.83
Net present value (NPV)	$0.00						
Internal-to-the-firm value	**$100.00**	**$87.19**	**$74.66**	**$61.88**	**$48.41**	**$33.85**	**$17.80**

expected future cash flows, is always higher than the market value. Figure 9.1 shows the internal-to-the-firm value and the market value through the life of the equipment based on the information in Table 9.1.

Implicit in the constancy of expectations is the assumption that deviations from market value early in machine life (through notional *under*-charging) will be recovered later in machine life. This is not a deliberate plan to buildup commitment value through sunk costs, but is rather a reflection of the fact that pricing for the *product* must be a constant in a competitive market when there is no market-recognized difference in product whether it is produced by an old or a new machine.[4]

The net effect of applying constancy of expectations for capital usage to undifferentiated product markets is to establish a difference between the internal-to-the-firm value and market value, and this difference represents a sunk cost. Further, it places an incentive on firms to use equipment for its full life since early disposal at market value means capital losses.[5] Early disposal also puts whole-of-project returns at risk because second-hand equipment purchased at market price can provide the same services as new equipment at a lower capital rental rate.[6]

Even if a third party enters the equation, the capital decision problem remains. Assume, for example, that a third party offers long-life equipment on short-term hire at the same rental rate as for long-term hire and with no commitment on the part of the user. Users would pay the same (average) rental rate for new equipment as for older equipment. Such a business is

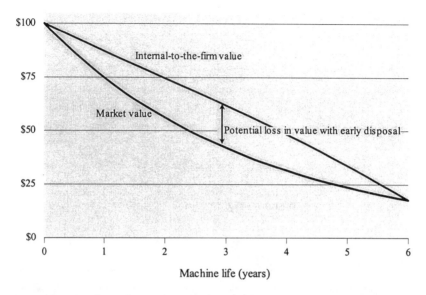

Figure 9.1: Market value and internal-to-the-firm value

vulnerable to competition from other suppliers offering lower rates on rental of (just) older equipment. Thus, circumstances such as this will exist in the market place only if there is a non-equilibrium environment (offering opportunities for entrepreneurial gains). This third-party rental business is then the subject of the capital decision being analysed in this book. The problem is not resolved, just transferred – although gains from trade are possible if the party offering the short-term hire is in a more favourable position to absorb the risk.[7]

Only two outcomes can emerge from Figure 9.1:

1. for long-term commitments, any termination of capital usage prior to the expected period results in a loss in value; or

2. capital can be 'rented' for the same long-term period on the assumption of rolling short-term commitments. This will facilitate no loss in value on exit (a costless exit?); however, it incurs a capital rental cost that is higher than average initially and that varies over time, following the lower of the two lines in Figure 9.1.

The importance of this for capital decisions is paramount.

The term of commitment cannot be overlooked in any theory of capital investment choice. 'Value' in a decision framework concerns the changes between the time when entrepreneurs *de-homogenize* their money capital until the time when they are in a position to recover their capital in a 'free' form (that is, as money). The assumption of costless exit at any time (as suggested in contestable market theory) effectively makes 'capital' a variable cost, and the capital choice problem that is the subject of this book ceases to exist.[8]

Market Environment for Entrepreneurial Opportunities

Consider now a new market offering entrepreneurial capital investment opportunities. This market is distinctly *not* a contestable market. Baumol *et al.* (1983, 491) go to some pains to highlight the 'static equilibrium' nature of the contestable market model as opposed to the entrepreneurial choice model being developed here which is clearly dynamic in character. Actors acknowledge that the market is changing, and profits are dependent on the correctness of entrepreneurial expectations and the decisions flowing therefrom with regard to these changes.

At least three characteristics distinguish the market assumed in this model from the contestable market of Baumol *et al.* (1982):

1. *Influence of fixed costs* In a contestable market, fixed costs are irrelevant because it is assumed that a new entrant to the market can instantly match an incumbent firm's output. Any shortfall in output by the new entrant results in fixed costs per unit higher than the incumbent's. In the model which follows, output (market offtake) is unknown. Further, existing market participants are distinctly aware that new entrants may hold expectations of output substantially different (more optimistic) than themselves. Indeed, in the presence of sunk costs such an expectation *even if proved incorrect* presents a strategic threat that influences capacity choice.

2. *Sunk costs* are closely and inversely related to time duration and are larger in the short run than the long run. This issue has already been discussed (p. 140) above.

3. *Production-specific assets* The market setting in this model is poorly developed. Market-based supply of the product is subject to uncertainty, and at least some of the investment in uncertainty reduction remains proprietary to the firm (reputation, R&D, for example).

Nevertheless, these attributes are not necessarily enduring, particularly in a market that is changing. As equipment wears out and is replaced with equipment and methods of a slightly (or substantially) different nature, the relative advantage accruing to an incumbent reduces. The analysis does not preclude actual competition. All that the analysis requires is that actors' decisions on capital investments be informed by expectations whose time frame is significant in relation to potential losses in capital value.

Baumol *et al.* (1983) acknowledge this time aspect and instructively use the example to highlight the differences between fixed costs and sunk costs, and the difference between *economic* and technological notions of sunk cost. A business can be subject to high fixed costs but low (or even non-existent) sunk costs if it can arrange precommitments for its outputs prior to making commitments to capital inputs. In a contestable market:

> it is sufficient that the process be rapid enough so that the entrant does not find his investment vulnerable to a retaliatory response by the incumbent. *The length of this time period is not exclusively a technological datum, but is also the result of business practice and opportunities in the market in question.* This period can be as long as the longest period for which it is credible for buyers to commit their patronage. (Baumol *et al.*, 1983, 493; original emphasis)

Thus, indirectly, Baumol *et al.* define the entrepreneurial choice decision in terms of risk, since such a precommitment situation is tantamount to complete satisfaction of the reservation criterion – in other words, *no risk*. This surely is an objective of entrepreneurial choice, though not necessarily to the exclusion of entrepreneurial profits. The decision being analysed here can be more appropriately framed as an attempt *in the absence of the contestability conditions* to *minimize* or reduce the time period of unbalanced commitments at the conclusion of which the entrepreneur is able to exit costlessly (or, in Hayekian terms, to recover his or her money capital in a 'free' form). The minimization or reduction of this time to one consistent with his or her expectation is the precondition to choice focused in the efficiency dimension on profit maximization.

Case Study

Chapter 6 sets out four main categories of entrepreneurial activity. This case study, which is extended through Chapters 10 and 11, uses just one of these categories: the production of a good external to the firm (a new 'market' good) where previously production was completely internal to firms.

Entrepreneurial profits are possible in this scenario through applying known technologies with volume efficiencies not available in the internal-to-the-firm mode. The style of the entrepreneurial opportunity is unimportant for the illustration; what is relevant is that at the time entrepreneurial choice decisions are being made, market characteristics are unavailable. Choices must be made on ill-informed expectations that recognize the arrival of information over time and the changes that accompany this.

Entrepreneurial profits are built upon the difference between the long-term cost of production, including capital, and the market price. This difference is not constant through time, and it will be different for different levels of output. Thus expectations on the likelihood and timing of price changes and demand changes is the major factor underpinning entrepreneurial choice and, ultimately, entrepreneurial profits.

In the case study, the decision-maker is presented with a choice between two different technologies. Each technology allows a range of outputs by varying secondary capital and operating inputs. The larger-scale technology offers lower cost but is applicable only with higher output.

The case study is based around a large excavator loading one or more trucks, and assumes that the production process involves three elements:

1. a primary capital good (the excavator), which is the technological defining element of the process. The range of outputs associated with this technology is defined both technologically and economically. For this primary capital good it is assumed that in the event of changes in the plan the disposal of it implies a substantial loss in value to its next most appropriate use;

2. a secondary capital good or multiple units thereof (the trucks) which work only in association with the primary capital good and are sized to match it. Additional units result in additional production but at a declining marginal rate. This secondary capital is also potentially subject to loss in value following premature disposal;

3. 'pure' variable costs (the operating costs – fuels, tyres, labour) used jointly with the secondary capital and whose remuneration is based only on the number of hours worked.

Table 9.2 sets out the capital and operating costs of the two sets of technology.[9] The effective machine life is independent of production because new equipment makes older equipment redundant after this time even if it is not physically worn out.

Table 9.2: Capital equipment base costs

Technology and equipment description	Initial capital cost ($)	Operating cost ($/hr)	Effective life (years)
A Excavator: 19 cu.m. front-end loader	2,380,000	271.00	6
Truck: 120-t capacity, rear dump	1,099,000	144.44	7
B Excavator: 22 cu.m. hyd. excavator	4,709,000	315.38	6
Truck: 153-t capacity, rear dump	1,350,000	167.20	8

This three-part model – fixed (primary) capital, secondary capital, and operating costs – represents a wide range of industry processes. Transport companies have fixed infrastructure (warehousing, distribution, workshop facilities) coupled with secondary capital (trucks, trains, aircraft) that undertake the main production role using variable operating costs (labour, fuel, electricity). Manufacturing plants consist of primary capital (factory buildings, transport infrastructure) coupled with secondary capital (the machine tools) and operating costs. In each of these cases the primary capital places limits on the productive capacity of the secondary capital. Output within a range is achieved by relative inefficiency of the primary capital at the low end of the range and relative inefficiency of the secondary capital at the high end of the range. The fully variable operating costs also influence capacity choice, with, for example, overtime work at higher cost being offset by higher utilization of capital.

Production beyond the high end of the range requires either duplication or multiplication of the primary capital accompanied by additional secondary capital – where the technology is already at maximum efficient size – or changeover to a new technology. New technology means investment in a different style of primary capital and frequently also means different secondary capital. Thus within a *technology* costs of production follow the characteristic U-shaped curve, but within an *industry* the cost function is L-shaped. Within the industry, costs decrease with increasing scale until the maximum scale technology is reached and thereafter increasing outputs require replication with constancy in costs.

The case study is also similar to standard neoclassical models. Nicholson (1992) describes a three-part model which yields a total cost curve following the same cubic shape – the most common model used in simple competitive pricing models.[10] The primary difference, as will be set out below, involves consideration of capital *not* as a homogeneous quantity with some easily determinable rental rate, but as a heterogeneous quantity whose value is a function of its relationship with other elements of the process and of the changing expectations associated with the complete process.

The two technologies were analysed using an operating situation in use in large-scale mines around the world. Output is a function of the equipment interaction. The complete interaction of the excavator and the trucks was simulated by computer. The simulation included variability in machine availability on an individual machine basis; variability in loading and hauling cycles; interference between trucks; and queuing of trucks waiting to be loaded. As more trucks are deployed, interference and queuing become more pronounced. Thus the declining marginal productivity with output recognized in the classic microeconomic models was faithfully accounted for. The analysis was undertaken using a sophisticated computer simulation program employed by the mining industry.[11] Such simulations employ randomness, so deterministic results are not possible. Nevertheless, calculations were analysed to a high level of precision, with production data accurate to within 1 per cent of the long-term (one year or more) expected result. Previous studies by the software developer have confirmed the precision and consistency of such calculated results through numerous field trials.

Figure 9.2 shows the total output and declining marginal productivity for Technology B, associated with matching of an increasing numbers of trucks with the excavator. Similar calculations were undertaken for the other technology.

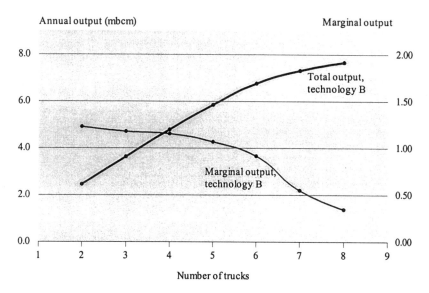

Figure 9.2: Output and productivity

The following section uses the information from the simulation to replicate the neoclassical cost of production curves as they are typically presented, assuming continuous functions and implicit rental rates for capital.

NEOCLASSICAL COST CURVES: A RECONSIDERATION

The traditional presentation of cost curves, following Viner (1931), has a certain technology that is capable of yielding output over a defined range. The applicability of any one technology is a function of the price and the availability of other technologies at higher or lower rates of output.

In this traditional presentation, total costs are represented by the relationship:

$$TC_q = \alpha K' + \upsilon K_q + \omega L_q$$

where:

TC_q	Total cost of producing output q
$\alpha K'$	Total cost of (fixed) capital elements (independent of q)
υ	Price of one unit of (variable) capital K
K_q	Amount of (variable) capital necessary to produce output q
ω	Price of one unit of labour L
L_q	Amount of labour necessary to produce output q

Figure 9.3 sets out the total cost curves in this form for the two technologies in the case study. In Figure 9.3 annual operating costs (represented by labour in the traditional model) have been determined by multiplying actual hours by the hourly rates from Table 9.2. Total costs which include these operating costs and taxes are based on revenues or implied selling prices which will yield a 15 per cent after-tax return on capital over a nominal 12-year project life. The choice of the 15 per cent rate is consistent with the hurdle rates mentioned in Chapter 1. Such a rate implies some background level of uncertainty which in this initial model is assumed to be the same across all choices. The assumption of constant annual costs implies expectations consistent throughout the life of the investment.

The form of the total cost curve in Figure 9.3 is consistent with the Viner

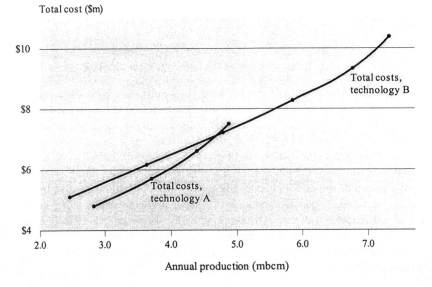

Figure 9.3: Total cost curves

model. Technology A has lower costs at lower outputs but higher costs at higher outputs compared to Technology B. The assumption of continuity implies that whole trucks do not necessarily have to be purchased with each increase in production – parts of a truck can be 'rented' for part of the time at the same rate applying to any other capital to achieve any desired level of output.

The average and marginal costs of production for these two illustrative technologies are shown in Figure 9.4. In this figure, a smooth curve has again been drawn between actual points of production associated with discrete numbers of trucks. The presentation in the above figures is consistent with the traditional model. Under this formulation, the appropriate output level is determined by simply equating marginal revenues with marginal costs.

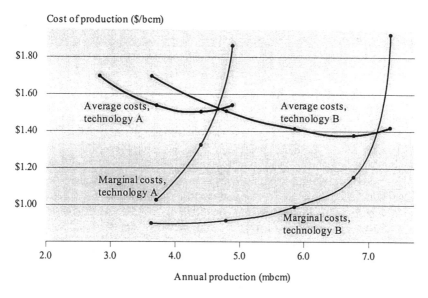

Figure 9.4: Average and marginal cost curve, technologies A and B

In the standard models of production the excavator is the only fixed element of capital. The secondary capital, the trucks in this example, are assumed to be a fungible commodity, with no sunk cost. Certainly, adding another truck to the fleet may not be as difficult as changing the fleet over to another complete technology, but these secondary capital elements also involve sunk costs whose effects are dependent on the duration of commitment.

As described above (p. 142), rental rates for secondary capital whose output is insensitive to age will not normally be independent of the duration of commitment. For entrepreneurial choice, this means that continuous functions in (secondary) capital such as are shown in Figure 9.4 do not exist. Costs reflecting secondary capital utilization will be higher whenever this secondary equipment is only part used – either because of poorer capital utilization within the firm or because of market-based capital rental which reflects that market-based changes in capital value are different to internal-to-the-firm value.

Of more importance for the model under discussion is the impact of joint production involving (secondary) capital and labour. An additional truck can be readily *under*-used, but when in use it demands fixed proportions of labour and other consumable expenses. Without denying the possibility of rising marginal costs due to *variable* factors (operators working overtime, for example), the model makes no explicit attempt to draw out such a characteristic. It assumes that when equipment is fully utilized there is no scope for additional production through overtime use. Joint production in this model yields no clear trend in the direction of variable costs.

It is worth noting a subtle but important aspect of the shape of the marginal supply curve in how competitive market prices and outputs are arrived at. If the supply curve is rising due to variable costs only (overtime work, for example), then the Marshallian partial equilibrium position can be arrived at readily by trial and error – that is, through actual practice. No great distinction need be made between an actor's *expectation* of where this supply/demand balance will fall and where it falls in practice, since action or planned action would be the same. Where supply price rises due to capital increments that cannot be reversed without loss of value, action *ex post* may be subject to substantially different economic forces than planned action. The mechanism for arriving at a price that equates supply with demand is substantially more complicated.

The extension of the model to explicitly present capital in this heterogeneous, non-fungible form is undertaken in the next chapter.

NOTES

1. '[C]apital is not an amorphous mass but possesses a definite structure, ... it is organized in a definite way, and ... its composition of essentially different items is much more important than its aggregate "quantity"' (Hayek, 1941, 6).
2. The development of the case study is described on pp. 144–7 and the representation of this case study in standard form is set out on p. 147.
3. Akerlof (1984) notes that in established markets – used cars, in his example – *market* values reduce dramatically once an asset is no longer new. Yet there is no logical reason why purchasers should undergo a similar sudden drop in their *private* valuation the minute the vehicle is removed from the showroom. Akerlof provides an explanation for this well-recognized phenomenon, based on information asymmetries. If an asset is to be employed continuously within a firm over an expected long-term period there is no internal

information asymmetry. Unless there is a change in expectation where a market transaction becomes likely, there is no logical reason why the internal-to-the-firm value has to mirror market value.

4. If there is a market-recognized difference, then competition will be likely to differentiate the market to exploit this difference. In rental cars, for example, a new car is valued more highly than an older car, yet the age of the car does not figure highly (if at all) in the booking procedure. Nevertheless, there is discrimination. Companies with a mix of cars in their fleet offer better-quality cars to their frequent customers, and other companies (for example, Rent-a-wreck) will differentiate by offering only older cars at cheaper prices.

5. Capital 'losses' are here taken to mean losses in the economic sense (that is, sale at a value less than the present value of expected future cash flows), not accounting losses. There would be no accounting losses with sale at market values in this example.

6. A vigorous market in second-hand equipment would appear to undermine the model being presented, since this implies that poorer returns from under-charging early in machine life cannot be recovered in later machine life, thereby 'forcing' differentiation in product pricing. Such an outcome only follows where output and operating costs of second-hand equipment are no different to newer equipment. In most cases where vigorous markets in used equipment do exist, the age at point of sale of the equipment is where productivity and operating costs, when combined with capital rental rates, equates at the margin to average costs for the same equipment from new to the date of disposal, discounting of costs considered.

7. This sort of market response has started to emerge with large-scale mining and construction equipment over the last decade: whereby equipment manufacturers in conjunction with financial intermediaries do offer long-life equipment on commitment terms less than machine life, with rental rate premiums substantially less than individual companies can justify applying to use the same equipment for the same period. In this case, equipment manufacturers only have their opportunity cost of the equipment at risk, and through their control of spare parts have sufficient control on the used equipment market to ensure that such practices do not erode the market for new equipment.

8. If 'ultra-free entry' markets ('contestable' markets, following Baumol *et al.*, 1982) are widespread, then the decision problem that this book addresses is largely without foundation. Shepherd (1984) also questions the extreme nature of assumptions necessary to sustain an argument of zero sunk costs that underpin the contestable market approach and notes that research 'has provided no cases of ultra-free entry into markets where incumbents hold substantial market shares' – the condition under study that suggests sustainable entrepreneurial profits. Given that every actor contemplating capital investment choice has an economic incentive to find every means possible to exit costlessly in the event of expectational 'error' the fact that 'no cases of ultra-free entry' have been found is significant.

9. Costs imply typical conditions in North America, current at time of writing.

10. '[I]t is assumed that initially the TC [total cost] curve is concave; although initially costs rise rapidly for increases in output, that rate of increase slows as output expands into the mid-range of output. Beyond that middle range, however, the TC curve becomes convex, and costs begin to rise progressively more rapidly. One possible reason for such a shape for the total cost curve is that there is some *third* factor of production (say, the services of an entrepreneur) that is fixed as capital and labor usage expands. In this case, the initial concave section of the TC curve might be explained by the increasingly optimal usage of the entrepreneur's services' (Nicholson, 1992, 340). The well-known cost curves of Viner (1931) also use a three-part (cubic) form.

11. The software used for this analysis was (is) TALPAC (an acronym for Truck and Loader Productivity Analysis and Costing), a program developed by Runge Pty Ltd, supplied to and used in mining sites throughout the world. Preliminary financial analysis was also undertaken in TALPAC. Financial simulations and options pricing analyses were undertaken in Microsoft Excel using Visual Basic.

10. Model with capital heterogeneity

The extended model set out in this chapter draws from Lachmann's recognition that capital resources are *heterogeneous*, not necessarily in a physical sense but in their use, and in his conclusion that '[f]or most purposes capital goods have to be used jointly. *Complementarity* is of the essence of capital use' (Lachmann, 1978, 3).

Chapter 9 introduced the problem by contrasting the treatment of capital and labour in the standard neoclassical construct (that is, as the primary arguments in a production function) with the treatment in this book. Four assumptions of the neoclassical construct were noted:

1. that the function is continuous and differentiable;

2. that capital is represented as capital *services* – as an implicit rental rate rather than as a specific item requiring decision;

3. that uncertainty can be ignored or is consistent across choices; and

4. that expectations are constant and consistent with current prices and costs of production.

In the first section of this chapter the first two constraints are relaxed. Where capital is applied in non-divisible steps and cannot be acquired and disposed of without loss of value, production functions are not continuous. The marginal cost curve – the primary decision guide – takes on a form substantially different from the typical neoclassical presentation. This changed form leads to different incentives and different outcomes even for actors with constant expectations and with marginal costs equating to marginal revenues.

With continuous production functions in contestable markets, decision-making is uncomplicated. But once capacity decisions are not continuous and result in lock-in for some time, decision-making is not so unambiguous. Entrepreneurial expectations place constraints on capacity choice. Marginal cost, in so far as it applies to capital, is a *function* of entrepreneurial expectations and is itself seldom easy to define. Compared to the full-information-fully-competitive ideal, the outcome demonstrates sub-optimum output constrained primarily by uncertainty rather than by marginal returns alone.

CAPITAL HETEROGENEITY AND COMPLEMENTARITY

The extension of the model to present capital explicitly in heterogeneous, non-fungible form is undertaken in this section. As with Chapter 9, this chapter examines only the production or supply side of the entrepreneurial capital investment decision and draws conclusions remote from demand side or strategic influences.

The capital-based model recognizes that secondary capital associated with any technology is also a heterogeneous, poorly fungible commodity. Capital is acquired in increments. Exit prior to the expected time results in loss of value. Figure 10.1 shows the same information relating to Technology A as is shown in Figure 9.4, except in this instance recognizing that:

- production cannot be achieved using just half a truck. A whole truck must be purchased once the capacity of the previous fleet size has been exhausted. If this truck cannot be fully used, then the fixed costs associated with it have to be borne by the entire fleet. Average costs reflect partial utilization of trucks and *include* recovery of capital associated with the truck;

- marginal costs cannot faithfully portray step increments in capital since the first unit of production following a previously fully utilized fleet effectively incurs an infinite marginal cost. The marginal costs in Figure

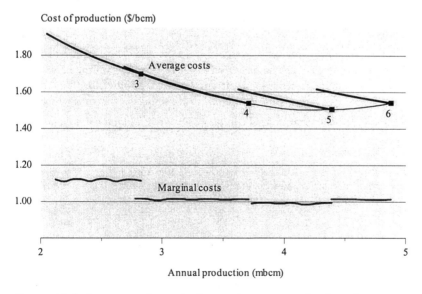

Figure 10.1: Average and marginal operating costs, technology A

10.1 effectively show just marginal operating costs and exclude secondary capital effects.

The marginal cost in Figure 10.1 is the short-run cost, assuming that the secondary capital is fixed. Marginal cost, following this definition of overlooking secondary capital, provides little assistance for even short-run decision-making regarding optimum output levels. Even where secondary capital is in place (and assumed fully sunk) beyond the optimum, it should still be used.

Figure 10.1, showing just marginal *operating* costs, exhibits no rising trend and contrasts with Figure 9.4 which shows a distinctly rising trend. In this example – and arguably across a large spectrum of the economy – rising marginal costs are entirely due to the inefficiency in return on secondary capital. To portray these secondary capital effects faithfully and to show their impact on decisions regarding capacity choice, the marginal cost must be calculated using each increment of capital as the starting point.[1]

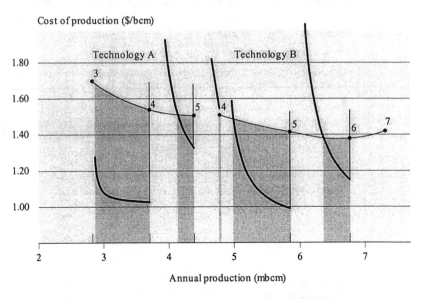

Figure 10.2: Marginal costs with capital, technologies A and B

Figure 10.2 shows marginal costs calculated in this way. It is the same situation as Figure 9.4, but with secondary capital correctly portrayed as a step function. In this figure, points marked adjacent to the number of trucks (3, 4, 5 and so on) represent the fully utilized fleet of that size. Such a fleet offers no scope for production increase without the addition of another truck.

Marginal costs are not just from one increment of production to the next but represent the change in total cost on a per unit of production basis from the previous fully utilized fleet.

Figure 10.2 stands in stark contrast to Figure 9.4. From the standpoint of secondary capital investment, this is the *ex ante* characterization of marginal cost. Indeed, the same shape of curves apply whether it is primary or secondary capital being considered.

The rising marginal cost lines in Figure 9.4 are the connections of the end points of each of the *declining* marginal lines from Figure 10.2. The shaded areas are viable zones of production expansion considered *ex ante*: if actual output falls within these zones following purchase of the additional truck, then average costs of production decline.

How are the declining marginal cost lines and shaded zones in Figure 10.2 to be interpreted? From the *ex ante* viewpoint considering expanded production, two conclusions are directly evident:

1. Each increment of capital is added (and production expanded) according to the expectation that output will fall within the shaded area. The decision regarding the increase in output is *ceteris paribus* harder the closer the production approaches the optimum for any one technology. The shaded areas represent smaller and smaller targets for the correctness of expectations.

2. The viability of expanded production (within the shaded areas) is defined by marginal costs less than expected marginal revenue. In Figure 10.2 this cut-off was based on average costs being reduced. Nevertheless, even with expected marginal revenue at some higher expected level (say, $1.70 per bcm), the relative inelasticity of the volume/price (cost) relationship means that the zones of viable production are relatively insensitive to price.[2]

Once production has been expanded, the viability of *remaining* in production does not follow the shaded zones because marginal costs are then different. This is a different problem – a capital divestment problem – that follows the same logic as this model but subject to a different set of costs.

The relationship between capacity choice and price set out in Figure 10.2 is dramatically different to the standard model. The difference stems from the indivisible nature of the capital. In the standard model, output expands smoothly with price increases because of the assumed capital rental and rising supply cost due to variable costs. Entrepreneurial expectations play only a minor role.

In the capital heterogeneity model above, *price* plays a minor role. In the absence of any change in expectations, changes in market price yield little or no change in output. Even substantial changes in price (marginal revenue) change the shaded zones very little. On the other hand, a change in expectation (increased confidence that additional output can be sold) can lead to decision, even with no change in price.

This is not to say that price has no influence in an entrepreneurial decision to make the marginal investment. The primary mechanism is a roundabout one. If price changes become institutionalized – they are sustained at a higher level for some time – then actors will revise their perception of the market, and these (revised) expectations can lead to the decision to invest.

APPLICABILITY OF THE CAPITAL HETEROGENEITY MODEL

The conclusion that price plays a minor role and expectations the major role seems reasonable in the case of capital at the start of the production chain, where almost all capital goods are unique to the production process and have high sunk costs. But is the same conclusion valid where well-developed markets exist for secondary capital goods and sunk costs are proportionally lower?

Also, the example in Figure 10.2 involves a relatively small number of trucks (secondary capital) whose output is quite sensitive to the efficiency with which they interact with the excavator. The fixed (primary) capital is paramount. Arguably, a more normal case is where secondary capital is the most important element. A trucking company with hundreds of trucks is one such example. In this case, does not the expectational problem apply only to the 'last' few secondary units? If so, perhaps industry-wide output is still likely to be very close to optimum?

Influence of Well-developed Markets

This section looks at the case where secondary capital is the most important element in the capital-intensive process. It looks at the influence of well-developed markets in capital goods, particularly focusing on expectations, the mix of secondary versus primary capital, and the influence of sunk costs. This assessment is presented by way of a new but similar study.

Foreshadowing the result, the expectational problem becomes *more* acute rather than less so as secondary capital assumes a larger role. The analogy is the tragedy of the commons.[3] In this analogy, the apparent return to marginal capital narrowly considered is dramatically different to the true marginal return, and this effect is more dramatic but less obvious the larger the number of participants in the common.

Even with competitive markets, sunk costs associated with 'capital' elements remain the critical ingredient in decision-making.

To illustrate the case where secondary capital is the crucial element in the process, a new excavator/truck model has been analysed. In this model, up to 16 trucks have been matched with the excavator, with the capital and operating costs associated with the trucks accounting for more than 80 per cent of the cost of production. This is like saying that 80 per cent of the airline business is tied up in owning and operating the planes and just 20 per cent associated with fixed facilities. The average and marginal cost curves are shown in Figure 10.3.

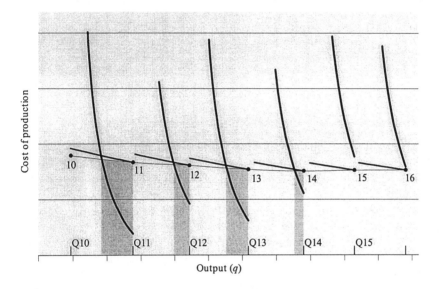

Figure 10.3: Cost curves focused on secondary capital

For clarity, the vertical marginal cost lines representing fully utilized fleets have been omitted. Again, the shaded areas of Figure 10.3 show the same characteristics as in Figure 10.2. Connecting the end-points of the declining marginal cost lines results in a rising marginal cost line in the same form as the standard models.

The indivisibility of each capital increment again means that each increment must be more fully utilized to justify its acquisition as production approaches the long-term optimum level. The utilization presents a narrower and narrower window of expectation. Moreover, the inelasticity of the volume/price (cost) relationship on the zone of viable production is more acute. Expectations play an even more important role in determining the output decision than they do in a case where secondary capital is of lesser importance.

The average and marginal cost curves shown in Figures 10.2 and 10.3 were derived from an expectation of a long-term investment (in this case, a 12-year project life). How important is this 12-year expectation when there is a well-developed market in capital goods?

The importance of expectations is directly related to the likelihood of loss in the event they are found incorrect. Yet the observation that business people routinely make investments extending over decades does not mean that such investments are dependent on expectations extending over this complete time (although this would be the conclusion in the general equilibrium, perfect competition world).

Figure 9.1 gives the initial clue to the answer. In this figure, and from Table 9.1, an exit from the investment after one year means a 14 per cent loss in capital value. The original expectation posited a capital value of $87.19 at the end of year 1, whereas a sale into the market only yields a $75 return. Put another way, the annual rental charge of $29.32 would need to be 42 per cent higher in year 1 to ensure no loss in the event of exit. An expectation unfulfilled after two years represents a 25 per cent loss in capital value on exit, with an average rental charge 31 per cent higher for each of the two years necessary to ensure no loss. In the event that such changes are likely, how would this influence the choice in the first place? The influence on choice is fundamental. With no entrepreneurial profits the risk of loss in capital value exists throughout the life of the capital good.

Figure 10.4 shows the same situation as Figure 10.3 for the change from a 12-truck fleet to a 13-truck fleet, but also showing the marginal cost of production up until the year of downsizing, including capital losses associated with disposal of the capital.

The cost of the marginal production in Figure 10.4 derives from the difference between the *market-determined* method of calculating capital value and the internal-to-the-project form. This result is partially dependent on how market values are estimated, of course. Yet the result must always apply in markets where there is no recognized difference in product, whether it is produced by an old machine or a new machine: the cost of exiting early must always be higher than the cost of staying in for the full duration.

If the market-determined value was ever *higher* than the internal-to-the-project value, then the continuation of the project is in any case a less-viable option than exiting. Such a case does not represent an *option* on exit: it signals non-viability of project continuation. Such a case is valid *ex post*, but could not be the basis of investment *ex ante*. *Ex ante*, it must be *the* plan, not an option to some less viable plan.

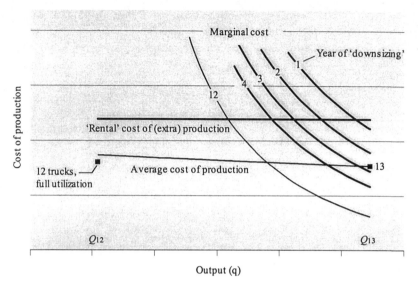

Figure 10.4: Cost of production with 'downsizing'

For illustrative purposes a horizontal 'rental cost of production' line has also been drawn in Figure 10.4. This assumes a well-developed market for secondary capital at a 'rental' rate 30 per cent greater than the equivalent rate for fully utilized capital in the rest of the model. The 30 per cent figure is the assumed market premium for commitments of a short- rather than long-term nature. The 30 per cent premium on capital 'rental' translates into an 11 per cent higher overall cost. Actors with uncertain expectations can rationally pay this premium for some time if it allows reduction in uncertainty regarding their expectations on offtake and duration.

Well-developed markets for capital do not provide costless exit strategies, but they do play an important role in honing expectations. Figure 10.4 suggests that the actor must be satisfied that the thirteenth truck can be fully utilized for at least three years to make the investment viable. Perhaps he or she thinks that there is a 30 per cent chance that this might not be so. Under the temporal utility model, the 30 per cent chance of loss may fail to satisfy the reservation criterion, despite the fact that entrepreneurial profits will be generated if the truck is fully used beyond the three years. The presence of a well-developed market in this capital, even at higher rental cost, allows market demand to be *tested*. Results from the testing (*actual* production) will change the expectation. Rational decision-makers who follow the temporal utility model can expend resources to do this testing even at the expense of efficiency (higher 'capital' costs for the duration of the 'tests'). Refinement of expectations can lead to subsequent investment.

Lest this example be considered unrepresentative, it is worth noting that the mix of secondary capital-type elements and purely variable costs is seldom as narrowly defined as in this example. Upon examination, many costs that appear to be variable are actually of a secondary capital nature and frequently are often more fully sunk than physical capital.[4] Labour costs involve significant components that do not vary with use: training and recruitment, hiring costs, and certain minimum levels of benefits, for example. Electricity usage is frequently based on a two-part tariff. When these things are considered, true variable costs play an even lesser role, and the impact of the step function associated with secondary capital effects becomes even more pronounced.

Uncertainty, Expectations and the Time Element

Whilst the marginal cost of production with each capital increment is lowest when capital is committed for the full duration, this does not necessarily mean that it must be committed for this full duration to be viable. Indeed, this period up to the point where the entrepreneur can recover his or her capital in a 'free' form is simply the precondition to induce commitment. The entrepreneur does not actually have to recover his or her capital at this time – he or she merely has to be in a position to do so within some market setting.

As equipment gets older (beyond some point), the difference between private value and market value becomes less significant. The recovery of capital in a free form becomes less of a burden. Where the production process is made up of groups of capital (the trucks, the excavator) each with a different life, sunk costs will fluctuate. Sunk cost minima will correspond to periods just prior to capital replacement: 'The expiry of a single commitment may therefore bring large numbers under review and cause a great jump in immediately escapable cost' (Lewis, 1948, 12).

Figure 10.5 examines the impact of this fluctuation in sunk cost. Prepared using the same information as Figure 10.4, it looks at how long expectations regarding output have to be sustained for production increments to remain viable. It assumes that the additional truck can be fully utilized, but not necessarily for the full 12-year project life. Marginal costs of production are the equivalent costs *now* of the marginal production, assuming the entrepreneur could exit the investment at market prices after the time shown. The sooner such an exit is viable, the lesser risk he or she is taking in extrapolating expectations into the future.

Since trucks in this example have an eight-year life, disposal (or non-renewal) of a truck after eight years represents the lowest-cost exit strategy.

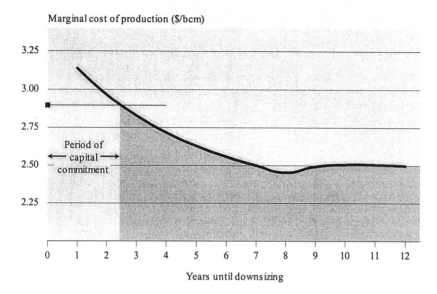

Figure 10.5: Sustainability of expectations for marginal investment

Considered *ex ante*, exit prior to this time is viable depending on the marginal revenue. From Figure 10.5, at a marginal revenue of $2.89 an investor must be confident that he or she can fully use the truck for at least 2.5 years. Disposal of it at market value after this time still represents a viable investment, and full utilization under these conditions beyond 2.5 years results in entrepreneurial profit.

Thus periods of commitment and optimum levels of output are functions of the correctness of expectations. Imperfect expectations cause actors to choose output levels less than optimum, and at this output level there are always (expected) entrepreneurial profits at the margin. Imperfect expectations do not result in output levels distributed either side of the neoclassical perfect information mean level.

Chapter 11 examines this scenario further and addresses the question of how imperfect expectations are accommodated in the market, and how rational actors choose the appropriate level of production.

NOTES

1. Lewis (1948, 12) highlights the difficulty in establishing the appropriate marginal cost to apply for decision-making: 'There is no such quantity as "the marginal cost" of output; there is not even a simple choice between two quantities, short- and long-run cost; there is a large variety of costs to choose from, depending merely on how far ahead you choose to

look.' And, as pointed out in Chapter 9, 'how far ahead you choose to look' means the period of commitment towards some technology, not a time period necessarily fixed by physical characteristics.

2. At a marginal revenue of $1.70 per bcm, the threshold for viable production only changes about 1 per cent for every 5 per cent change in price.

3. For a useful description of the tragedy of the commons, see, for example, Henderson (1993), 88–91.

4. Shepherd (1984, 580fn) recognizes R&D, advertising to establish brand loyalty, and training to create special workers skills in this category.

11. Capital decisions: choices between strategies

In this chapter the model explicitly examines one of the distinctive characteristics of rational choice set out by Arrow (1958, 61) 'stress[ing] the sequential nature of many choice situations; [and that] choices are frequently extended in time, with a choice at one stage having an effect on choices at a later stage.'

This penultimate chapter drops the final assumption of choices whose characteristics can be explicitly understood *ex ante*. It recognizes that each choice is actually a choice to set upon a certain *strategy* whose ultimate value is dependent on follow-up decisions in later periods. Initial choices include imbedded options to change. The value of these real options cannot be assumed from their mere recognition without also accounting for the *rule* an actor must use to exercise them. In the presence of uncertainty whose stochastic characteristics are *not* known, these rules must consider not just the timing and magnitude of change compared to the cost of exercise, but also the mechanism that the actor uses to form expectations of future change.

THE ENTREPRENEURIAL DECISION: WHERE TO PRODUCE?

In the neoclassical general equilibrium world, the decision of how much to produce is trivial. Output is determined by the point at which marginal revenues equate to marginal cost.

In the world where demand curves are unknown and changing and the marginal cost is a function of an entrepreneur's expectations, the decision of how much to produce is more complicated. Nevertheless, action is only meaningful amongst alternatives that are under the actor's control. By extension, the focus of attention must be towards those activities that are *most* under the actor's control. Four factors, ranked in suggested order from most to least are briefly considered:

1. *Output* Ex ante the limits of production (or, at least, *maximum* capacity choices) are totally under an actor's control.

2. *Expectations and uncertainty* Uncertainty can always be reduced at a cost in efficiency, and the decision point for this trade-off is under the actor's control. There is a short-term (before investment) and a longer-term aspect to this choice problem. Prior to investment, the trade-off is focused on the proportion of outcomes yielding returns less than the cost of capital which can be regarded as relatively fixed. In the longer term, demonstrated performance also offers scope for reduction in the cost of capital.

3. *Price/marginal revenues* Short-term supply inelasticities allow some monopoly power to existing producers and scope for marginal revenues to be different to price. Even in a competitive market, an exogenous change that affects all producers equally does not require all producers to *react* equally. The extent to which other producers' reactions can be pre-empted or influenced offers scope for relative gain.

4. *Costs of capital* Performance consistencies stemming from correctness in expectations and anticipation of market changes lower the long-term costs of capital.

Consider again Technology B in Figure 10.2. The marginal cost curves for this technology are reproduced to a different scale in Figure 11.1, focusing in this instance on a planned investment in a fifth truck. This figure can now be used to examine the impact of expected price, the cost of capital, and expectations (volume and timing) on capacity choice and the decision to invest.

Consider first the influence of price. The neoclassical perfect-competition model suggests that if marginal costs are less than the long-run average cost minima then additional output can be sold with no expectational uncertainty. The model in Figure 11.1 yields quite a different result. The expected output must fall within the shaded zone for investment to be viable, and changes in price about the average have little impact on the range of outputs defining this zone. Given an assumption that all output can be sold, price has virtually no impact on the decision to invest. At full capital utilization, marginal investment is not only viable, but offers entrepreneurial profit. Price would have to change dramatically – fall to below $1.00 from 'current' levels of $1.50 – to *stop* investment proceeding. Under this model, small changes in prices *independent of changes in expectations* make almost no impact on investment.

There is a caveat to this result. The market under study is not an equilibrium market, and (in the short term at least) actors face downward-sloping demand curves. Marginal revenue does not have to equal price in such a market. In a single-price market, small reductions in price induced by small increases in supply may effectively mean marginal revenues

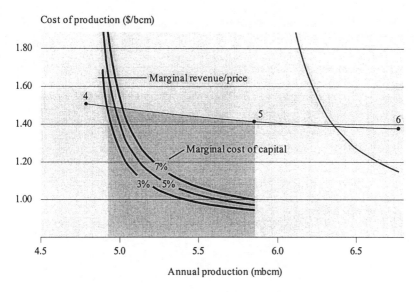

Figure 11.1: Costs of production, technology B

substantially below price. Expansion to, say, 5.5 mbcm per year in Figure 11.1 is viable so long as marginal revenue exceeds $1.04 per bcm. Yet in a single price market a relatively small 6 per cent *average* price reduction (to $1.43 per bcm) means a marginal revenue of only $0.90 per bcm – a marginal revenue that makes the investment non-viable.

Consider, second, the impact of the cost of capital. Start again from the assumption of high capital utilization. The cost of capital enters the calculation by way of the discount factor applied. Lower discount factors mean lower costs and a larger target zone where expanded production is viable. Since the cost of capital is strongly related to the interest rate in the general economy, this sensitivity has a direct relationship to monetary influences on the business cycle that have been the subject of debate throughout this century.[1]

Under the model shown, fully utilized capital has marginal costs substantially below average costs. In this case, the reduction in unit cost associated with a reduction in the cost of capital has little impact. Actors would proceed regardless of the cost of capital if they were convinced that all the output could be sold. If they were not fully convinced that all the output could be sold then reductions in cost associated with reductions in the cost of capital would make little change to the target zone that is the focus of their expectations. Only in an ultra-competitive economy, where marginal costs of production are very close to average costs, would changes in the cost of capital make any significant difference to the decision to invest.

This leaves just the third element – entrepreneurial expectations – as the primary influence on the decision to invest. The decision to invest is seen to be one of how reliably expectations are held regarding output (that is, capital utilization), and how many years the expected output conditions can be sustained.

Without developing a theory of entrepreneurial expectations, Figure 11.2 looks at a sample range of output conditions (capital utilization) and the number of years these must be sustained prior to potential disposal of the capital at market prices. It suggests the minimum boundary of expectations necessary to induce an entrepreneur to invest. The shaded areas effectively represent a successful investment, considered *ex ante*.

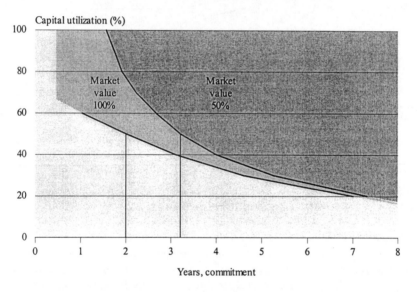

Figure 11.2: Expectations necessary to induce investment

There are two lines drawn in Figure 11.2. The lower line represents the case where there are well-developed markets and an easy exit strategy in case expectations turn out to be wrong. The upper line represents the case where just 50 per cent of the market price is recoverable in the event of exit from the market. It is included to demonstrate the effect of opportunity cost or commitment power on expectations. For example, to induce investment an entrepreneur must be convinced that the capital can be at least 50 per cent utilized for a period of two years, even where there is a competitive market in the capital good. Poorer utilization, fewer options for change or fewer competitive markets in capital inputs reduce the size of the shaded areas. The entrepreneur is committed for a longer period of time – or must be satisfied to take on such a commitment before decision.

The absence of a competitive market in capital inputs, if this is to be the exit strategy, locks in a 50 per cent utilized investment for a period of 3.2 years, or 60 per cent longer than if easier exit strategies (resale price at 100 per cent of market value) are available. This period of commitment is the crucial element in the entrepreneurial choice problem. It is dependent on the *continuing* opportunity cost (value of the next best alternative available through the life of the capital good) rather than the *ex ante* value of the choice.

The neoclassical model with no uncertainty in expectations could be characterized two ways. On the one hand, using a perfect-information, perfect-foresight conception, it is equivalent to a single point on the top right-hand corner of this graph at 100 per cent utilization over eight years. On the other hand, using a contestable market conception, it has a *continuing* opportunity cost represented by a vertical line at time zero – imperfect knowledge and foresight, but a zero-cost, instantaneous exit strategy.

When uncertainty is expressed in the Hayekian terms – of the time it takes until an entrepreneur is in a position to recover his or her capital in a 'free' form – the decision takes on new dimensions. Substantial differences are evident even amongst alternatives that offer entrepreneurial profits and are far removed from the neoclassical equilibrium position. Without change in expectations, reductions in the cost of capital and higher notional prices of the product are very blunt mechanisms for inducing capital investment leading to additional capacity.

OPTIONS, STRATEGY AND CAPITAL VALUE

This section drops the final constraint set out in the introduction: of choices whose characteristics can be explicitly understood *ex ante*. It recognizes that each choice is actually a choice to set upon a certain *strategy* whose ultimate value is dependent on follow-up decisions in later periods. Alternatives are valued more highly if they allow an actor more influence or more freedom to choose over yet-to-be-encountered circumstances requiring change. 'Options' are part of the 'liberty' dimension in Buchanan's (1993) argument. They are the counterpoint to what he calls the Aristotelian or efficiency dimension. The equivalent Aristotelian dimension in the capital choice problem is the productivity of resource usage, typically represented by the *expected* return on investment.

The market value as one of these options has already been discussed. But an exit strategy (the 'option' at any time) of reselling capital at market prices is not the only fall-back position and is seldom the most attractive alternative course of action. One reason why such abandonment options are problematic is that at the time when this alternative is drawn upon it is likely that *other* producers will be considering the same thing. The option is shared. Historical market values are not necessarily a reliable guide to market values forming part of an exit strategy.

Trigeorgis (1996) identifies six types of real[2] options that decision-makers can make use of in addition to the option to abandon already discussed. These seven types, summarized from Trigeorgis with comments framed using the temporal utility model, are:

1. *Option to defer* This option compares the alternative to 'proceed now' with the alternative to 'wait and then proceed'. Such a choice was discussed in Chapter 7. With the arrival of information over time the present value of deferred choices planned with greater efficiency with the (then) known information can exceed the present value of the same choice proceeded with immediately.

2. *Time-to-build option* This option involves a series of outlays. Each outlay sets in place production capability plus conditions for subsequent (reduced) outlays involving production. The example involving rental of secondary capital in Chapter 10 is one such time-to-build option.

3. *Option to abandon* This option has been extensively discussed above.

4. *Alter operating scale* This option does not lead to more refined expectations but it explicitly values alternatives that are *less sensitive to imprecise expectations*.

5. *Option to change (switch inputs or outputs)* This option is analogous to the option above. It pertains to the imprecision of expectations regarding the type and cost of inputs and outputs. Imbedded options to change are essential ingredients in long-life machines used for fashion goods, for instance.

6. *Growth options* Similar to time-to-build options, these options recognize that certain actions (R&D for instance) can be narrowly focused on the project at hand, or more broadly focused. The option explicitly values the externalities from a more broadly focused approach where these externalities can be retained within the firm.

7. *Multiple interacting options* This is a recognition that combinations of options – for example, one that offers downward protection, and one that offers revenue enhancement – can have a combined value exceeding the sum of the separate parts. Options increase the reliability in achieving planned returns, and in addition to improving the return on investment on

the project at hand a demonstrated history of capitalizing on this approach can also lower the cost of capital.

The objective in this section is to consider the value of this option approach from the standpoint of the temporal utility model and the influence of expectations on option value.

Real Options and the Temporal Utility Model

The quantitative origins of real options derive from the seminal work of Black and Scholes (1973) and Merton (1973) in pricing financial options. There are a number of assumptions deriving from these origins that cannot be automatically applied to real options within the capital investment decision problem. The assumptions have to do with whether the source of the option is exogenous or endogenous, shared or proprietary, and costly or costless.

First, however, some terminological clarification is in order. Options on financial assets follow the finance literature and equate uncertainty (or variability) with *risk*. The validity of this approach was discussed and acknowledged in Chapter 3 wherein the differences to the cases under study in this book were also highlighted. Simply put, a valid statistical understanding that 35 out of 10,000 convenience stores will burn down in the ensuing year (a *class* probability statement) is categorically different to an actor's perception of the value of his or her one convenience store adjacent to the fireworks on new year's eve. Real options have to do with this second case (of *case* probability), and uncertainties associated with single projects can be fitted within a class probability framework only by assuming away many choice decisions that are the essence of the problem and the foundation of option value.

Risk in the discussion that follows means the potential exposure associated with outcomes whose achieved return on investment falls short of the cost of capital.[3] Increases in uncertainty (increases in the variability of outcomes) which automatically mean greater risk in the financial options world only mean greater 'real' risk if they increase the scope for outcomes whose return on investment is less than the cost of capital. Thus the twin requirements for choice under the temporal utility model are particularly relevant in any discussion on options value. Value in the efficiency dimension – the *expected* return on investment – is meaningful only subject to the constraint that the risk (or reservation) precondition is satisfied, and 'options' affect both of these dimensions.

Consider now an example similar to Trigeorgis (1996)[4] and Pindyck (1988) involving the simplest no-cost option: the management option to change.[5] Like the example set out in Alchian (1950)[6] this option recognizes that in the face of some negative exogenous impact, the investment can be changed to minimize the effects. Likewise, in the face of some positive exogenous impact the investment can also be changed to achieve gains. Such a case is portrayed in Figure 11.3.

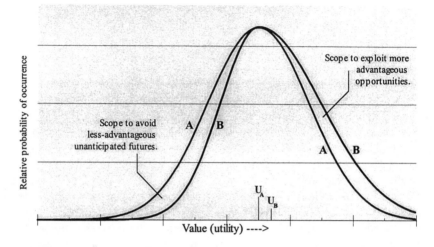

Figure 11.3: Value of zero-cost option

As these authors rightly point out, even if the 'most likely' outcome is unaffected by management's scope to adapt, the option introduces an asymmetry in the curve. The 'most likely' (or *modal* value) result is U_A in both cases. Yet the 'strategic' NPV (or *mean* value, U_B) is greater for case B. In Figure 11.3 the difference between U_B and U_A represents the value of the option.

Such a construct potentially leads to a rather curious result. If, in the neoclassical world, choices are valued according to the subjective expected utility model, then costless options combined with increasing uncertainty may actually *enhance* investment returns. More uncertainty means *more* investment, so long as management has the scope to adapt to it. Pindyck (1988) and Roberts and Weissman (1981, quoted in Leahy and Whited Whited, T.M., 1995, 2) have examined models that suggest this counter-intuitive outcome.

This result is plausible if options are costless and proprietary, and increased uncertainty does not lead to increased risk (in the sense defined by the temporal utility model). Yet the temporal utility model applied in a competitive market economy suggests that the conditions for *increased* investment to flow from increased uncertainty are highly unlikely.

Figure 11.4 shows the same two curves as Figure 11.3, with alternative B shifted to the left – indicating an endogenized *costly* option to change. The notional cost of the option changes the modal value from U_A to U^*_B, but after accounting for the asymmetry results in a 'real' value of U_B.

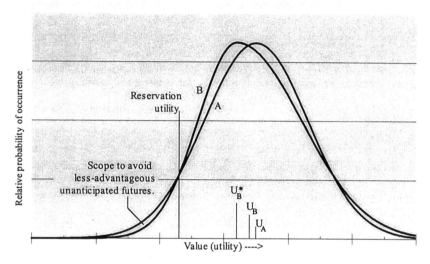

Figure 11.4: Costly options valued with the temporal utility model

In Figure 11.4 alternative A represents a choice with no scope for change except for exogenous or automatic options such as the option to abandon. Alternative B includes an additional option, built into the capital investment choice at a cost, which provides for more alternatives in the event that future outcomes turn out unfavourably.

Real options, including management's option to change, have a cost. In the example quoted previously (see note 8 of Chapter 6), Packard (1995) quotes an instance of an electronics factory designed as a general-purpose building (at some presumed extra cost) so that in the event of failure of the main plan it could be turned to some alternative use. That the 'management option to change' is *not* costless is even better illustrated in the case of investments employing large amounts of project debt financing. Project debt finance always includes covenants that limit the scope for change. In these circumstances the presence of value-enhancing *potential* change cannot be presumed a sufficient condition for removal of these restrictions.[7]

For increased uncertainty to generate *increased* investment, the option to change must also be at least partly *proprietary*. In a competitive market economy, non-proprietary (shared) options also benefit competitors, and the net direction of forces is ambiguous. Increased uncertainty may *reduce* competition from others not already in the market, and this may result in higher pricing and entrepreneurial profits for existing participants but no net increase in output.

In the neoclassical world, risk is synonymous with variance. Assets (or at least, assets in the *financial* markets) are automatically devalued if their returns are subject to greater variance. Counterbalancing this, the asymmetry associated with options to change moves some of this increased variance into improved (expected) value. But there can be no presumption that the loss in value due to the increase in variance is less detrimental than the improvement in expected value due to the option asymmetry. In the temporal utility model, the impact is unambiguous.

In an economy subject to uncertainty, actors will not engage in projects that are *more* risky than their own preferences dictate. These cases have already been discussed at length. But in a *competitive* economy, entrepreneurs are also unlikely to engage in projects that are *less risky* than their own preferences dictate. In these cases they will seek out ways to enhance economic returns up to the point when their reservation utility is just satisfied. An increase in the debt/equity ratio is one way to achieve this. To the extent that there are such opportunities, this suggests that investments will be pursued to the point where, for individual private actors, at the margin all investments just satisfy this risk-based or 'reservation' criterion.[8] Any increase in uncertainty will unambiguously make some previously marginal choices unattractive.

Results evidenced in Figure 11.4 can be summarized thus:

1. The notional cost of the option ($U_A - U^*_B$) – the change in most likely outcome – is partially offset by the asymmetry. The real cost ($U_A - U_B$) – the change in 'mean' outcome – will *ex ante* always be less than the notional cost.

2. Under the temporal utility model, an endogenized costly option can reduce risk (the scope for outcomes to the left of the reservation line). For potential choices constrained by this precondition, such options will result in increased investment even to the detriment of the *expected* return on investment.

3. Under the temporal utility model, economy-wide increases in uncertainty that start from a competitive state of affairs are unambiguously detrimental to investment. Even if the increase in uncertainty makes no change in the most likely outcome, both alternatives with and without the option have increased proportions of potential outcomes to the left of the reservation line. Some projects that were previously unconstrained by the reservation criterion will now become constrained, but *no* projects previously constrained will become viable, unless the change in uncertainty is also accompanied by some *increased* ability to adapt.[9]

Increases in uncertainty under this model imply that:

1. Actors will seek out additional options to be able to adapt, at some *ex ante* cost in *expected* return, until the profile of potential outcomes again satisfies the precondition. For the same planned capacity choice, the amount of capital will be greater, or the efficiency of the capital will be less. Alternatively, investment decisions will be stalled until mechanisms can be found that trade-off the now-possible *enhanced* outcomes against the increased likelihood of detrimental outcomes.

2. In the presence of uncertainty or in an expanding economy, the value of an option to invest in an irreversible process (or a process involving high sunk costs) is greater than in a stable economy. Since this option is effectively exercised when the investment decision is made, firms will make fewer investments than they otherwise would in a more stable market environment. This result is similar to the Pindyck (1988, 983) result that 'firms should *hold* less capacity than they would if investment were reversible or future demands were known'.

3. In the presence of uncertainty or in an expanding economy, production technology choices favour those alternatives that *include* endogenous, proprietary options to change. Many endogenous options to change involve additional capital expenditures to facilitate such future changes and the value of this additional capital is not evident by observing current outputs. For *observable* capital investments, therefore, apparent capital efficiency will be lower and capacity investment will be greater than it otherwise would be in a more stable market environment.

Some of these theoretical results have already been mentioned in the review of empirical work in Chapter 7.

Expectations and Option Value

Financial options are subject to no ambiguity as to when they should be exercised. European financial options cannot be exercised until maturity, and Merton (1973) has shown that it is never optimal to exercise an American call option early.[10] The value of financial options is independent of human decision-making once it is assumed that the stochastic characteristics of the underlying asset are unchanging. This is not the case with real options.

This difference has been dramatically illustrated throughout history. Firms exercise their option to abandon at the bottom of a market cycle[11] when they become convinced that its underlying characteristics have changed. Others who are convinced that the underlying characteristics have not changed buy the assets and, if they are correct, make entrepreneurial profits. The assumption that actors value real options and exercise real options based on some *exogenously* determined independent characteristic leaves many of the most important business decisions unexplained.

The value of a real option derives from the recognition that the path about to be followed may turn out to be wrong. Exercising the option means a second decision: to deviate from the path currently being followed. Rational actors must also recognize that this decision too might be wrong. The value of the option is reduced by the uncertainty in capitalizing on its potential value in the face of the same kinds of changes that gave it value in the first place.

Consider again the case of the option to purchase a fifth truck in the example in Figure 11.1 (see page 165). At an *expected* market offtake of 5.26 mbcm per year – held constant for the duration of the investment – the purchase of the fifth truck is more viable than a precommitted choice limited to just four trucks. Traditional (static) capital budgeting suggests that the five-truck case should be selected.

If, however, the market offtake is unknown prior to commitment and may turn out to be more or less than this expected amount, then there is value in waiting for such a characteristic to be revealed. An initial commitment for four trucks placed in production will test market reaction and reveal the 'true' market characteristics (at least for this first example). The fifth truck can be purchased in the following year if the actual offtake is such as to make the additional capital purchase viable.

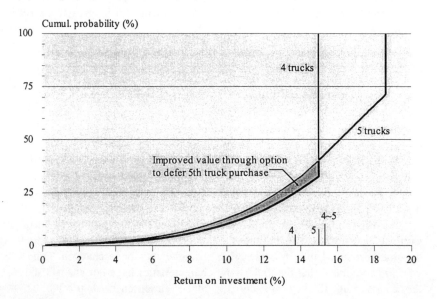

Figure 11.5: Value of real options to change

'Low' outcomes mean that the fifth truck is deferred forever. 'High' outcomes mean that the truck is purchased and the extra value captured. This case, assuming that market offtake is fully revealed during the first year and constant thereafter for the duration of the investment, is shown in Figure 11.5.

In Figure 11.5[12] market offtake once revealed is *constant* (there is no performance variability), but *ex ante* is only known in a probabilistic sense. In this case, the offtake has an expected value of 5.26 mbcm per year, normally distributed, with a standard deviation 20 per cent about this expected value.

Table 11.1 sets out the net present value and internal rate of return for the available choices.

Table 11.1: Option value (traditional approach)

Alternative (description)	Net present value at 5% cost of capital ($)	Internal rate of return (%)
Ex ante values, at the *expected* offtake		
'Fixed' 4 trucks	5,940,000	15.00
'Fixed' 5 trucks	7,492,281	16.16
Ex ante expected values		
'Fixed' 4 trucks	5,155,496	13.70
'Fixed' 5 trucks	6,758,284	14.99
4 trucks, with option to expand	6,829,659	15.32
Value of option to expand/defer ($)	1,674,163 or 71,375	

The example set out in Figure 11.5 and in Table 11.1 is the traditional approach. The uncertainty only applies to the original capital expenditure decision and performance of the investment and follow-up decisions (to exercise the option) are not subject to any uncertainty. Despite these limitations, the example illustrates two important points:

1. Whenever there is variability there is scope for asymmetry of outcomes. The *ex ante expected value* is always less than the *ex ante* value of the *expected* outcome. Market offtake above the expected offtake typically cannot be accommodated because of capacity limitations, whereas the corresponding offtake below the expected offtake results in less-than-average returns that cannot be avoided because of sunk costs. In the example, this effect decreases value by 10 per cent to 13 per cent. The impact of this is more pronounced with each increase in variability.

2. In the traditional presentation, the value of an option is a function of how it is framed. In this example, the option could be framed as a four-truck choice with an option to expand (valued at $1,674,163, or 24.5 per cent of the whole value of the choice) or as a five-truck choice with an option to defer (valued at $71,375). From an economic viewpoint there is no framing problem. The value of any choice is always based on the next most attractive alternative that might have been chosen.

The value of an option increases with increasing uncertainty, since its asymmetry potentially allows positive outcomes to be capitalized on but negative outcomes to be avoided. But it is important not to confuse the value of an option (increasing with uncertainty) with the value of the whole project to which the option relates. For 'whole' projects, uncertainty introduces its own asymmetry which works in the opposite direction. Figure 11.6 illustrates both these effects using the same example.

Return on investment (%)

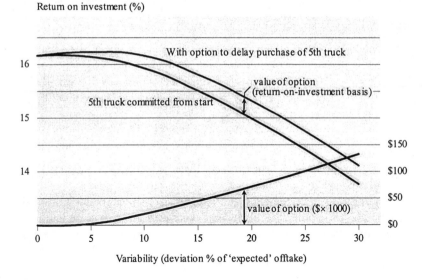

Figure 11.6: Value of real option under increasing uncertainty

In Figure 11.6 the standard deviation of market offtake was modelled in the range 0 to ± 30 per cent about the expected value. Without any option to defer, increasing uncertainty always reduces the expected return. *With* the option to defer, the trend with increasing uncertainty is also unambiguously negative; however small increases in uncertainty beyond the deterministic case can lead to *increases* in expected return. The five-truck case has capacity beyond that required for the base case, and for small increases in demand this can be capitalized on.

Nevertheless, such outcomes are unusual and unlikely to be a feature of a competitive economy since they require the existence of unsold marginal production when prices are above marginal cost.

As a model of real-world decision-making, there are two significant shortcomings in this traditional 'real options' presentation:

1. The example assumes that all uncertainty is resolved after the first year, and that thereafter output is constant. Yet in the real world, as fast as one endogenous change comes to be understood another may come to influence the situation at hand. Even truly exogenous influences may not be stable in their influence on the choice. Many treatments of real options fail when uncertainty cannot be so resolved and the financial options solution of waiting until maturity (when all uncertainty disappears) is not possible. Thus every choice must also accommodate the on-going variability – the *performance* variability – whether it is understood or not understood, and this variability introduces permanent asymmetry in the performance of investments, not just in the *initial* choice characteristics.

2. Strategic choice – the decision to *exercise* the options – is also subject to this performance variability. Even if the variability characteristics are completely exogenous and independent of the project at hand, the knowledge that this is so has to be endogenously determined.

When the above influences are considered, two outcomes follow:

1. Expected returns that allow for performance variability must always be less than expected returns that do not allow for performance variability.

2. Variability causes imprecision in the timing and exercise of options. Signal extraction problems resulting from endogenously derived expectations mean that sometimes the option is exercised when it should not be and sometimes the option is not exercised when it should be. This imprecision in expectations reduces the value of the option. It acts in the opposite direction to the typical impact of uncertainty on option value.

This section analyses the impact of performance variability (cyclicity, noise) on value through the twin influences of capacity constraint asymmetry and imprecision in option exercise. The model adds cyclical and noise characteristics to the previous example as set out in Table 11.2.

The expectations model is not meant to be comprehensive, but is aimed at capturing some of the more common influences in the economy. In particular, the model assumes yearly decision-making but expectations modelled quarterly to try to capture the interrelationship between the noisy real-world (quarterly) signals and the more stable requirements for

Table 11.2: Simulation data, expectations modelling

Component of model	Simulation characteristics used
'True' mean annual offtake	5.264 mbcm ± 20% (std. deviation, normal distribution)
Cyclical characteristic:	
Length of cyclical influences	From 11 to 19 quarters (mean 15 qtrs, uniform distribution)
Amplitude of cycles	Peak quarterly production offtake ± 25% above/below mean
Cycle starting point (Year 0)	45 deg. ± 45 deg. (uniform distribution)
Random 'noise'	± 10% of mean production offtake, applied quarterly

production and capital budgeting. Though simulated market demand varied quarterly, actual production was modelled only on an averaged four-quarterly basis (assuming that inventory changes smoothed out the differences).

The model also simulated the starting point of the cycle. The starting point is important for two reasons. Initial investments are usually timed to capture the benefits of earlier cyclical upswings. However, this means that choices to upgrade (purchase the fifth truck), being delayed at least one year, have an increased probability of presentation after the market has started to turn down.

Actors' decisions to exercise or not to exercise an option depend on their perception of future conditions. Without developing a comprehensive theory of how actors form expectations, this model assumes that they form these endogenously, using an adaptive approach.

Whilst such an approach leaves many aspects of the expectations formulation problem unaddressed, it is still valid in this instance because in the model the underlying characteristics *are* stable and past experience *is* an unbiased indicator of future outcomes. The criterion for choice (to exercise the option or to decide *not* to exercise the option) using this adaptive approach suggests that the expectations so formed will possibly be *more* reliable than most real-world applications.

In the temporal utility model, choice requires both risk or 'confidence' elements, and an 'expected return' or *efficiency* element. Three criteria derived from quarter-by-quarter experience in the model are assumed to be necessary prior to any decision to exercise:

1. Predicted future offtake must be above the threshold for viable investment. This is the expected return or efficiency element.

2. The model predicts offtake using an OLS regression of past offtake. Thus the reliability of how an actor can predict *current* conditions is the most valuable confidence indicator of future predictions. The model looks at the residuals from this regression and requires that actual offtake must be

within the range –5 per cent to +15 per cent of predicted offtake in the quarter in which the decision is to be made. This is the primary risk, or confidence element.

3. Increasing offtake: This condition requires that quarter-to-quarter offtake must increase, or at least not decrease by more than 1 per cent from the previous quarter. This is a secondary confidence element. It reflects the influence of short-term confidence on decisions and, if not satisfied, normally results in decision deferral to the immediately following quarter.

Decision-makers can choose to exercise the option (purchase the fifth truck) at any time, not just after the first year. In a cyclical market, if an opportunity to upgrade is missed in one cyclical up-turn (due, say, to insufficient confidence in expectations), then several years later similar cyclical conditions may allow upgrading at that time.

Obviously in the real world entrepreneurs use more information than the above to make such decisions; however, when imposed on a cyclical market with noise, even these fairly innocuous constraints mean that there are only certain periods when potential choices can satisfy the conditions. The decision and production strategies were simulated using a Monte Carlo technique for approximately 10,000 cases over the full range of predicted market offtakes. The results from this simulation, in the form consistent with Figure 11.5, are shown in Figure 11.7.

Variability causes a substantial reduction in value across almost the full range of potential outcomes.

Two influences are at work in Figure 11.7. The first is the reduction in value directly associated with the performance variability. This reduction in value comes from below-average variations not being counterbalanced by the above-average outcomes and in this example amounts to approximately 6 per cent loss in value. The second influence is due to the way that variability causes incorrect choices for expansion – either through expansion when it is not truly warranted (as annotated in Figure 11.7), or refraining from expansion when it is warranted. In this example this influence amounts to approximately 4 per cent loss in value.

Table 11.3 sets out the numerical results from the simulation. This table corresponds to Table 11.1 in the previous example where the noise and variability were absent.

Performance variability is a fact of life. But the loss of value due to incorrect choices to exercise or not to exercise options is an *ex ante* avoidable cost that has to be compared to alternative ways to accommodate the uncertainty. In this case, the 4 per cent loss in value appears to be sub-optimum, since a rule of 'always buy the fifth truck' results only in a 1 per cent loss in value (the fixed 5 truck case in Table 11.1 has only 1 per cent

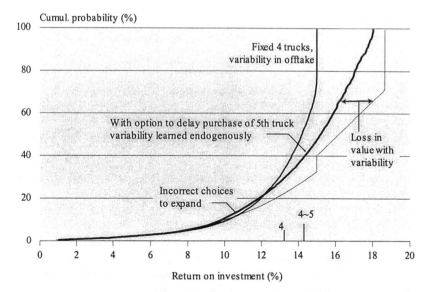

Figure 11.7: Uncertainty impact on project and option value

lower NPV than the best case). The result suggests that, in this case, an actor with no freedom to choose whether or not to buy the fifth truck would be better off *ex ante* than someone with *more* information and the freedom to make the choice at the time.

The conclusion above is unusable in real life because only in a simulation can the reliability of rules for expectations formulation be examined. Nevertheless, it points to an important implication for how capital investments subject to uncertainty are valued. It suggests that the value of capital investment strategies subject to follow-on choices may be much more a function of expectations formulation than *ex ante* expected value (assessed in the efficiency dimension) as traditionally considered. Such a result is surely not uncommon in the real world, where business people by acting have ended up being worse off than if they had let some current situation run its course.

Table 11.3: Option value including variability and expectations

Alternative (description)	Net present value at 5% cost of capital ($)	Internal rate of return (%)
Ex ante expected values		
'Fixed' 4 trucks	4,841,995	13.25
4 trucks, with option to expand	6,164,815	14.31

Whilst the availability of options and strategic choices adds potential and often unrecognized value to capital investment choices, the realization of this value is integrally linked to the variability and the ability of decision-makers to formulate rules for the proper exercise of the strategic choices after the original investment decision. In the absence of robust rules, the resulting outcomes may result in returns which offer no improvement over the case where commitments that otherwise might have been delayed are made at the very start.

IMPLICATIONS

This chapter and the previous two chapters have set out a model of capital investment choice, explicitly focusing on the indivisibility of capital, the influence of sunk costs, and the complementarity of capital within a production process (secondary capital) with capital that is the defining element of the process (primary capital). The evaluation has been built on a competitive but non-equilibrium framework.

In this model, the driving force for capital investment decisions is entrepreneurial expectations concerning market offtake for the envisaged production. In particular, the importance of expectations is reflected in the time it takes and potential *changes in value* from when an entrepreneur invests his money capital until he or she is in a position to recover the capital again in a 'free' form (that is, as money). The case study, developed realistically from current capital investment decisions in the earthmoving industry, suggests that even with capital investment projects extending over more than ten years, the critical time element when capital values are at risk is only of the order of two to three years.

According to the model, capital investment decisions are primarily a function of the reliability of expectations within this two- to three-year time frame. Capital investment decisions are positively influenced by the presence of well-developed markets in capital goods, by increases in prices and by reductions in interest rates, though these influences appear to be minor.

Capital investments are unambiguously negatively affected by increases in uncertainty (without changes in offtake expectations), and observable capital investments in environments of uncertainty are characterized by relative over-capitalization (at least in respect to *current* output).

Capital value is enhanced by the presence and recognition of options to change, and the value of options (though not the value of the investment) increases with increasing uncertainty. Where uncertainties are not exogenous to the production and decision process, the value of options is decreased due to signal extraction and strategic influences on how they are exercised.

NOTES

1. See, for example, Mises (1971) and Hayek (1931) for the Austrian explanation of the business cycle deriving from this source.
2. 'Real' options are distinguished from financial options because they apply to capital assets rather than financial assets. For a more comprehensive analysis of the theory of real options, see, for example, Dixit and Pindyck (1994); Trigeorgis (1996); Pindyck (1988); Brennan and Schwartz (1985); and McDonald and Siegel (1986).
3. Chapter 3 compares 'risk' from an individual, entrepreneurial perspective with risk in the neoclassical world.
4. See Trigeorgis (1996, 123) for a series of graphs similar to Figure 11.3.
5. This option to change is not necessarily a no-cost option (see discussion below).
6. This example was also discussed at length in Chapter 3.
7. Since debt finance for major projects is normally sourced from multiple financial consortia, the removal of restrictions by agreement amongst the members of these consortia is subject to many of the prisoners' dilemma style of problems common in the public choice literature – even when the proposed changes are to the benefit of all parties. The financing of the Channel Tunnel, for instance, was drawn from over 200 banks and other finance institutions. In such a case, strategic behaviour directed against other members of the consortia (say, by using veto power) may offer private benefits to one party that exceed the benefits deriving from the improved financial viability of the project itself.
8. The neoclassical general equilibrium conditions in the macroeconomy equate economy-wide marginal value to price. Under the temporal utility model, the equivalent general equilibrium condition is equality of *risk* at the margin, with marginal value (in the efficiency dimension) equating to price only as a secondary effect.
9. Such a case could be envisaged, for example, if the increase in uncertainty is due to an act of war and was clearly perceived to be so.
10. Where there are dividends, the optimal point of exercise will be immediately prior to the dividend, and this may make a difference if the maturity date does not coincide with the dividend.
11. Recognized *ex post*.
12. This figure (and also Figure 11.7) is presented as a *cumulative* probability distribution rather than a *relative* probability distribution that is used in Figure 11.4 and elsewhere in the book. Relative probability distribution curves cannot be faithfully represented in cases where a single point value rather than a range of values represents any fixed probability of outcomes (for example, in the four-truck case, approximately 67 per cent of outcomes yield exactly 15 per cent return on investment).

12. Summary and conclusions

This book started with the observation that large capital investment decisions within firms are only rarely profit maximizing under the traditional neoclassical definition. It suggested that 'agency' interpretations of this were only a partial explanation, and that an explanation based on *uncertainty* could lead to this result even with agents (the firm's managers) being truly representative of the firm's owners.

The book sets out a comprehensive model of the capital investment decision process within a firm, assuming a dynamic competitive market environment. Analysis is founded on definitions of capital, risk, and uncertainty from a value-based, opportunity-cost perspective.

Value-based Concept of Capital

In the value-static world of general equilibrium, there is little to separate the *value* of capital from the physical goods that form part of any process leading to this value. The book works from a *non-equilibrium* setting. Capital investment decisions are decisions aimed at exploiting the differences between 'value' as it might be understood in a well-developed market (or *near* 'equilibrium') setting, and 'value' as it is understood using the private knowledge and action capability of the actor within a changing market. The book proceeds from a value-based framework and makes no attempt to differentiate between physical changes leading to changes in value, on the one hand, from informational changes and externalities that lead to changes in value, on the other.

'Capital' in this book is the *value*, assessed in the present, attaching to something envisaged in the future. The value is associated with certain goods (capital *goods*) combined with resources, institutional structures and a plan within some market framework that, when combined, make up an actor's expectation towards this future coming to realization.

Risk and Uncertainty

Knight (1921) distinguishes between events that are capable of actuarial treatment (which he called 'risks') and events not capable of such treatment (which he called 'uncertainty'). Neoclassical economic theory is almost always concerned with risk according to the Knightian definition, and has very little to say about events that are not capable of actuarial assessment.

The primary focus in this book concerns choice amongst alternatives not capable of actuarial assessment, hence these traditional definitions are unhelpful. The book adopts a layman's concept of choice involving risk: the scope to make a wrong decision, and the exposure associated with the outcome resulting therefrom. This 'real' risk applies even if the probabilities cannot be actuarially determined.

Uncertainty

Uncertainty, on the other hand, does not necessarily mean risk. It refers to some outcome whose value is not definitely known or cannot be determined in advance. Uncertainty may arise on economic grounds because information is not free: an additional drillhole to resolve some uncertainty in orebody definition may not yield enough knowledge to offset the cost. Alternatively, uncertainty may be an inherent characteristic unable to be resolved by known technology or additional expenditure (due to the weather, for instance). Uncertainty may or may not be assessable in some actuarial manner. Further, since 'value' is a subjective concept, *outcomes* with no uncertainty can yield uncertain *value* where an actor is unsure how the pursuit of some choice will translate into utility for him- or herself. Uncertainty is characterized by some distribution of potential values, rather than one unique value. Uncertainty in capital investment choice also means conceptually unknowable elements, uncertainty in *expectations* and uncertainty (and cost) in *discovering* whether elements are indeed varying in predictable ways or not.

Risk

Risk (or 'real' risk) is the potential exposure associated with an outcome whose value falls short of some minimum expectation. Even with a great deal of uncertainty, there is not necessarily risk if the value resulting from all the possible outcomes still exceeds this minimum. On the distribution of values characterizing uncertainty, an outcome involving risk is one that falls on the adverse side of some 'reservation' line: a line denoting satisfaction or continued satisfaction of certain preferences corresponding to some minimum utility of the actor.

An actor who chooses to go mountain climbing *instead of* staying home and reading a book (the most attractive alternative foregone) is taking a risk only by way of the *difference* in potentially unfavourable outcomes between the two alternatives. The Knightian concept of risk is definable independent of choice. 'Real' risk requires choice. 'Real' risk is a meaningless concept independent of the opportunity cost.

Choices Between Strategies

The objects of choice in a 'capital' framework are alternative *strategies*. Actors are choosing between one path into the future (and the complete future opportunity set implied with that path) and some other path. Each strategy includes desirable and undesirable attributes subject to uncertainty, the fulfilment of which is at least part-influenced by the actor him- or herself. Choice between alternative strategies implies a mechanism to rank these attributes comparatively, including the scope to influence their fulfilment.

A major theoretical work in the book involves development of the *temporal utility model*: the conceptual framework for understanding choice problems where choice is between alternative *strategies* and uncertainty associated with these alternative strategies is undefinable in probabilistic terms. The major elements of this model are:

1. Choice under uncertainty cannot be characterized as a *simultaneous* weighting of the utilities attaching to the set of possible outcomes. It is a *sequential* process where issues that are ranked more highly in an individual's preference order receive first consideration.

2. For human action, value is a term that is meaningful only between objects of choice, and constitutes only those elements that differ between choice alternatives. There is no 'total' concept of utility. For choice, 'utility' relates only to the *differences* between choice alternatives.

Several outcomes derive from this model:

1. Risk is concerned with issues that are ranked more highly in an individual's preference order and that are assessed first. Reconciliation of these risk issues – focusing on only a sub-set of the choice attributes – is a *precondition* to utility maximization (where *all* attributes are considered).

2. By requiring actors to value only the *difference* between choice alternatives, the model ascribes for human action a computational requirement far reduced and arguably far more realistically grounded than previous models.

3. Investment in information is rational if it reduces the scope for potentially unfavourable outcomes, *even if* it makes no difference *ex ante* to the *expected* utility of choices. This is a significant shift from most neoclassical models which suggest that investment in information is rational only if there is an *ex ante* gain in expected utility to offset information costs.

When applied to investment projects within firms, the distribution of utilities in the temporal utility model is replaced by a distribution of returns to investment. The cost of capital constitutes the benchmark against which attributes exhibiting risk are measured.

Iterative Choice Process

The book examines a comprehensive process of decision-making. The process is an iterative one and does not require decision-makers to start with a fully developed rank-ordered set of preferences.

Decision-making starts with preferences only broadly defined, and these preferences constitute the initial rules of evaluation. It proceeds with successive rounds of evaluation. Each round involves information-seeking and the rejection of unsuitable alternatives according to currently understood rules. Before proceeding to the next round, decision rules are refined and enhanced, and elements no longer relevant to the remaining choice set are discarded. Rules therefore become endogenous to the process.

The institutionalized structure of rules and the mechanisms to implement them form a primary role in uncertainty reduction and efficiency enhancement. Yet gains in efficiency come at the expense of freedom to change, and the application of a rule derived from a *class* of activity may be sub-optimal for individual cases. In an institutionalized corporate decision environment, the successive evaluation and rejection of alternatives under an evolving structure of rules leads to outcomes that are path dependent. This process is a major explanation for the observed non-profit-maximizing result, though it does not necessarily suggest that more efficient results are achievable given information available *ex ante*.

Models of Capital

A model of a production process involving capital is developed. The model explicitly focuses on the indivisibility of capital, the influence of sunk costs, and the complementarity and heterogeneity of capital within a production process. The model uses the notion of capital *within* the process ('secondary' capital) and capital that defines the process ('primary' capital). The evaluation has been built on a competitive, but non-equilibrium framework.

Three important outcomes flow from the model:

1. The driving force for capital investment decisions is entrepreneurial expectations concerning market offtake (capital utilization) for the envisaged production. Increasing price is only an indirect force in promoting increased production. Uncertainty in these expectations has a

significant influence, with the scope for incorrect outcomes increasing as output levels approach the long-run average cost minima.

2. Capital investments are unambiguously negatively affected by increases in uncertainty (without changes in offtake expectations), and observable capital investments in environments of uncertainty are characterized by relative over-capitalization (at least in respect of *current* output). Empirical work supports this model.

3. The model includes a comprehensive development and analysis of the value of options to change. Capital value is enhanced by the presence and recognition of these 'real' options, and the value of options (though not the value of the investment) increases with increasing uncertainty. In option valuation, the contribution of expectations formulation is vital. Unlike financial options that are usually subject to no uncertainty as to when they should be exercised, the uncertainty associated with the exercise of real options substantially influences their value. With signal extraction difficulty and strategic influences, outcomes that allow for no change can be more efficient than alternative strategies pursued by rational actors allowing such change. This too is an important explanation for observed non-profit-maximizing results, though it does not necessarily suggest that more efficient results are achievable given information available *ex ante*.

An additional and related outcome from the model involves the difference between internal-to-the-firm valuation of capital goods and the market value of those goods. With consistency in expectations throughout the planned equipment life, internal-to-the-firm value does not have to reflect market value for this capital except when equipment is bought and sold. With uncertainty in expectations, or changing expectations, costs of production must reflect the value of the capital in its now more likely alternative use. 'Costs' (in the correct economic use of the term) increase and investment is reduced.

The capital model promises significant advances in the way capital investment alternatives are understood and in the way decisions are made within firms.

References

Abel, Andrew B. (1983), 'Optimal investment under uncertainty', *American Economic Review*, 73, 228–33.

Abel, Andrew B. and Eberly, Janice C. (1995), 'Optimal investment with costly reversibility', NBER Working Paper Series, no. 5091, Cambridge, Mass.: National Bureau of Economic Research.

Abel, Andrew B., Dixit, Avinash K., Eberly, Janice C. and Pindyck, Robert S. (1995), 'Options, the value of capital, and investment', NBER Working Paper Series, no. 5227, Cambridge, Mass.: National Bureau of Economic Research.

Ainslie, George (1992), *Picoeconomics: The Strategic Interaction of Successive Motivational States within the Person*, Cambridge: Cambridge University Press.

Akerlof, George A. (1984), 'The market for "lemons": quality uncertainty and the market mechanism', in *An Economic Theorist's Book of Tales*, Cambridge: Cambridge University Press.

Alchian, A.A. (1950), 'Uncertainty, evolution, and economic theory', *Journal of Political Economy*, 58 (June), 211–21.

Alchian, A.A. (1968), 'Cost', in *International Encyclopaedia of the Social Sciences*, vol. 3, New York: Crowell Collier & MacMillan, 404–15.

Allais, Maurice (1979), 'The foundations of a positive theory of choice involving risk and a criticism of the postulates and axioms of the American school', in M. Allais and O. Hagen (eds), *Expected Utility Hypotheses and the Allais Paradox*, Dordrecht, Holland: D. Reidel.

Allais, M. and Hagen, O. (eds) (1979), *Expected Utility Hypotheses and the Allais Paradox*, Dordrecht, Holland: D. Reidel.

Arrow, Kenneth J. (1950), 'The difficulty in the concept of social welfare', *Journal of Political Economy*

Arrow, Kenneth J. (1951), 'Alternative approaches to the theory of choice in risk-taking situations', *Econometrica*, 19, 404–37.

Arrow, Kenneth J. (1958), 'Utilities, attitudes, choices: a review note', *Operations Research*, 5, 765–74; reprinted as Kenneth J. Arrow 'Individual choice under certainty and uncertainty', in *Collected Papers of Kenneth J. Arrow*, Cambridge, Mass.: Harvard University Press, 1984.

Arrow, Kenneth J. (1974), 'General economic equilibrium: purpose, analytical techniques, collective choice', *American Economic Review*, 64, 253–72.

Arrow, Kenneth J. (1979), 'The division of labor in the economy, the polity, and society', in Gerald P. O'Driscoll (ed.), *Adam Smith and Modern Political Economy*, Ames, Iowa: Iowa State University Press, 153–64.

Arrow, Kenneth J. (1984), 'Individual choice under certainty and uncertainty', in *Collected Papers of Kenneth J. Arrow*, Cambridge, Mass.: Harvard University Press.

Arrow, Kenneth J. and Debreu, Gerard (1954), 'Existence of an equilibrium for a competitive economy', *Econometrica*, 22, 265–90

Baldwin, C.Y. and Meyer, R.F. (1979), 'Liquidity preference under uncertainty: a model of dynamic investment in illiquid opportunities', *Journal of Financial Economics*, 7, 347–74.

Baumol, William J. (1982), 'Contestable markets: an uprising in the theory of industry structure', *American Economic Review*, 72 (March), 1–15.

Baumol, William J., Panzar, John C. and Willig, Robert D. (1982), *Contestable Markets and the Theory of Industry Structure*, San Diego, Cal.: Harcourt Brace Jovanovich.

Baumol, William J., Panzar, John C. and Willig, Robert D. (1983), 'Contestable markets: an uprising in the theory of industry structure. Reply', *American Economic Review*, 73 (June), 491–6.

Becker, G.S. (1962), 'Irrational behaviour and economic theory', *Journal of Political Economy*, 70, 1–13.

Becker, G.S. (1981), *A Treatise on the Family*, Cambridge, Mass.: Harvard University Press.

Bernanke, Ben S. (1983), 'Irreversibility, uncertainty, and cyclical investment', *Quarterly Journal of Economics*, Feb., 85–106

Bernoulli, D. (1738), 'Specimen theoriae novae de mensura sortie' in *Commentarii Academiae Scientiarum Imperiales Petropolitanae*, vol. 5, pp. 175–92; trans. A. Pringsheim as *Die Grundlage der modernen Wertlehre: Versuch einer neuen Theorie der Wertbestimmung von Glucksfallen*, Leipzig: Duncker & Humblot, 1896, 60 pp.

Black, F. and Scholes, M. (1973), 'The pricing of options and corporate liabilities', *Journal of Political Economy*, 81 (May–June), 637–59.

Bliss, C.J. (1975), *Capital Theory and the Distribution of Income*, Oxford: North-Holland Publishing.

Böhm-Bawerk, Eugen von ([1921]1959), *Capital and Interest*, South Holland, Ill.: Libertarian Press.

Brainard, William, Shoven, John and Weiss, Laurence (1980), 'The financial valuation of the return to capital', *Brookings Papers on Economic Activity*, 2, 453–502.

Brealey, Richard A. and Myers, Stewart C. (1991), *Principles of Corporate Finance*, New York: McGraw-Hill.

Brennan, Michael J. and Schwartz, Eduardo S. (1985), 'Evaluating natural resource investments', *Journal of Business*, 58 (2), 135–57.

Buchanan, J.M. (1969), *Cost and Choice: An Inquiry in Economic Theory*, Chicago: University of Chicago Press.

Buchanan, J.M. (1981), 'Introduction: LSE cost theory in retrospect', in J.M. Buchanan and G.F. Thirlby (eds), *LSE Essays on Cost*, New York: New York University Press.

Buchanan, J.M. (1992), *Better than Plowing, and Other Personal Essays*, Chicago: University of Chicago Press.

Buchanan, J.M. (1993), 'Property as a guarantor of liberty', in C.K. Rowley (ed.), *The Shaftesbury Papers, 1* Aldershot, UK: Edward Elgar.

Buchanan, J.M. (1994), 'The return to increasing returns: an introductory summary' in J.M. Buchanan and Yong J. Yoon (eds), *The Return to Increasing Returns*, Ann Arbor, Mich.: University of Michigan Press.

Buchanan, J.M. and Thirlby, G.F. (eds) (1981), *LSE Essays on Cost*, New York: New York University Press.

Buchanan, J.M. and Yoon, Yong J. (1994) (eds), *The Return to Increasing Returns*, Ann Arbor, Mich.: University of Michigan Press.

Caballero, Richard J. and Pindyck, Robert S. (1992), 'Uncertainty, investment, and industry evolution', NBER Working Paper Series, 4160, Cambridge, Mass.: National Bureau of Economic Research.

Carlton, Dennis W. and Perloff, Jeffrey M. (1994), *Modern Industrial Organization*, New York: HarperCollins.

Chew, Soo Hong and Waller, William (1986), 'Empirical tests of weighted utility theory', *Journal of Mathematical Psychology*, 30, 55–72.

Choi, Young Back (1993), *Paradigms and Conventions: Uncertainty, Decision Making, and Entrepreneurship*, Ann Arbor, Mich.: University of Michigan Press.

Cox, John C. and Rubinstein, Mark (1985), *Options Markets*, Englewood Cliffs, N.J.: Prentice-Hall.

Cramer, G. (1728), Letter to Nikolaus Bernoulli, in D. Bernoulli (1738), 56–60.

Cramer, H. (1930), 'On the mathematical theory of risk', *Forsakringaktie-bolager Skandia*, 2, 7–84.

Crew, M.A., Jones-Lee, M.W. and Rowley, C.K. (1971), 'X-Theory versus management discretion theory', *Southern Economic Journal*, 38(2), 173–84

Danziger, S., van der Gaag, J., Smolensky, E. and Taussig, M. (1982), 'The life cycle hypothesis and the consumption behaviour of the elderly', *Journal of Post-Keynesian Economics*, 5, 208–27.

Davidson, P. (1991), 'Is probability theory relevant for uncertainty? A Post Keynesian perspective', *Journal of Economic Perspectives*, 5(1), 129–43.

Davis, Steven J. and Haltiwanger, John (1992), 'Gross job creation, gross job destruction, and employment reallocation', *Quarterly Journal of Economics*, 107, 819–64.

Debreu, Gerard (1959), *Theory of Value: An Axiomatic Analysis of Economic Equilibrium*, London: Yale University Press.

Demers, Michel (1991), 'Investment under uncertainty, irreversibility and the arrival of information over time', *Review of Economic Studies*, 58, 333–50.

Dewey, Donald (1965), *Modern Capital Theory*, London: Columbia University Press.

Dixit, Avinash K. and Pindyck, Robert S. (1994), *Investment under Uncertainty*, Princeton, N.J.: Princeton University Press.

Eberly, Janice C. (1993), 'Comment on Pindyck and Solimano (1993)', in *NBER Macroeconomics Annual, 1993*, Cambridge, Mass.: National Bureau of Economic Research and MIT Press.

Einhorn, Hillel J. and Hogarth, Robin M. (1986), 'Decision making under ambiguity', in R.M. Hogarth and M.W. Reder (eds), *Rational Choice: The Contrast between Economics and Psychology*, Chicago: University of Chicago Press.

Fama, Eugene F. (1980), 'Agency problems and the theory of the firm', *Journal of Political Economy*, 88 (2), 288–307.

Fama, Eugene F. and Jensen, Michael C. (1983), 'Agency problems and residual claims', *Journal of Law and Economics*, 26 (June), 327–49.

Ferderer, J. Peter (1993), 'The impact of uncertainty on aggregate investment spending: an empirical analysis', *Journal of Money, Credit, and Banking*, 25, 30–48.

Fisher, I. ([1906]1965), *The Nature of Capital and Income*, New York: A.M. Kelley

Ford, J.L. (1987), *Economic Choice Under Uncertainty: A Perspective Theory Approach,* New York: St. Martin's Press.

Friedman, M. (1953), *Essays in Positive Economics,* Chicago: University of Chicago Press.

Friedman, M. and Savage, L.J. (1948), 'The utility analysis of choices involving risk', *Journal of Political Economy,* 56, 279–304.

Greene, William H. (1993), *Econometric Analysis,* New York: Macmillan.

Hall, Robert E. (1993), 'Comment on Pindyck and Solimano (1993)' in *NBER Macroeconomics Annual, 1993,* Cambridge, Mass.: National Bureau of Economic Research and MIT Press, 313–16.

Hartman, Richard (1972), 'The effects of price and cost uncertainty on investment', *Journal of Economic Theory,* 5, 258–66.

Hartman, Richard (1976), 'Factor demand with output price uncertainty', *American Economic Review,* 66, 675–82.

Hayek, F.A. (1931), *Prices and Production,* London: Routledge.

Hayek, F.A. (1941), *The Pure Theory of Capital,* London: Routledge & Kegan Paul.

Hayek, F.A. (1945), 'The use of knowledge in society', *American Economic Review,* 35(4), 519–30.

Hayek, F.A. (1952), *The Sensory Order,* Chicago: University of Chicago Press.

Hayek, F.A. (1967), *Studies in Philosophy, Politics, and Economics,* Chicago: University of Chicago Press.

Hayek, F.A. (1973), 'Rules and order' in *Law, Legislation and Liberty,* vol. 1, Chicago: University of Chicago Press.

Henderson, David R. (1993), *The Fortune Encyclopaedia of Economics,* New York: Warner.

Herrnstein, R. (1961), 'Relative and absolute strengths of response as a function of frequency of reinforcement', *Journal of the Experimental Analysis of Behaviour,* 4, 267–72.

Hey, John D. (1991), *Experiments in Economics,* Cambridge, Mass.: Basil Blackwell.

Hicks, John R. (1933), 'The application of mathematical methods in the theory of risk', lecture presented at Econometric Society in Leyden, Sept.; quoted in Sinn (1989).

Hicks, John R. (1939), *Value and Capital,* Oxford: Clarendon Press.

Hicks, John R. (1974), 'Capital controversies: ancient and modern' *American Economic Review*, May, reprinted in J.R. Hicks (1977), *Economic Perspectives: Further Essays in Money and Growth*, Oxford, OUP, 149–65.

Hicks, John R. (1979), *Causality in Economics*, New York: Basic Books.

Hogarth, Robin M. and Reder, Melvin W. (eds) (1986a), *Rational Choice: The Contrast Between Economics and Psychology*, Chicago: University of Chicago Press.

Hogarth, Robin M. and Reder, Melvin W. (1986b), 'Introduction', in Hogarth and Reder (eds), *Rational Choice: The Contrast between Economics and Psychology*, Chicago: University of Chicago Press.

Hurn, A.S., and Wright, Robert E. (1994), 'Geology or economics? Testing models of irreversible investment using North Sea oil data', *Economic Journal*, 104, 363–71.

Ingersoll, Jonathan E. Jr and Ross, Stephen A. (1992), 'Waiting to invest: investment and uncertainty', *Journal of Business*, 65, 1–29

Kahneman, Daniel and Tversky, Amos (1979), 'Prospect theory: an analysis of decision under risk', *Econometrica*, 47, 263–91.

Keynes, J.M. (1921), *A Treatise on Probability*, London: Macmillan.

Keynes, J.M. (1936), *The General Theory of Employment, Interest and Money*, New York: Harcourt, Brace; London: Macmillan.

Kirzner, Israel M. (1973), *Competition and Entrepreneurship*, Chicago: University of Chicago Press.

Knight, Frank H. (1921), *Risk, Uncertainty and Profit*, Chicago: University of Chicago Press

Kreps, D.M. (1988), *Notes on the Theory of Choice*, Boulder, Col.: Westview Press.

Kuhn, Thomas S. (1970), *The Structure of Scientific Revolutions*, Chicago: University of Chicago Press.

Lachmann, L.M. (1971), *The Legacy of Max Weber*, Berkeley, Cal.: Glendessary Press.

Lachmann, L.M. (1975), 'Reflections on Hayekian Capital Theory', reprinted in D. Lavoie (ed.), *Expectations and the Meaning of Institutions*, London: Routledge, 1994.

Lachmann, L.M. (1978), *Capital and its Structure*, Kansas City: Sheed Andrews & McMeel.

Lange, O. (1943), 'A note on innovations', *Review of Economics and Statistics*, 25, 19–25. Reprinted in *Readings in the Theory of Income Distribution*, Philadelphia, 181–96; quoted from Sinn (1989).

Lashley, K.S. (1951), 'The problem of serial order in behaviour', in L. Jeffress (ed.), *Hixon Symposium on Cerebral Mechanism in Behaviour*, New York, quoted in F.A. Hayek (1967, 49).

Leahy, John V. and Whited, Toni M. (1995), 'The effect of uncertainty on investment: some stylized facts', NBER Working Paper Series, no. 4986, Cambridge, Mass.: National Bureau of Economic Research.

Lewis, W. Arthur (1948), *Overhead Costs*, New York: Rinehart.

Lindberg, E.B. and Ross, S.A. (1981), 'Tobin's *q* ratio and industrial organization', *Journal of Business*, 54, 1–33.

Locke, John ([1693]1995), *An Essay Concerning Human Understanding*, New York: Prometheus Books.

Lucas, Robert E. (1966), 'Optimal investment with rational expectations', in Robert E. Lucas and Thomas J. Sargent (eds), *Rational Expectations and Econometric Practice*, Minneapolis, Minn.: University of Minnesota Press (1981).

Lucas, Robert E. (1986), 'Adaptive behaviour and economic theory', in R.M. Hogarth and M.W. Reder (eds), *Rational Choice: The Contrast between Economics and Psychology*, Chicago: University of Chicago Press, 217–42.

Lucas, Robert E. and Prescott, Edward C. (1971), 'Investment under uncertainty', *Econometrica*, 39(5), reprinted in Robert E. Lucas and Thomas J. Sargent (eds), *Rational Expectations and Econometric Practice*, Minneapolis, Minn.: University of Minnesota Press (1981), 67–90.

Machina, Mark J. (1987), 'Choice under uncertainty: problems solved and unsolved', *Journal Economic Perspectives*, 1(1), 121–54.

Markowitz, H. (1952), 'Portfolio Selection', *Journal of Finance*, 7, 77–91.

Markowitz, H. (1970), *Portfolio Selection: Efficient Diversification of Investments*, 2nd edn, London: Blackwell.

Marschak, J. (1938), 'Money and the theory of assets', *Econometrica*, 6, 311–25.

Maslow, A.H. (1943), 'A theory of human motivation', *Psychological Review*, 50, 370–96.

Mazur, J.E. (1986), 'Choice between single and multiple delayed reinforcers', *Journal of the Experimental Analysis of Behaviour*, 46, 67–77.

McDonald, Robert and Siegel, Daniel (1986), 'The value of waiting to invest', *Quarterly Journal of Economics*, Nov.

Merton, R.C. (1973), 'Theory of rational option pricing', *Bell Journal of Economics and Management Science*, 4(1), 141–83.

Meyer, Willi (1986), 'Beyond choice', in I. Kirzner (ed.), *Subjectivism, Intelligibility and Economic Understanding*, New York: New York University Press, 221–35.

Miller, David (ed.) (1985), *Popper Selections*, Princeton, N.J.: Princeton University Press.

Mises, Ludwig von (1966), *Human Action*, 3rd rev. edn, Chicago: Henry Regnery

Mises, Ludwig von (1971), *The Theory of Money and Credit*, trans. from earlier German editions dating from 1924, New York: Foundation for Economic Education.

Morrison, Catherine J. (1993), 'Investment in capital assets and economic performance: the US chemicals and primary-metals industries in transition', *Journal of Business and Economic Statistics*, 11(1), 45–60.

Neyman, J. and E.S. Pearson (1933), 'The testing of statistical hypotheses in relation to probabilities *a priori*', *Proceedings of the Cambridge Philosophical Society*, 29, 492–510.

Nicholson, Walter (1992), *Microeconomic Theory: Basic Principles and Extensions*, 5th edn, New York: Dryden Press.

Niehans, J. (1948), 'Zur Preisbildung bei ungewissen Erwartungen', *Schweizerische Zeitschrift fur Volkswirtschaft und Statistik*, 84(5), 433–56.

O'Driscoll, Gerald P. (ed.) (1979), *Adam Smith and Modern Political Economy*, Ames, Iowa: Iowa State University Press, 153–64.

Oi, Walter Y. (1961), 'The desirability of price instability', *Econometrica*, 29, 58–64.

Packard, David (1995), *The HP Way*, New York: HarperCollins.

Pareto, V. (1909), *Manuel d'economic politique*, Paris: Girard.

Peters, Thomas J. and Waterman, Robert H. (1982), *In Search of Excellence: Lessons from America's Best-run Companies*, New York: Warner.

Pindyck, Robert S. (1988), 'Irreversible investment, capacity choice, and the value of the firm', *American Economic Review*, 78(5), 969–85.

Pindyck, Robert S. (1993a), 'A note on competitive investment under uncertainty', *American Economic Review*, 83(1), 273–7.

Pindyck, Robert S. (1993b), 'The present value model of rational commodity pricing', *Economic Journal*, 103, 511–30.

Pindyck, Robert S. and Solimano, Andres (1993), 'Economic instability and aggregate investment', in *NBER Macroeconomics Annual, 1993*, Cambridge, Mass.: National Bureau of Economic Research and MIT Press.

Popper, Karl R. ([1934]1959), *The Logic of Scientific Discovery*, New York: Harper & Row, originally published as *Logik der Forschung*, Berlin: Springer, 1934; Reprinted in David Miller (ed.), *Popper Selections*, Princeton, N.J.: Princeton University Press, 1985.

Ramsey, F.P. (1931), 'Truth and probability', in *The Foundations of Mathematics and Other Logical Essays*, London: K. Paul, Trench, Trubner.

Roberts, Kevin and Weissman, Martin L. (1981), 'Funding criteria for research, development, and exploration projects', *Econometrica*, 49, 1261–88.

Robinson, Joan (1941), 'Rising supply price', *Economica*, new series, 8, 1–8.

Romer, Paul M. (1990), 'Endogenous technological change', *Journal of Political Economy*, 98(5, part 2), 71–102.

Rowley, C.K. (ed.) (1993), *The Shaftesbury Papers, 1*, Aldershot, UK: Edward Elgar.

Roy, A.D. (1952), 'Safety first and the holding of assets', *Econometrica*, 20, 431–49.

Runge, I.C. (1996), 'Capital and uncertainty', unpublished PhD dissertation, Fairfax, Va: George Mason University.

Samuelson, Paul A. (1983), *Foundations of Economic Analysis*, Enlarged edn, Cambridge, Mass.: Harvard University Press.

Schelling, T.C. (1967), 'Economics and criminal enterprises', *Public Interest*, 7, 61–78.

Schelling, T.C. (1981), 'Economic reasoning and the ethics of policy', *Public Interest*, 63, 37–61.

Schoemaker, Paul J.H. (1980), *Experiments on Decisions under Risk: The Expected Utility Hypothesis*, The Hague: Martinus Nijhoff.

Schwartz, Marius and Reynolds, Robert J. (1983), 'Contestable markets: an uprising in the theory of industry structure: Comment', *American Economic Review*, 73, 488–90.

Shackle, G.L.S. ([1949]1952), *Expectation in Economics,* 2nd edn, Cambridge: Cambridge University Press.

Shackle, G.L.S. (1983), 'The bounds of unknowledge', in J. Wiseman (ed.), *Beyond Positive Economics*, London: Macmillan, 28–37; reprinted in Shackle (1988).

Shackle, G.L.S. (1988), *Business, Time and Thought: Selected Papers*, ed. S.F. Frowen, New York: New York University Press.

Shepherd, William G. (1984), '"Contestability" vs. Competition', *American Economic Review*, 74, 572–87.

Simon, Herbert A. (1979), 'Rational decision making in business organizations', *American Economic Review*, 69(4), 493–513.

Simon, Herbert A. (1986), 'Rationality in psychology and economics', in R.M. Hogarth and M.W. Reder (eds), *Rational Choice: The Contrast between Economics and Psychology*, Chicago: University of Chicago Press, 25–40.

Sinn, Hans-Werner (1989), *Economic Decisions Under Uncertainty*, 2nd ed, Heidelberg: Physica-Verlag.

Smith, Adam, ([1776]1976), *An Inquiry into the Nature and Causes of the Wealth of Nations*, Oxford: Oxford University Press.

Stigler, George J. (1951), 'The division of labour is limited by the extent of the market', *Journal of Political Economy*, June, 185–93.

Stigler, George J. (1961), 'The economics of information' *Journal of Political Economy*, 69(3), 213–25.

Stigler, George J. and Kindahl, J.K. (1970), *The Behaviour of Industrial Prices*, New York: National Bureau of Economic Research.

Stiglitz, Joseph E. and Weiss, Andrew (1981), 'Credit rationing in markets with imperfect information', *American Economic Review*, 71, 393–410.

Strydom, P.D.F. (1986), 'The economics of information: a subjectivist view', in I. Kirzner (ed.), *Subjectivism, Intelligibility and Economic Understanding*, New York: New York University Press, 288–94.

Summers, Lawrence H. (1987a), 'Investment incentives and the discounting of depreciation allowances', in Martin Feldstein (ed.), *The Effects of Taxation on Capital Accumulation*, Chicago: University of Chicago Press.

Summers, Lawrence H. (1987b), 'Corporate capital budgeting practices and the effects of tax policies on investment', in Martin Feldstein (ed.), *Taxes and Capital Formation*, Chicago: University of Chicago Press.

Thaler, Richard H. (1986), 'Comments on Simon, on Einhorn and Hogarth, and on Tversky and Kahneman', in R.M. Hogarth and M.W. Reder (eds), *Rational Choice: The Contrast Between Economics and Psychology*, Chicago: University of Chicago Press.

Tirole, Jean (1993), *The Theory of Industrial Organization*, Cambridge, Mass.: MIT Press.

Tobin, James (1969), 'A general equilibrium approach to monetary theory', *Journal of Money, Credit, and Banking*, 1, 15–29.

Trigeorgis, Lenos (1996), *Real Options: Managerial Flexibility and Strategy in Resource Allocation*, Cambridge, Mass.: MIT Press.

Tversky, Amos and Kahneman, Daniel (1986), 'Rational choice and the framing of decisions', in R.M. Hogarth and M.W. Reder (eds), *Rational Choice: The Contrast Between Economics and Psychology*, Chicago: University of Chicago Press, 67–94.

Viner, J. (1931), 'Cost curves and supply curves', reprinted in R.V. Clarence (ed.), *Readings in Economic Analysis*, Cambridge, Mass.: Addison-Wesley Press, 1950, vol. 2, 31–5.

von Neuman, J. and Morgenstern, O. (1947), *Theory of Games and Economic Behaviour,* 2nd edn, Princeton, N.J.: Princeton University Press.

Witt, Ulrich (ed.) (1992), *Explaining Process and Change: Approaches to Evolutionary Economics*, Ann Arbor: University of Michigan Press.

Wald, A. (1939), 'Contributions to the theory of statistical estimation and testing hypotheses', *Annals of Mathematical Statistics*, 10, 299–326.

Wald, A. (1950), *Statistical Decision Functions*, New York: John Wiley.

Weitzman, Martin L. (1983), 'Contestable markets: an uprising in the theory of industry structure. Comment', *American Economic Review*, 73 486–7.

Williamson, O.E. (1964), *The Economics of Discretionary Behaviour*, Chicago: Markham.

Winter, S.G. (1975), 'Optimization and evolution in the theory of the firm', in R.H. Day and T. Groves (eds), *Adaptive Economic Models*, New York: Academic Press.

Winter, S.G. (1986), 'Comments on Arrow and Lucas', in R.M. Hogarth and M.W. Reder (eds), *Rational Choice: The Contrast Between Economics and Psychology*, Chicago: University of Chicago Press, 243–50.

Zeckhauser, Richard (1986) 'Behavioural versus rational economics', in R.M. Hogarth and M.W. Reder (eds), *Rational Choice: The Contrast Between Economics and Psychology*, Chicago: University of Chicago Press, 251–65.

Index